By STUART SHERMAN

CRITICAL WOODCUTS
POINTS OF VIEW
THE GENIUS OF AMERICA
AMERICANS

CHARLES SCRIBNER'S SONS

CRITICAL WOODCUTS

CRITICAL WOODCUTS

BY

STUART SHERMAN

ILLUSTRATED WITH PORTRAITS ENGRAVED
ON WOOD

BY

BERTRAND ZADIG

CHARLES SCRIBNER'S SONS
NEW YORK · LONDON
1926

TO

IRITA VAN DOREN

CONTENTS

Contents

ILLUSTRATIONS

INTRODUCTORY

HAVING carved these twenty-six critical impressions, and having arranged them with various odd intentions in three little galleries, I am to stand for a few moments in the vestibule, exhibiting the artist and chatting about his exhibition with the visitors, the purpose being to lure the curious onward and to satisfy the incurious at the door.

In the present state of criticism, I fancy that most of my visitors will interest themselves in the subjects and not in the treatment, just as, to compare great things with small, the casual visitor at the Metropolitan standing before the portrait of an eminent American falls into a revery on Mr. Rockefeller rather than on John Sargent. But as the object of my appearance here is to remind the public that even the crudest sketches imply the existence of an artist, this is clearly the occasion for the drumming up, if possible, of a little interest in the workshop and in the point of view at which these "woodcuts" were made.

It has been intimated to me that this book shows significant changes in my point of view and in my opinions. Perhaps it does. If so, I trust that some reviewer, hostile to change, will go patiently through the essays, collect the evidence, compare it with the previously accessible evidence, and point out my aberrations and inconsistencies. I have never taken a vow to carry any opinion unaltered to the grave; and if it can be proved to-night that I have learned absolutely nothing since morning, I shall be dismayed.

The first duty of a commentator on current literature, as it appears to me, is to present a fairly full and veracious report of what is going on. He will have his own convictions regarding the permanent value of various parts of the contemporary spectacle; and, inevitably, they will "show through" in his report. But his first duty is not to exploit his own predilections; it is rather to understand the entire "conspiracy" of forces involved in the taste of his day. What is "important" now and never may be so again has a charm for him which he would think it a kind of baseness and disloyalty not to admit and record.

He conceives of literature perhaps as a river, himself as a scout seeking for the main channel of intellectual and emotional activity in his own tract of time, recurring constantly to the point where the full rush of living waters comes in from the past, and eagerly searching for the point where the flood breaks out of the backwater and through the dams, and streams away into the future. He is always sounding and essaying to discover where the water is deepest now. He tries to characterize the most promising navigators, their crafts, their cargoes. When he concerns himself with historical figures, he seizes upon those who, by reason of some vital congruity, are felt by us as "modern" and pertinent to our present occasions.

In the back of his mind is the knowledge that an annual chronicle so composed will outweigh the sum of the diurnal entries; his work will come together in the end, and constitute a picture of his age and its tendencies.

I am talking much of pictures, and, on very high authority, I understand that Mr. Joel E. Spingarn now classes me as a belated convert to the theory of expression for expression's sake. I have now and have always had a lively interest in the arts of expression; and yet I am not conscious of any alteration in my ancient conviction that all human activities have, up their sleeves, an ulterior object and ultimate justification in happier living; and that it is rather specially the "function" of critics to be engaged in an incessant untiring exploration in quest of "the good life."

The important change of which I am conscious is in the intensity of my conviction that no man should state very emphatically what "the good life" is until he has found it. Too much theory about it and too many preconceptions obscure the vision. The best criticism is of a concrete and inductive habit. The wise critic attempts on all possible occasions to keep his theoretical and didactic mouth shut and all his other faculties open, here, there, and everywhere, for all the reports and rumors of positive charm and joy in things and people, as the most indubitable tokens that they are participators in some degree of that "good life" which he is seeking.

A suspense of judgment regarding the complete outlines of the ideal, need involve no abdication of discrimination and judgment. But these elements in the critic's report will, in proportion as the report itself becomes "artistic," be more and more implicit, will be conveyed insensibly along with the characterization of the subject, will be felt by the reader immediately as elements in his own response to the subject.

In my exploration for the "virtues" of men, I have learned that patient search usually discovers some refreshing virtue wherever there has been exhibited any unusual display of energy. As I revisit my three little galleries, I am impressed by the abundance and variety and high interest of the vital powers exhibited there. Taking my "sitters" one by one, I rather think that my main intention has been to feel strongly the unique life in all these men and women from Sherwood Anderson to the Known Soldier, and to communicate the impetus of it, in a sort of blind faith that "where there is life there is hope," and where there is power there is virtue.

The essays in this volume were all printed in "Books," the literary supplement of the *Herald Tribune*, in 1924 and 1925. The title was suggested by my admiration for the swift cutting art of the original and present illustrator, Mr. Bertrand Zadig, who, under the constant temporal stress which urges a contributor to journalism to do well promptly, has accomplished with the graving tool what I have tried to do with the pen.

CRITICAL WOODCUTS

FIRST GALLERY

I

Sherwood Anderson's Tales of the New Life

WELL, here is Sherwood Anderson again with another disquieting tale, "Dark Laughter."
He is a man rather difficult to make out or to "size up," externally or internally, and one shouldn't go at it too hastily. Your eyes take an impression of him distinct enough: middle height, middle age, a compact, square-shouldered person in rough tweeds, dark blue flannel shirt, and bright-colored tie drawn through a ring or fastened, perhaps, with a horseshoe pin. He stands squarely on his feet, no shifting or teetering. His well-molded head, strong-featured, firm-mouthed, substantial in all its dimensions, sits squarely on his shoulders. In speaking—his speech is mild and slow— his eyes light up quickly with humor; but in silence they are somber with a shadowy introversion. In repose the lines of the face set austerely. I fancy the head would have appealed to the sculptors who limned the tougher-minded of the Cæsars. But this visual impression is inadequate. His secret aspiration, I believe, is to be "preeminent in being more sensitive to everything going on about him than others could possibly be."

He is from the fat Midlands—born, he rather thinks, in Camden, Ohio, in 1877, of a shrewd hard-working mother and a father who was a romantic braggart and a liar. In his youth he haunted race-

[3]

tracks and conceived a passion for thoroughbred
horses. Then he knocked around a bit on farms, in
mines, in factories, in paint shops, drug stores
and harness shops, working at one thing and
another. But he is distinctly from Chicago, too,
from the Chicago of Mr. Darrow and Mr. Masters
and Mr. Sandburg and Margaret Anderson, from
roaring, odorous, fuliginous Chicago, where poets
are obliged to yell if they are to be heard above
the booming of big business, the bellowing of the stock-
yards, and the bass drums of advertising conventions.
Also he is from New York, where intellectual Villagers
draw a little away from Wall Street to discuss anarchy
and perfect love over synthetic gin and spaghetti.
But finally he is from the left bank of the Seine, where
one can sit all day on the boulevard talking of line
and color and the virtues of words, with enthusiastic
foreigners of American birth who regard George
Moore, Marcel Proust, James Joyce, D. H. Lawrence
and Gertrude Stein as the brightest constellation in
heaven. Yes, he is from the fat Midlands, but decidedly he has been a passionate pilgrim.

I wish to write an introduction to the works of Mr.
Anderson for the benefit of correspondents who inquire: "When will the country begin to sicken of this
flood of literary rot from the corn and hog belt?" But
the devil—to borrow his own favorite literary exple-
tive, he doesn't make it easy for me!

Recently he has been down the Mississippi Valley,
down the river, living in New Orleans, I believe. He
has been getting the "feel" of all that rich, crude,
rough, profane tract of land and water which Huckleberry Finn traversed and navigated in his ingenuous
youth. He has been down in the heart of our trans-

Sherwood Anderson

planted Africa, and the spell of dark blood, the careless gusto of dark laughter, the magic of spontaneous and instinctive people, have been invading him. Mark Twain had told what the great river meant to a boy. What if he, Sherwood Anderson, should tell what it means to a man? What if he should attempt to suggest in some fashion how the national culture, the national letters, might be vitalized, vivified, if the national imagination assimilated its materials? It is obvious that some such undercurrent of thought was running in his mind when "Dark Laughter" took shape. His imagination has been roving southward for warmth, color, abandon.

But, as I have already remarked, "the devil!" He might have found a better symbol for the expedition, mightn't he? Here is Mr. Anderson reciting me another story about a man who has run away from his wife! I think he overworks that symbol.

This time it is a journalist with literary aspirations and a wife who writes for the popular magazines. At times they have in some "arty" people who talk about art. But they never touch the heart of the matter, with their palaver about "word-slinging." The beginning of art is to know what people think and feel. The time comes when he can stand it no longer. He runs away. He wanders around in the South; finds work painting wheels in an automobile wheel factory; consorts with a jocund fellow workman and his wife who are very jolly and lively and spontaneous when they are on their cat-fishing expeditions and are a little drunk, the two of them. Then the eye of his employer's wife falls upon him— etc. In fact, they flash together as abruptly as the electricity of earth and sky.

[7]

The first chapter of this book, which is just four pages long, seems to me as consummate a piece of art as the first chapter of "Pride and Prejudice," which also occupies four pages; and the rest of the book is keyed up to that pitch. I am not comparing Sherwood Anderson's narrative soliloquy with Jane Austen's dramatic method. I am comparing merely and exclusively the skill with which two fine craftsmen handle their tools, the ravishing economy of their means, the intensity and poignant reality of their effect. But when I have said a good word for fine workmanship, and have invited curious and shocked readers to take down their "Pride and Prejudice" and compare its first chapter with the first chapter of "Dark Laughter," what else shall I say to commend the suspicious material and theme of the Midwesterner's tale to the favorable attention of correspondents who are sick of "literary rot from the corn and hog belt"?

Shall I fall back upon the earlier novels? The first, "Windy McPherson's Son," 1916, is another tale of a runaway. Nothing enchants Mr. Anderson like a runaway. Windy McPherson is a self-made Midwestern business man whose successful career breaks down in the middle; he decamps and goes vagabonding and carousing through various sordid adventures in search of a meaning for a life that rang hollow, seemed empty. He finds his meaning in some adopted children.

In "Marching Men," 1917, Beaut McGregor runs away from his success in law to find a life-purpose in drilling men to march; he knows not why they should march or whither, but in the form and order and rhythm of marching there is something which to his chaos-maddened soul is profoundly right.

Hugh McVey, the inventor in "Poor White," 1920, runs away from his bride, leaps from the window to avoid her embrace.

Webster, the tub manufacturer in "Many Marriages," 1923, runs away from his wife and his business—elopes in the dusk of the morning with his stenographer; and when this novel appeared Mr. Canby made something of a sensation by comparing Webster's flight with the departure of Christian in "Pilgrim's Progress" from the City of Destruction.

The shorter tales, "Winesburg, Ohio," 1919; "The Triumph of the Egg," 1921, and "Horses and Men," 1923, are filled with restless fugitives. Images of escape hitherto have been the dominating shapes in Mr. Anderson's imagination, and for reasons some of which are now obvious.

The central fact in his life, when you come to understand it, is this: Till he was nearly forty years old he was engrossed in the all-American game of getting on in the world. He was in the "advertising game"—making it go, too, one understands—why not? with that Cæsarian chin, that rudder-like nose, those devouring eyes. But midway in this mortal life he walked out of business into art. Midway in life he had the sort of experience which makes the crisis in many of Tolstoy's novels—a kind of uprushing profound despair over the oppressive emptiness of his busy, successful existence, a kind of desperate need of finding some soul-satisfying meaning in the clangorous scheme of things. He had the Dantean experience of losing his way in an "obscure wood" and meeting a "lion" which drove him from his path, drove him in

[9]

scornful flight from the familiar path. And now, not
to enter into detail which may be found most capti-
vatingly set forth in "A Story Teller's Story," after
only ten years in letters he finds himself in the front
line of the "new literary movement" in America and,
in certain respects of his craft, one of the most interesting men writing English. For him, at least, what
happened within him at forty was epoch-making.
Relatively speaking, nothing that happened before
mattered till the "illumination" of his middle years
broke over it.

I should like to see Sherwood Anderson "whole" and
in relation to this literary movement in which he is
now active. Rigorous teachers seized my youth and
taught me some phrases about the desirability of seeing things steadily and seeing them whole. But experience has taught me that it is exceedingly difficult
to see steadily and whole any object which is alive
and moving rapidly. Our object is very much alive
and is moving rapidly. I mean by our object that
group of American writers which is most conspicuously
engaged in the "advance of letters."

Some of them affectionately salute Theodore Dreiser
as their shaggy spiritual Father, as the path-breaker
who went before them and with heavy stumbling tread
opened the way to Truth and Life. Some trace their
descent from Walt Whitman and Mark Twain. Some
neither know nor inquire who their spiritual Grandfather was. But all of them, with increasing clearness as to what they are about, are seeking, in divers
ways, to end the dwindling reign of "the New Englanders" over the American conscience and the American imagination. They seek to pull out all the unused
stops in the organ of national consciousness. They

seek to use powers that have been denied, starved, suppressed. They seek to make the voice of contemporary letters adequately express the color and passion of contemporary life. Perhaps I should add that with the general purpose of the movement, as here stated, I am heart and soul in sympathy, however impatiently I may have contemplated some of its bungling preliminary operations.

To this movement Sherwood Anderson brings a number of gifts, some of which were not abundant in it before his arrival, gifts which should be of inestimable service to it. I don't really know where to begin enumerating them nor which of them to single out as his prime distinction. But I rather think it is an allotropic form of the religious spirit which particularly appeals to me in him. It is something inward, close to his heart, regulating his other powers, and giving edge and intensity to his perceptions.

Externalized, this central passion signally flames forth in his white-hot zeal for craftsmanship. This Midwestern ex-advertising man with the inscrutable poker-player's face is down on his knees, is in sackcloth and ashes, is shattered and in tears when he finds himself in the presence of superbly perfect workmanship. The man is in love, desperately in love, with perfection. And that passion puts humility into his heart, and grace, and reverence, and the fragrance of adoration. That is one gift.

Another is that he possesses the idiom of American colloquial speech beyond most living writers—Ring Lardner perhaps excepted; and he has had the tact and the taste and the patience to work with the colloquial idiom and the colloquial tune till he has lifted them above the level of slang and made of them a sound literary medium, original and savory. In his first two books, "Windy McPherson's Son" and "Marching Men," it is present but not fully developed; in the rest of them he is master of a singularly intimate and vital style, a delicate instrument for telling the truth about the agitations of the heart in the presence of much unvisited beauty.

Another gift is that he is a natural born story teller, who has scornfully rejected standardized tricks and formulas and has steadily perfected and subtilized his art, and devoted it to expressing secret crises in the mind and in the feelings which only a delicate and subtle art can explore. I seem to remember that he was credited with being a follower of "the Russians" before he had made the acquaintance of them. If so, it was a natural error. Notably in his short stories one has the sense that one is envisaging restless naked souls in the moments which contain, as the Russian masters of the short story think, all the real significance of lives, dead else.

Another of his gifts is that he is tremendously American and is glad of it. He is no booster or braggart, save in the purely poetic Whitmanian sense. Like Whitman, he is too profoundly conscious of all that is vile and shoddy and vicious and sodden and ugly in the American scene. But in his moments of elation he, too, feels that, with all his imperfections on his head, and with all the roily turbulence within, he is "the typical American" of our day. I love his cry of defiance as a Chicago poet, in his "Midwestern Chants." Leave us alone, is the burden of it: "We want to see if we are any good out here, we Americans from all over hell." The men and manners and soil, yes, even the profanity, of his native land are a gay riot in his blood and a sweetness under the tongue as they were to Mark Twain when he first came out of the West.

Another of Sherwood Anderson's gifts.—Now, I must apologize, I suppose, for calling this a gift. He possesses what some of the younger critics devoutly hoped had gone out: he possesses "high seriousness." He has made no secret of it. From his first book to his latest he has appeared as a passionate seeker for the meaning and purpose, the inmost meaning and purpose, in this driving, noisy, smoky, ugly, hungry, monotonous, wearying civilization in which we welter.

Finally, Sherwood Anderson is or has been a mystic—I think a genuine mystic; and time after time he has been in moments of almost ecstatic "awareness," when through the arid channel of existence meaning swept like a spring freshet and all the dusty cobwebbed windows of the house of life were filled with colored flame, like a sordid tenement transfigured by some casual felicity of the sunset.

I know perfectly well that I cannot expect modern readers to follow me when I say that my interest in this ex-advertising man from Chicago and my understanding of him are due in considerable measure to my youthful addiction to a queer book by a mediæval Italian—a fierce, quarrelsome, disreputable, probably sensual and certainly vagabond fellow who wrote a book about the Beatific Vision and another, *Vita Nuova*, in which he describes, among other visions, this:

Methought I saw in my chamber a cloud of the color of fire, within which I discerned a Lord of aspect fearful to whoso should look upon him; and he seemed

[13]

to me so joyful within himself that a marvelous thing it was; and in his words he spoke many things which I understood not save a few, among which I understood these: *Ego Dominus tuus.* In his arms meseemed to see a person sleeping, naked, save that she seemed to be wrapped lightly in a blood-red cloth. . . . In one of his hands it seemed to me that he held a thing which was all on fire; and it seemed to me that he said these words to me: *Vide cor tuum.* And when he had remained a while, it seemed to me that he awoke her that slept; and he so far prevailed upon her with his craft as to make her eat that thing which was burning in his hand; and she ate it as one in fear.

God knows what our psychoanalysts would make of this naked lady eating a man's heart; but it was once generally understood to express something of the fiery ecstasy in which this Italian vagabond entered upon a new spiritual life; and I wish modern readers who are under the spell of psychoanalytic quacks might have it in mind when they attempt to classify the day dreams of Sherwood Anderson. As for myself, for the moment I will say only that time after time he has caught and reported fragments of spiritual meaning beneath our struggle—more or less stolidly, more or less handsomely, refined and concealed—our struggle for existence.

Many of Mr. Anderson's associates in the movement have intimated—some of them have vehemently affirmed—that life has no inner meaning and purpose. And I myself have long been inclined to believe, with Conrad, for example, that life's meaning is only in the figure or pattern which human volition marks and holds in place upon the surface of infinite chaos and darkness. Perhaps I have been too rarely a mystic, too arrogantly rationalist. For Sherwood Anderson, at any rate, the meaning of life is something that the rational mind can hardly lay hold upon. Only in the "moments" which are, he thinks, the prime subjects of the story teller's art, the meaning comes clamoring through the senses, through all the senses, out of the unfathomable inwardness of life.

Symbolism just now is very much the mode in the movement, but Sherwood Anderson has always been a symbolist, feeling from the outset the necessity of storming sluggish sensibilities with a new set of images, strange, extravagant and grotesque, symbols of an experience otherwise intransmissible.

I insist on this because it is absurd to approach such a book as "Dark Laughter" or, indeed, any of his books, as if they were ordinary "realistic" novels attempting to picture the detail and circumstance of contemporary society. His books are stories of housefronts falling down; stories of men walking out of houses and closing the doors behind them; stories of men walking up railroad tracks into the night; stories of women racing through corn-rows; stories of souls fleeing out of nowhere into nothing; stories of barren breasts opened to the night; stories of arms outstretched to enfold the fugitive wind; stories of persons bathing, with a passionate eagerness to be washed and made clean, with tears and with prayers, with water and with blood, for some mystical union with the spirit of life.

Since the day when he himself decided that he cared nothing about making money, and he went out of the factory and closed the door and entered a new room, and wrote at the top of a fresh ream of paper, *Incipit Vita Nova*—Here beginneth a new life—he has been,

[15]

I fancy, serenely indifferent to the instituted forms
of society. He has not railed at society, with the
satirists. He has been all absorbed in studying more
perfect means for expressing the strange joy in the
hearts of men and women when, at the ages of twenty,
thirty, forty and upward, they suddenly resolve not
to accept the world's price for tame acquiescence in
its routine, not to "fall for" a standardized ante-
mortem burial in respectability, but to strike out reso-
lutely for a personal life and a deeper awareness of
their own existence and its brief ripple in the coursing
stream of humanity.

We should approach Mr. Anderson as the impassioned interpreter of day-dreams, the day-dreams of
common people—newsboys, stableboys, washerwomen,
farmhands, sign painters, drug clerks, old maids,
small-town preachers, tub manufacturers, newspaper
men, and women with nothing to do but to wait for
their husbands to come home—the great masses of the
plain people, in their occasional hours of revolt against
what Stevenson declared is the destiny of most men:
"leading lives of quiet despair." He has an intimate
and quite extraordinary understanding of what goes
on in American plain people when they are groping
for an escape from "lives of quiet despair." Do you
wish he would keep that understanding to himself
or, at least, find some less disquieting way of uttering
it? You don't like his symbols?

I suppose Mr. Anderson knows how a late-Victorian
poet expressed his revolt against the enveloping gray-
ness of drab lives, "faces of all emotion purged, from
nothing into nothing urged." He imagined a mad
king proclaiming: "I heard an angel crying from
the sun for glory, for more glory on the earth." That

injured no one's sensibilities. It is in the grand style, I suppose. But Sherwood Anderson knows that stableboys, farmhands, and washerwomen, so far as they attempt to phrase a kindred urge, do not phrase it in that way. Their speech in this field is poor and meager. It is of the very essence of their misery that they cannot give it a name. They can only say, perhaps: "Oh, I feel so queer—*so* queer!" or "Hell, but I'd like a drink!" or "I want a woman." And if they act upon these urges they are likely to act in a way which only a man who understands very primitive signs and symbols could interpret as a cry for "glory, more glory, on the earth."

And yet I am sorry for any one who doesn't get the "glory" in a bit of the vernacular, like this:

Often he would go on talking for an hour maybe, speaking of horses' bodies and of their minds and wills as though they were human beings. "Lord help us, Herman," he would say, grabbing hold of my arm, "don't it get you up in the throat? I say, now, when a good one like that Lumpy Joe I'm swiping, flattens himself at the head of the stretch and he's coming, and you know he's coming, and you know his heart's sound, and he's game, and you know he isn't going to let himself get licked—don't it get you, Herman; don't it get you like the old Harry?"

It does me!

Well, there is what I have found of chief interest in Sherwood Anderson, and the only way to determine whether all these qualities are really in him or whether I have imagined them, is to read his books.

II

D. H. Lawrence Cultivates His Beard

D. H. LAWRENCE has been rushing through an evolution. When he first faced the public, he was open-faced, clean-shaven and looked at one squarely from big glowing eyes. Now he resembles a moujik, now he makes himself up to resemble a moujik as much as the heir of all the ages can—a shag of hair across the forehead, eyes alert, defiant, glinting like a squirrel's, snubby nose sniffing the air, and a big bush of a beard.

The beard is sacred. It is worn out of respect for the impulses from our "lower" natures, out of reverence for the Dark Gods which inhabit the Dark Forest of one's own being. As Mr. Lawrence wears the beard, it is intended also to suggest and symbolize his isolate and inviolable "otherness," "separateness," "maleness." He does not insist upon an exclusively male aristocracy. He respects also the isolate "otherness" of women who attain that form of self-realization. But for himself, he is a conscientious barbarian, a revolutionist in favor of a cultivated, individualistic, aristocratic barbarism. He wants to bring back the beard, and to rebuild the ancient barriers between the naturally and the artificially smooth-faced sexes. I am not sure when he first restored the beard to fiction, but there is a sacred beard in "Kangaroo" and a still more sacred beard in "St. Mawr"—a rather fasci-

D H Lawrence

nating book, which can be read easily enough but can hardly be taken in, with its full import, unless one has in mind everything that led up to it.

"Who is D. H. Lawrence, who, you think, would interest me?" So, sitting on the lid of cultivated English fiction, wrote Henry James to that able lookout for young talents, Mr. Hugh Walpole, in 1913, on the appearance of Mr. Lawrence's third novel, "Sons and Lovers." "Send him and his book along," he continued, "by which I simply mean inoculate me, at your convenience . . . so far as I can *be* inoculated." Next year, in his much-quoted essay on "The New Novel," James warily circled around Mr. Lawrence three or four times, without actually boarding him, with, I suspect, a dim septuagenarian presentiment that Mr. Lawrence was a power, and, potentially, an intensely hostile power. As he was. As he is. Mr. Lawrence admired *William* James: he wore a beard. Henry James was a smooth master of *bienséances*—smooth-faced and bland as a Roman prelate.

In 1922 Mr. John Macy, who, with characteristic generous enthusiasm, had flung up his cap for "Sons and Lovers," ranked Mr. Lawrence with Meredith and Hardy, and declared that he knew of no other writer of his generation "endowed with his great variety of gifts." In 1923 Dr. Joseph Collins, psychologist and alienist, allured to the task by Mr. Lawrence's obvious interest for the psychoanalyst, avowed that he once had had high hopes of this man, but he added sternly that Lawrence had "sown in glory and raised in corruption," that his instincts were perverted and that it was a pity the British did not "annihilate every trace of him."

In 1924, Mr. Herbert Seligman carried on the defense in a little monograph, "D. H. Lawrence, An American Interpretation," of which the main contention, couched in very mixed metaphors, is that Mr. Lawrence is a great genius who is striving to do our Western world good. Mr. Seligman's expression of this thought is memorable: "D. H. Lawrence, like a well tempered chisel or some sharp boring instrument, goes to America's vitals, not to destroy but to strip off the lies and duality and subterfuges that prevent its voice singing out." One doesn't ordinarily use a "boring instrument" as a stripping instrument, but when by such an operation one can get "singing" out of a nation's "vitals" one shouldn't be too particular.

Something there is discussable and even exciting in Mr. Lawrence. There is much of England and Europe in him, and quite a bit now of Australia and the United States. The World War is in him and a violent individualistic reaction against war and the pressure of mobs and the crush of democracies upon the "isolate" self; see "Kangaroo." There is much current emotion and contemporary psychological interpretation of it in him. He appears to possess abundant energy and drive and more and more definiteness of purpose and direction. It is surmised in some quarters that the future is going his way and that he is close at its heels. Of the little group with the "bloom" on them, which James discussed a dozen years ago, he seems still as well worth watching as any. If what he will do next cannot be surely predicted, that is a considerable element in our interest.

This much can be said with assurance: His novels do not leave you where they found you. They have designs upon you. They quicken your consciousness, enlarge your capacity for feeling. They invade you, pluck at you, pervade you, stir the centers of emotion, as Mr. Seligman suggests—or else they produce a reaction of repugnance and send you out slamming the door after you, as Dr. Collins has done. Mr. Lawrence has this token of genius, that he affects readers as Whitman, Hardy and Dostoievsky affect them: He makes flaming disciples, on the one hand, and on the other hand he allures a certain number of temporary devotees, who subsequently shudder away from him as from the brink of a precipice and the roar of chaos.

I suspect this second group is composed of those who were first charmed by the luxuriance of natural beauty in his earlier novels and then shocked by the frank insistent association of beauty in his poetry and elsewhere—in "Amores," "Tortoises," and "Birds, Beasts and Flowers"—with Alma Venus, the generative and reproductive forces in nature.

For my own part, I came to him in his strenuous and somewhat yeasty middle period, between "Rainbow," 1915, and "Kangaroo," 1923, when he was troubling our censors with things which they were probably incapable of understanding, such as "Women in Love" and "Aaron's Rod." Though I felt immediately the power and the seriousness of intention in these books and their unfitness for children and censors, I was—by reason of an antecedent inoculation—nearly immune to them, very little stimulated by them till "Studies in Classic American Literature" struck me by its original critical force and interested me in the course of Mr. Lawrence's development. The two books in which I felt most his captivating charm and his substantial power as a novelist were "The White Peacock" and "Sons and Lovers."

The undebatably potent and enthralling virtue in

Mr. Lawrence and the central source, I think, of his power as a writer is his marvelous awareness of life in nature. To a limited extent he responds to the life in people, particularly in deep, vital, inarticulate people. The articulate life of people in society he regards as mainly tedious. But he responds as if there were no barrier between him and the life which pulses in beasts, birds, flowers, clouds, the sea and the spumy star clusters of the Milky Way. Arnold called Wordsworth "a priest of the wonder and bloom of the world." It is a beautiful phrase, but it should have been reserved for D. H. Lawrence. Wordsworth was an interpreter of the contemplative *mind*. Wordsworth saturated nature with purely human emotion, he filled the woods with the "still sad music of humanity," he tinted the skies with a divine benevolence not their own. Mr. Lawrence does not taint the air with human preconceptions or "pathetic fallacies." And to reward him for his disinterested adoration of the multitudinous spirit of life, the "thing in itself," it seems as if life had let him penetrate into intimacies unknown even to those who have made most boast of her confidences.

One might illustrate the point by quoting innumerable lovely things from his record of the bright intoxicating passage of the seasons over the English land. But our question here is not primarily a question of beauty, and not at all a question of conventionally recognized beauties. It is a question of life and the adorableness of life. It is a question of life discovered afresh by a sixth sense—life magically rendered, rippling and quivering under the impulse of the *élan vital*. To illustrate Mr. Lawrence's incessant captures of moving life I could ask nothing more conclusive than this:

I met George tramping across the yard with a couple of buckets of swill, and eleven young pigs rushing squealing about his legs, shrieking in an agony of suspense. He poured the stuff into a trough with a luscious gurgle, and instantly ten noses were dipped in, and ten little mouths began to slobber. Though there was plenty of room for ten, yet they shouldered and shoved and struggled to capture a larger space, and many little trotters dabbled and spilled the stuff, and the ten sucking, clapping snouts twitched fiercely and twenty little eyes glared askance, like so many points of wrath. They gave uneasy gasping grunts in their haste. The unhappy eleventh rushed from point to point trying to push in his snout, but for his pains he got rough squeezing and sharp grabs on his ears. Then he lifted up his face and screamed screams of grief and wrath into the evening sky.

If the reader will pause now and thoughtfully consider the *point of view* at which the phrase "with a luscious gurgle" was written he will be close to one secret of Mr. Lawrence's incomparably vital interpretations of nature. He sees nature with a vision more intuitive than was possessed by even those "clear Greek eyes" which Heine envied Goethe for possessing. He looks at nature for nature's sake, acknowledging nothing superior, nothing equal. Nature through the eyes of the old god Pan—fecund, fair and flecked with blood, without sentiment, but passionately urgent. Nature, with humanity standing back, fearful of interruption, holding its breath, not to stir the down, not to hurry the drifting mist, not to mar the pale bloom on blue plums, not to drown the whisper of the grass, not to alarm the thrush molding the mud of her nest with her breast, not to quicken the little heart of the rabbit palpitating under the brown fur, not to lose the faint tinkle of stubble, not to dim the light in the moth's eye.

The second conspicuous interest of Mr. Lawrence's work he believes is intimately and profoundly related to the first. I refer, in general, to the erotic interest and, in particular, to his searching, exhaustive and exhausting exploration of certain phases of sexual attraction and sexual repulsion, and the bearings of these violent and excessive emotions upon human conduct. Where and how he acquired the psychopathic lore which fills the pages of "The Rainbow," "Women in Love," "The Lost Girl," "Aaron's Rod" and "The Captain's Doll" I shall not inquire. It is clear that for a dozen years he has been a "specialist" in that form of violent "love," which, as he says, is to be regarded rather as a "duel" than as a "duet," as a bitter and shattering clash of contending egotisms—"wildcats in a red-hot iron cage."

This tract of Mr. Lawrence's labors is before us. It is just as well to take an intelligent attitude toward it. Whether we wish it or not, Mr. Lawrence's remorseless studies in sex psychology will no more be annihilated by wishing than sex will be annihilated by wishing. These studies are dangerous to the young; sex is dangerous to the young. The men and women in these novels, exclaims Dr. Collins, can be referred to definite abnormal types, easily recognized and named by the psychopathologist. But that supplies no principle for annihilating Mr. Lawrence's novels. Doubtless Dr. Collins has often seen in hospitals or insane asylums men easily recognizable as of the type of Orestes or King Lear or Othello. We don't dispose of Othello by saying "epilepsy," or of King Lear by saying "senile dementia," or of Orestes by murmuring "paranoia." The critical attitude, commendable for young and old, is to recognize Mr. Lawrence's studies of excessive and perverse passion for *what they are*. Classify them, name them, see them clearly, and then these books may be as safe and useful on the shelf as a labeled bottle of carbolic acid.

To adult readers moderately acquainted with European literature, with Tolstoy and Dostoievsky, with Zola and Flaubert and the Goncourts, with Ibsen and Strindberg and with D'Annunzio, there is little that is novel in Mr. Lawrence's representation of the various erotic furies. In "The Triumph of Death," for example, D'Annunzio worked out for readers of a generation ago, the entire course of exactly such passions as rage through "Rainbow" and "Women in Love." D'Annunzio's sophisticated and megalomaniac poet-hero aspires through sexual excess to a state of the "soul" which shall "surpass carnal sensibility and communicate itself to an ultra-sensible element of the inner being." He is an aristocrat, his mistress is of the peasantry, and, through her lower animal nature, he hopes to enter into communication with every form of natural life. In a short time, however, he discovers that the central ingredient of his relation to his mistress is hatred—"the mortal hatred of the sexes which is at the bottom of love." He recites to himself the words of the Preacher: *Non des mulieri potestatem animae tuae*—Give not power over thy soul into the hands of a woman. He begins to frame for himself a "male" ideal of physical force, robust health and savage joy. He struggles to assert himself against the woman, and has a premonition that he will never attain complete "self-realization" except by killing

[27]

her. And the book ends with the appropriate mortal consummation of sex-antagonism: the two of them, locked in a last embrace, roll fighting over a precipice.

Mr. Lawrence's "Women in Love" is, psychologically, identical in most important respects. He introduces this variation of his Alpine scene: Gerald Crich releases the throat of Gudrun, when he has her nearly choked, with this reflection: "As if he cared about her enough to kill her, to have her life on his hands."

The story of violent and egotistical loves faithfully, remorselessly told is always, I am inclined to believe, as "moral" as hell fire or Holy Writ—"Her guests are in the depths of hell." And Mr. Lawrence impresses me as a far more austere "moralist" than D'Annunzio. As I have said elsewhere, my abiding impression from these books of his middle period is a sense of his "studious, remorseless revelation of what a horrible, devouring mania sexual passion may be: how involved with mortal fear, and with cold, probing curiosity, and with murderous hatred. . . . He is coming to the conclusion that—for men, at any rate—passional surrender is not the greatest thing in the world . . . and that the romanticists have all been on the wrong track in representing as the height of human experience that ecstasy in which one individuality is merged and absorbed in another. This is an aspiration toward death and disintegration, from which the inevitable reaction is disgust. The virtue of a man is to preserve his own integrity and to resist the dissolution of union. 'When he makes the sexual consummation the supreme consummation, even in his secret soul,' says Mr. Lawrence in his 'Fantasia of the Unconscious,' 'he falls into the beginnings of despair.'"

"St. Mawr" carries on, from there, Mr. Lawrence's

"criticism of life." It carries on his moving representation of the soul's fiery struggle for independent selfhood, for individuality. In this case, the chief pro-
tagonists are women. From the first Mr. Lawrence
has been a feminist—of a sort. In "The White Peacock," he speaks with profound insight of Lettie's determination to ignore her own self and to empty her
potentialities into the vessel of another:

This peculiar abnegation of self is the resource of
a woman for the escaping of the responsibilities of
her own development. Like a nun, she puts over her
living face a veil, as a sign that the woman no longer
exists for herself: she is the servant of God, of some
man, of her children, or may be of some good cause.
As a servant she is no longer responsible for herself,
which should make her terrified and lonely. . . . To
be responsible for the good progress of one's life is
terrifying.

"St. Mawr" is a shorter novel than Mr. Lawrence is
accustomed to write—only 222 pages, unencumbered
by dissertations or digressions. Its tempo is much
brisker. The narrative moves at a swift canter. The
characters are sharply and brilliantly drawn, *so far
as needful for their function, and only so far*. The
novel is not a contribution to contemporary "realism,"
and should not be so approached. It is a piece of symbolism, which is, however, so well written that, if you
are a child, you are at liberty to read it as if it were
the story of a horse, of a superb golden stallion, who
rears and throws his rider.

But St. Mawr is a symbolical horse as Melville's
Moby Dick is a symbolical whale. It is Mr. Lawrence's
hobbyhorse. Readers of his "Studies in Classic Amer-

ican Literature" will remember that he interpreted
the whale as the subconscious seven-eighths of man's
life, what goes on beneath the twinkling surface of intelligence, "the deepest blood-being of the white race."
The golden stallion has exactly the same significance:
he is the deepest instinctive "blood-consciousness." It
may be noted in passing that the big bay stallion in
"Sons and Lovers," the red Arab mare in "Women in
Love," and the horses which thunder ominously
through two or three pages of "Rainbow" are steeds
of the same stable. See also Plato's horses.

The characters arrange themselves in a scale beginning with the horse, and *descending*, according to their
degrees of "blood-potency," to Flora, who is an ordinary woman of the social world. Next to the horse is his
own groom, Lewis, who is a dark, silent, shaggy mystical Welshman with a sacred beard; he understands
the horse, speaks to him in Welsh and is in perfect
sympathy with him. There is a second groom of mixed
Mexican and Indian blood; he is almost as sympathetic. Then comes the mother, Mrs. Witt, from
Louisiana, inheriting a strain of dark Welsh blood
through her grandmother: having exhausted society,
despising most of the human animals, including her
son-in-law, she admires the horse and shares his spirit.
Next comes Lou, the daughter, an American girl, much
Europeanized, very sophisticated. At twenty-five she
marries an artist, the best thing in sight, handsome,
healthy, with a desire for a fashionable success in London. Lou buys St. Mawr for her husband, hoping that
he will ride the splendid creature with effect. The
husband, Rico, has outgrown horses, doesn't like St.
Mawr, and the golden stallion has ·an instinctive repugnance for him. Ill managed, St. Mawr throws his

rider and breaks several of his bones. The lowest character in Mr. Lawrence's scale is Flora, who after the accident seizes upon Rico for a lover, and proposes to buy, castrate, and tame the horse. The immediate upshot of the affair is that mother and daughter fall in love with the horse and with the grooms and carry them off to America.

A superb creature, St. Mawr, if one knows how to ride him.

If one has but the merest rudiments of symbol-reading, the main meanings of all this and subsequent developments will be clear enough. The story is excitingly told, independently of its meanings. But it is obvious that this symbolical novel is intended to be mordantly satirical, as well. Mr. Lawrence's first theme is the emancipation of the two American women from the perfunctory type of men, and their adventure in quest of an independent selfhood. His second theme, pervading his entire conception of the tale, is his own profound revulsion from polite tea table literature, his sense that the English scene is exhausted, his quest for a newer, younger land in which, as George Moore would say, to "enwomb" a vital art.

The concluding chapter, in a slackened tempo, pictures the last refuge of Lou and her mother: an abandoned, rat-pestered, goat-ruined ranch in the mountains of the American Southwest. I know what Mr. Lawrence means by that, but I believe in leaving something to the imagination of readers. To mine, I recommend reading "St. Mawr," and thinking it over for some time before deciding whether or not it is a deeply suggestive piece of symbolism.

III

Willa Cather and the Changing World

WILLA CATHER has published a new novel, "The Professor's House." If I should say no more than that, I should have said enough to send all discerning readers in search of a copy. Miss Cather is not merely one of those rare writers who have taken a vow never to disappoint us. She is also one of the true classics of our generation. She is not merely entertaining. She is also important. Her work has a vital center, and its contours become steadily more distinct. It will become clear to us presently that she has been expressing these last ten or fifteen years a new sense of values which we are all gradually and often unconsciously beginning to accept. She has been clarifying for us our sense of what we have in common with the generation before 1900, and our sense of the points at which we have departed from the old paths.

Each of her novels has been a desired event, of which one could safely predict nothing but a style with the translucency of sky; a beauty, cool, grave, pervasive; deep feeling under perfect control; and a criticism of life both profound and acute—a criticism which deals as nobly with the simple elements as with the fine complexities of human experience.

"The Professor's House" is a disturbingly beautiful book, full of meanings, full of intentions—I am sure that I have not caught them all. Everything in it has

Willa Cather

its own bright surface meaning. The publisher's announcement suggests that Miss Cather actually intended to describe academic life. She is here addressing herself, we are informed, "to those who do not know or who doubt the American youth, to those who may be interested in the environment which their sons and daughters find in college."

The novel does, to be sure, present Godfrey St. Peter—a man of mixed French and American ancestry —professor of European history in a state university near Lake Michigan; his wife, Lillian—a woman of some elegance and beauty, with whom he seems to have almost nothing to do; the two married daughters and their husbands; the seamstress, Augusta; the professor's favorite pupil, Tom Outland, explorer of cliff-dwellings and inventor, killed in the war, and a colleague or two. The professor has completed his life work, an eight-volume history of the Spanish Adventurers in North America. He has received a big money prize from Oxford. And the family is moving into the new house which he, or perhaps rather his wife, has built with the reward of his labors.

What happens after that point would strike me as inconclusive, slightly incoherent, and without vital thesis, if I did not regard "The Professor's House" as an Ibsenish title—as Ibsenish as "The Doll's House." There is more in this house than meets the eye; but let us consider first what meets the eye.

The professor's former house was a poor old place, lacking many modern improvements, inconvenient, and as ugly as a house could be. It had a tin bathtub which the professor used to renovate with porcelain paint. It had a garret study. The professor wrote his "Spanish Adventurers" in a wretchedly bare little room under the mansard roof, without filing apparatus, and heated by a most dubious old stove. The room was further encumbered by a number of ancient dress forms, and he had to share it at times with Augusta, the sewing woman.

Money comes to the family from the professor's prize and from the marriage of a daughter to a Jewish engineer, who has grown wealthy by exploiting a patent of Tom Outland's. All sorts of comforts and luxuries now are made available—cars, imported Spanish furniture, furs, jewels, wine, country houses, travel. The professor's wife and his children take with alacrity to the new standard of living; they blossom out; the wife renews her youth.

But the professor is a tree of which the trunk has been hollowed by fire. He is nearly burned out. He haunts the old home. He clings whimsically to the fleshless companions of his scholarly solitude—those old dress forms. He finds comfort in chatting with the antique sewing-woman; and she saves his life when he is on the point of asphyxiation from the fumes of the old stove, the fire of which has been extinguished by the wind.

Out of a large acquaintance with professors, I can testify that Professor St. Peter is not an ordinary professor. Ordinary professors do not reluct against exchanging a ramshackle old house for a luxurious new one. Professor St. Peter is rather a spirit than a man. He is a spirit saying good-by to something much larger than the ugly old square domicile in which his life work was accomplished. He is a spirit reluctantly bidding farewell to a generation of American life, to a vanishing order of civilization. I find "The Professor's House" echoing and vibrating with the cumu-

lative meaning of all the books in which Miss Cather
has sought to record the quest of her generation for
true romance, for the real thing, for that which enables
one to forget everything else, for that which uses and
consumes one adequately.

Miss Cather came out of a Western small town by
way of the University of Nebraska some twenty or
twenty-five years ago. From that statement alone one
can infer, with small probability of error, that she had
a good intelligent mother of "Puritan" upbringing;
that her father was something of a pioneer, and that
Miss Cather's early education was of what we call a
New Englandish cast, qualified by a Western environment and contacts with German, Swedish and Bohemian settlers on the prairies.

When the University of Nebraska had done its best
to kindle her curiosity and to open her mind, I infer
that she came East with literature and music in her
heart, and eagerly continued her education in Greenwich Village, in Paris, in London, and in many other
places at home and abroad.

For nearly twenty years I have fondly preserved a
second-hand impression of her before she was a famous
novelist. It was sketched for me by a college friend
of mine, Harry James Smith, who was killed in war
service. Many years ago, as a beginner in letters he
used to give me delightful gossip about the young
people who were in those days sharpening their pens
for literary adventure in New York. In my old memories young Miss Cather is sitting every morning on a
bench in Washington Square, reading Whitman's
"Leaves of Grass." I believe she repudiates this reminiscence as imaginary. But I am sure that she has sat
in Washington Square and that she has read "Leaves

of Grass." So I cling to the reminiscence for its symbolic truth.

Looking back through the seven novels to discover the newcomer from the West, I see a young Nebraskan, hungry from the austerities and rectitudes of a prairie home, reading the "Leaves of Grass" in the morning sunshine on a bench in Washington Square and dreaming of the western pioneers and of Paris, dreaming of a world richer, fuller, freer than our fathers knew, a world enriched by the development of perceptions of beauty which in them were but rudimentary, and enriched by the liberation of powers which they did not value or which they feared and suppressed. With that much by way of biography, one can in some fashion "account" for everything that she has written.

Her first book, "Alexander's Bridge," 1912, is more significantly hers than she admits. It is a short novel presenting a "crucial moment" in the career of Bartley Alexander. He was by the gift of the gods a tremendous natural force, a great man of action. He came out of the West and distinguished himself as a bridge builder. He married a fine woman of talent and fortune and settled firmly into the imposing structure of established society in Boston. But in his dangerous middle age his unexhausted youth fermented within him. He renewed a liaison of his student days with an Irish actress in London. When he returned to inspect his biggest bridge, then building, it collapsed and he was drowned in its ruin.

In 1922, eleven years after the composition of this tale, Miss Cather wrote an apologetic but extremely interesting preface for a new edition. She said that

the "subject matter" had originally attracted her, but
that she now recognized it as not her "own material,"
not the field in which she was master. So far as the
"subject matter" is concerned, I can't follow this explanation; she appears to possess the subject matter
adequately for her purposes. But so far as the treatment is concerned, I see a point in the apologetic
preface. She has tried to treat her theme in accordance with the New England tradition, established by
Hawthorne and more or less perpetuated by Mrs.
Wharton. She has moralized the story as Hawthorne
would have moralized it: the collapse of the bridge is
an obvious symbolical device for emphasizing the "collapse" of that pillar of society, Bartley Alexander.
In its form and outline, the tale looks like a tribute to
that rigorously established order to which Mrs. Wharton used to offer sacrifices.

Now, nowhere else in Miss Cather's work, I think, is
there any such tribute to "established society" as is
implied in the title and in the dominating symbolism
of "Alexander's Bridge." All her deepest sympathies,
as her subsequent novels prove, were with, not against,
Bartley in his revolt against the prison-house of respectability, in which he felt that the primal energies
of his nature were being progressively fettered and
wasted. But in this first book she actually lugs in a
professor of moral philosophy, a Professor Wilson, to
serve as spokesman for the ethical sense of his generation; and he—lightly, yet ominously—speaks of a flaw
in Bartley's nature which he once feared might lead
to disaster. In so far as the book is moralized in this
sense, it is out of line with Miss Cather's practice and
her convictions.

Yet in "Alexander's Bridge" itself, Miss Cather does

strike into her own theme and material, she begins her own characteristic comment on life, in these "mutterings" of Bartley to the professor of moral philosophy:

"After all, life doesn't offer a man much. You work like the devil and think you are getting on, and suddenly you discover that you've only been getting yourself tied up. A million details drink you dry. *Your life keeps going for things you don't want, and all the while you are being built alive into a social structure you don't care a rap about. I sometimes wonder what sort of chap I'd have been if I hadn't been this sort; I want to go out and live out his potentialities, too.*" [My italics.]

To live out one's potentialities: there is the clew to all Miss Cather's sympathies. There is her primary intuition of the "real thing," in harmony with which she has readjusted her entire scale of values. She sympathizes profoundly and intelligently with that aspiration. It is a major distinction of her work and of her literary generation. Her criticism of life, in both its negative and its positive aspects, springs from her sympathy with that aspiration, and from her intelligent repudiation of the repressive philosophy upon which Mrs. Wharton's established polite society, as well as the village society of New England, was based.

From polite society, Miss Cather turned abruptly in 1913 to one large division of her "own material" in "O Pioneers!" with which, for our purpose, we may immediately associate "My Antonia," 1918. In these books, she tells us that she did not "build" her story. The story shaped itself inevitably in a loose, anecdotal, yet intensely vivid and poignant memoir. Here she is dealing not with the domain of convention, but with the domain of necessity. She is presenting the Bo-

hemian, German, Swedish and native American farmers of Nebraska battling with the soil and the elements,
against heavy odds. This is her account of what life
is, and must be, at bottom. This is her picture of
"romance" in its most elementary form.

For pioneers, these books tell us, there is naught but
this: food, shelter, clothing and reproduction of their
species; just not to perish; just to hold one's own on
the hard bedrock of existence. In these conditions,
the primitive struggle suffices to call forth one's best
and one's utmost, and to make one oblivious of everything else—of all the graces and refinements and the
large awareness of the world in which later generations
endeavor to slake the thirsts of the soul.

Miss Cather has taken the pioneers into her brooding heart. She extenuates nothing, but she sets down
naught in malice. She cannot, like so many of our
jolly young novelists, write satirically or even bitterly
of the long, lonely roads that lead to Main Street or
of "the big, lonely country where people worked hard
with their backs and got tired like the horses, and
were too sleepy at night to think of anything to say."
In her, this elementary struggle, whether she contemplates its symbol in the plow standing in the black
furrows against the Nebraska sunset or in the shards
and flints of the vanished cliff-dwellers who left their
mournful vestiges under the turquoise heavens of New
Mexico and Colorado, evokes a mood of luminous
Virgilian sadness. No other American novelist, I
think, has treated this theme with a beauty so grave,
so wistful.

The heroine of "O Pioneers!" demands special mention as one of Miss Cather's important contributions
to contemporary "feminism." *Dux femina facti:* the

chief pioneer is a woman. Alexandra is one of several children on a poor Nebraska farm. On the death of her father she alone of the brood reacts positively and creatively to the new demands of circumstances. Her brothers plod in the old ruts. She strikes out. She has enough vital energy to shape a little the terms of her struggle for survival, to make of it a big thing, an inspiring and rewarding activity. She finds what "romance" life has for her in buying up unvalued and forsaken farms, adding quarter-section to quarter-section, and competing with men in all the details of farm management. In this she is a notable predecessor of Ellen Glasgow's heroine in "Barren Ground."

Alexandra is not inhuman, not emotionally stolid. She feels the normal woman's desires and needs. In the end she takes a husband. But in the end the husband's place in her life is perforce incidental. Before the time comes when he seems to fit in, she herself has already done, fully accomplished, what we used to call "a man's work in the world." Marriage for her is a side enterprise—as it is for a man. It cannot now fill her life to the exclusion of everything else. Her life is already full—all but full. She will live out her personal and domestic potentialities without interrupting the big constructive "romance," which for many years has occupied her mind and her imagination.

From the pioneers, Miss Cather turns to her second major theme in "The Song of the Lark," 1915, and in her collection of short stories, "Youth and the Bright Medusa," 1920. One theme develops, when it develops vitally, out of the other, as the pattern comes out on the waterpots of the cliff-dwellers. Vital romance has its roots in necessity. For Miss Cather there are two great things in the world, the struggle for existence, and the art which expands our measured interval with beauty or high passion till we forget that we must live and must die.

I am astonished to learn that there are still some intelligent persons who have not yet read "The Song of the Lark." It is absurd. "The Song of the Lark" is certainly near the top notch of American fiction. It seems to me one of the truest and profoundest studies of the mind and heart of a great artist ever written anywhere. It is a magnificent piece of imaginative realism. It is also, I believe, Miss Cather's most intimate book—the book which she has most enriched with the poetry and wisdom and the passion of her experience, and made spacious with the height and the depth of her desire.

It is the story of a Swedish pastor's daughter in Colorado, in whom there is gradually discovered a singing voice of the first quality. Gradually the voice is born in her. "Every artist," says her old German singing master, "makes himself born." Gradually she escapes from everything else till she is living to fulfil the possibilities of her talent—for that and for naught else. Then, as one of her lovers says, with a note of pity for himself, "she drifts like a rifle ball" to her object. All her childhood, all her labor, all her love, all her acquaintance with the wide world, her struggles, her frustrations, her triumphs—all are converted into music, into beauty. Everything else is incidental—as it is, as it must be—to every absolutely first rate artist. As for those who play with art, art plays with them. Thea does not play.

Nothing in contemporary fiction has stirred me, I think, quite so profoundly as the deep rich harmonies Miss Cather makes in this story by the interweaving of her life-preservative with her life-expansive themes in those marvelous chapters where she shows Thea musically assimilating, among the ruins of the cliff-dwellers, the history of humanity's struggle for survival.

In all the stories of "Youth and the Bright Medusa" you will find variations on the central theme in "The Song of the Lark." These are poignant tales of painters, sculptors, singers seeking their "real thing," and discarding the interpretations of polite society, the New England village, and Main Street. Their romance is the expansion of the allotted interval. Their motto, like that of the old play, is "all for love." The object of their one unfailing love is their art. Through all the disgrace and squalor of life, that remains clean and holy. The artist who will not give all is no true lover of his art, and his mistress will forsake him.

The war tried in vain to divert Miss Cather from the development of her theme. In "One of Ours," 1922, she did indeed write one of the stories of the World War. As a reward for this work she received the Pulitzer Prize for the novel which "best presents the wholesome atmosphere of American manners and manhood." I am not sure to what extent the judges were moved by the patriotic and military interest of the book. It is a sufficiently good war story. But war is not Miss Cather's "own material."

And, as a curious and ironic matter of fact, Miss Cather is much occupied in "One of Ours" with an implicit satire on "the wholesome atmosphere of American manners and manhood," and with exhibiting the superior literacy, intellectuality, æsthetic interest, friendliness, affability and geniality of German men

and women in the Ehrlich family at the University of
Nebraska. The young hero who goes to fight the
Germans has learned pretty much all that he knows
of the amenities of life from his German friends and
neighbors.

Miss Cather's hero is a Western boy from the farm
whose deepest impulses and aspirations have been frustrated by precisely what I suppose the founder of the
Pulitzer Prize imagined were essential constituents of
"the wholesome atmosphere of American manners and
manhood." They have been frustrated by the hard
frugality and thrift of prosperous American farmers;
by the influence of a narrow denominational religion;
by the average American man's contempt for gracious
manners, art and the things of the mind; by the narrow
mother and the narrower parson piously assuring a
warm-blooded, hungry boy that he will find his happiness "when he finds his Saviour"; by a chaste and
frigid wife who abandons her young husband in order
to nurse a missionary sister in China, etc.

Miss Cather has never been valuable to us as a
flatterer of "the wholesome atmosphere of American
manners and manhood." She has conspicuously served
us by showing just how and where this "wholesome
atmosphere" has corroded and wasted some of the
precious resources of life. She has served us by showing again and again how the "alien" elements in our
population—German, Swedish, Bohemian, Spanish,
Mexican, French—have utilized what "we Anglo-
Saxons" have suppressed and rejected.

Her next novel, "A Lost Lady," is a remarkable
case in point. Like "The Song of the Lark," this is
a story on her great theme of living out one's potentialities. But in this case the potentiality to which the

heroine gives all is not artistic, but personal and spe-
cifically erotic, and to a certain extent illicit. Mrs.
Forrester is a woman who, as we vulgarly put it,
"trades" on her charm, though what she gets in barter
is only adoration. She is animated and consumed by
the passion for giving and receiving pleasure, which
she uses incidentally as a means of refining the manners of those to whom she gives it. Her perfumes, her
rings, her furs, her voice, her eyes, her kindness, the
touch of her fine hand upon one's arm are all bewitch-
ing, penetratively seductive. She cannot bow or give
one a passing glance without establishing a personal
relation of an indescribable sweetness.

Mrs. Forrester is the radiant Venus Anadyomene
united in the holy bonds of matrimony to an honorable,
crippled, corpulent, big-jowled railway man who looks
and acts like Grover Cleveland. She is, in her own
sense, unflinchingly loyal to this fine old wreck. But
that is not enough for her. She is in her sense loyal to
all men. She gives the best of herself to them all, and
so she fascinates all men, and all boys, who come within
reach of her voice and eyes. Personal charm is her one
talent. In all circumstances, worthy and unworthy,
she lives out its potentialities. She uses it as the
musician uses music, to expand the allotted interval;
and, like a public performer of music, she wishes to
please all.

At the first reading of this book I did not lose my
heart to Mrs. Forrester. I happen to have a deeply
seated, perhaps ineradicable, prejudice against persons who desire to please everybody. Mrs. Forrester's
passion for pleasing everybody left her, I thought,
without that trait which is essential to pleasing people
who are at all particular: it left her without discrimi-

nation. It seemed to me to betray her as estrangingly
devoid of taste in personal relations. And when she
submitted quietly to the embrace of the hard-eyed,
carbuncled shyster Ivy Peters, I revolted from her
charm as young Neil revolted.

But Mr. Heywood Broun, winking with the indulgence of the Almighty at Mrs. Forrester's unconcern
about preserving "the wholesome atmosphere of American manners and manhood," assured me in print that
in Mrs. Forrester I should find the genuine "portrait
of a lady," which I had somewhere said was missing
from current fiction. And not Mr. Broun alone, but
all my acquaintances, academic persons, old maids,
hardened old New England bachelors of the austerest
virtue—all unite with Mr. Broun in surrendering to
her charm and admitting—the austere old bachelors—
that if they could have met anywhere in their generation a lady like Mrs. Forrester—well, their lives might
have been very different.

On a third reading I see how "A Lost Lady" fits
in with the main thesis of Miss Cather's work. Mrs.
Forrester is a symbolic figure. Her story is Miss
Cather's poem of personality and its values—its
powers, its too-little regarded powers. In her calling
she is as admirable as Thea is admirable in hers. She
used the rare talent intrusted to her. She gave all for
love. She consumed herself adequately in making personal relations charming. She illustrates, and her innumerable adorers illustrate, the coming around of our
generation to Browning's position in the much quoted
poem:

The sin I impute to each frustrate ghost
Is—the unlit lamp and the ungirt loin.

And now I think we are in a position to see a little more deeply into Miss Cather's extraordinary Professor and his extraordinary House. The Professor—he is the intellectual spirit of our American "Victorian Era." The old house, which he cannot persuade himself to leave—that is what our famous Young People call Professorial America. His wife and daughters and sons-in-law—they are the celebrated Younger Generation, building themselves new homes, enriched with all sorts of new devices which the professor values little. His mind and imagination have been occupied, splendidly occupied, in a long historical retrospect; his dream has always drifted backward to former glories, Spanish adventurers, Cliff-Dwellers, the storied past, which rises like a western mesa abruptly out of the flat present, affording his essentially romantic spirit a refuge and a retreat. And now the word is forward. Young people may go forward, seeking a new romance amid the realities of the modern world and all its dizzying change. But he has consumed himself. His fire is out. He is a superannuated figure in his times. He clings to the old dress forms. He chats with Augusta.

IV

Floyd Dell on the Coast of Bohemia

THE publication of a new novel* by Mr. Floyd Dell has for the second time within a week set me to reflecting ironically on this thought: "What a crew of political subversives our literary radicals are becoming!"

Suppose you are an impressionable young person, and suppose the current drastic criticism of American civilization has convinced you that our "bourgeois" society is uninteresting and unlovely—humdrum, hidebound, and tedious to the yawning point. You turn to writers who are busy making ideals for the younger generation. You turn to two of our novelists who, like their master, Mr. H. G. Wells, regard the novel as a branch of social dynamics, and what guiding beam is thrown on your pathway?

Mr. Sinclair Lewis, who was once thought to be tainted with Socialism, and who certainly has a rare talent for presenting human beings as members of organized society—Mr. Lewis has at last given us in "Arrowsmith" a novel which presents a clear-cut ideal and suggests a way out of the vulgar stress of a competitive money-making society. But what a way out! —to renounce the world for the quest of pure truth in the laboratory—a way prescribable only to solitary remorselessly energetic individuals dedicated to the

* *This Mad Ideal*, New York, 1925.

[49]

pursuit of science, capable of severing all social bonds in order to voyage through strange seas of thought alone.

Mr. Floyd Dell has also, in one way and another, acquired what young unacademic authors rather enjoy, a reputation for being dangerous to existing institutions. He has been in court under the espionage act, together with his editorial colleague, that passionate immitigable individualist, Mr. Max Eastman. He has had a book—"Janet March"—suppressed or withdrawn. He has written an admirable panegyric on John Greenleaf Whittier and other conscientious objectors. He has talked blithely of The Revolution, and has, for picturesque purposes, painted his eagerness to assist at the building of a barricade. In the spring of life a young man's talking lightly turns to social Utopias.

But talking is a privilege guaranteed by the Constitution—though it is not always upheld by the police. As Disraeli pointed out, it is "imagination," not talking, that "governs mankind." And Mr. Dell's imagination is thoroughly unsocialistic. He may, to be sure, join the Socialist party, because, being out of power, it is free from responsibility and rich in promises and because it contains a number of intellectual Jews who relish, as few "Anglo-Saxons" do, the excitement of talk, the intoxication of ideas, the exhilaration of protest. He may for an evening unite with them in discussing the redistribution of political and economic power. But the "inner form" of Mr. Dell's imagination is individualistic and anarchical. Everything in him that is deep and instinctive loathes the impositions of power, loathes regulated work, loathes regimentation, loathes forced co-operation and equaliza-

Floyd Dell

tion, loathes obligation. Mr. Dell loves freedom and spontaneity just as heartily as Mr. J. P. Morgan does.

In the twentieth century, all literary men of any sense, like all sensible kings and presidents, wish to show themselves friendly to the poor and the inarticulate. But Mr. Dell is a poet, and no real poet, so far as I have heard, was ever a real Socialist. He is not merely a poet! He has been hitherto almost exclusively a poet of the coast of Bohemia—simple, sensuous and passionate. He knows nothing except what he has intimately experienced. His imagination does not penetrate into the reality of the economic, social, and political structure of a state. He is a play-boy like John Synge's hero, so deeply enveloped in his personal dream of felicity that he scarcely notices his collisions with a sordid reality.

He was born in the land of suppressed desires, the romantic dreamland of west-central Illinois, in the little town of Barry, in 1887. Illinois suppressed his desires by forcing him to attend high school and study algebra for a while in a Mississippi River town; but he escaped out of that into the Agnostic Society and into the library, where he made his own education by reading Ingersoll and Shelley, Spencer and Omar, anthropology and Ernest Dowson, Ecclesiastes and Swinburne, Verlaine and "The Shropshire Lad," and dreaming of the Venus of Melos and the Discus-Thrower. Economic need suppressed his desires by forcing him to work in factories, then as a newspaper reporter in Davenport, Iowa, and subsequently as a literary editor for some years in Chicago, and finally in New York, on "The Liberator" and "The Masses."

But in his high-school days he had entered an avenue

of escape from bourgeois realities by thinking freely and writing verse. In 1913, he expressed his dream of a new feminine ideal in "Women as World Builders." In 1918, he published his dream of educational reconstruction entitled "Were You Ever a Child?" which sets forth the "new" educational notion of utilizing instead of killing off by the educational processes the child's personal and creative impulses. As in Chicago, so in New York, he escaped from journalism to the coast of Bohemia; he haunted artistic settlements; he was a pioneer of the modern migration to Greenwich Village; he frequented little theaters; he wrote much verse and several one-act plays; he published in 1924 a very readable collection of critical essays called "Looking at Life," which interprets current books and ideas from the point of view of a poet and an intellectual radical.

Mr. Dell's novels are four: "Moon-Calf," 1920; "The Briary Bush," 1921; "Janet March," 1923, and "This Mad Ideal," 1925. By a comparison of these books with the essays and the available biographical record, I have convinced myself that the first two of them, at least, are hardly to be regarded as fiction, are rather to be considered as confessions, like those of Jean Jacques. They constitute one continuous narrative of the adventures of Felix Fay from childhood through his first marital difficulties and adjustments, and they resemble the "Confessions" of Rousseau in many important respects.

They are poetic, in the sense that poetry is "impassioned recollection." They have the form and movement of autobiographical revery in a sensitive mind which feels a rhythm in its experience, sees pictures in its own life history and savors and idealizes its past. There is nothing here of the sociologist's notebook, nor of the overworked optic nerve of the photographer-realist. Memory has discarded everything that is not memorable, quick, delicious, pungent, or enchanting to the revisiting mind. There are reminiscences of childhood raptures here as exquisite as that passage in Rousseau in which he remembers how he and his father read romances together till they were reminded that it was morning by the swallows twittering under the eaves. Take, for example, this recovery of the child's delight in learning to read—not forgetting that Mr. Dell's impulse to revise educational method derives from this source:

He had been looking at his favorite picture in the Yellow Fairy Book. He had said to his mother so often: "Mamma, read me that part," that he knew the passage beside it almost by heart. He put his finger on the printed words, one after another, and spoke them aloud: "The—Prince—took—her—hand" —— He stopped, with the realization that he had been reading. It was so wonderful that the thought of it made him feel faint. He went back again with his finger, saying them hesitatingly. With a kind of fearful awe he proceeded down the page.

Yes, it was true—he could read. And suddenly he began to cry out in piercing tones, "Mamma! Mamma!"

She came running, her arms white with flour from breadmaking.

"I can read! I can read!" he cried.

After young Felix has learned to wander on short excursions into "the realms of gold" he has a curious fantasy one day in school while dreaming over how many yards of calico you can buy for $1.38 at 11½ cents a yard. He dreams that he is a fairy prince carrying a magic book containing answers to all secrets into "*a little house in the woods that nobody knew anything about.*"

That is good child psychology: to build a "secret house" seems to be an instinctive act with children as with birds. For days and weeks together, when the fit comes upon them, they will live in a fever of mystery and excitement about their hidden retreat. And a conservative may interpret this fever as a token of the profound naturalness of the passion for 'property.'

At the age of twelve Felix, who has passed through his doll period, enters his secret-house period, and finds in the garret, with a trapdoor, a secure hiding-place where he may read and dream. Presently Rose, the gardener's daughter, joins him there. He reads to her from Rousseau's "Confessions." They talk, they dance, they dream there. Sometimes they walk in the woods and recite poetry to each other. One night they slip out to the woods with bread and meat and build a fire and eat their supper, and lie watching the friendly stars for hours. They are too happy to sleep. "Nevertheless, at last they slept, and awakened chill and stiff, a little before dawn. They laughed cheerfully, each rather secretly frightened at their daring." Then they went home. It was all quite innocent—and childlike!

Was it really? Childlike, yes, very likely. But what is "innocence" at the ages of twelve and fifteen? —when the girl gives queer little kisses on the mouth, which begin fiercely and end abruptly with a laugh, and when the boy has already read Jean Jacques and

relishes the "frank sensuality" of "Venus and Adonis."
Let us for the present leave the question unanswered.
As Mr. Dell presents the incident, it is what is known
as an idyllic incident.

I have recited it in some detail because it is a kind
of prototypical symbol for Mr. Dell's entire vision
of the happy life. It recurs, in one form or another,
in each of his four novels. The end of every man's
desire, as he sees it, is to be one of two children playing
in a secret garret. In "The Briary Bush" the fairy
prince and princess find some equivalent for the garret
in the artist studios of Chicago, and then there is
the actual cottage in the woods where Rose-Ann on her
bridal morn bathes in a bank of snow. In "Janet
March" the substitute for the shepherd's cottage is
again a studio in Greenwich Village. In "This Mad
Ideal" there is a little "shack" on the hillside that "nobody knows anything about," where passionate friends
talk, read poetry and exchange kisses—innocent and
childlike.

> But the chief marvel of the wilderness
> Is a lonely dwelling, built by whom or how
> None of the rustic island-people know.
> .   .   .   .   .   .   ,
> This isle and house are mine, and I have vowed
> Thee to be lady of the solitude.

Everything that Mr. Dell has to tell us about the
summum bonum is in Shelley's "Epipsychidion." So
far as I can make out, none of his heroes or heroines
conceives of any object higher or more complex or extensive than a *solitude à deux* with most simple cooking
and sleeping apparatus—"all the romantic incon-

[57]

veniences"—in which two delicately attuned comrades of opposite sexes shall sit them down and, first having told the stories of their lives, i. e., their previous love affairs, shall recite poetry to one another; talk a little about art; perhaps write a poem or two and a one-act play about what happened to the children after the Pied Piper led them into the hill, and then, certainly, exchange many, many kisses of happy and irresponsible comradeship.

Money-making is not a serious consideration to any of these Babes in the Wood; though they are all pretty consistent atheists, they still cling to the thought that "the Lord will provide" something from the delicatessen shop in the next block. Artistic "creation" is not a consuming passion to them, but rather a recreation after many, many kisses begin to pall. Marriage is an incident, avoidable or unavoidable—to be considered as, at the best, an expedient and a convenience. Children are incidents, not ultimate objects, and they are to be accepted only when desired. For them the consummation and the fragrant flower of life is just the simple personal relationship of two people who, in the consciousness that they are, for the moment, sufficient one for the other, have run a finger of fire around themselves and their "secret garden" and shut the universe out.

Let us have a description of the quality of this ideal relationship from an "anonymous author" quoted in "Janet March":

I seek happy companionship in which what is vulgarly called passion shall have a dancing quality, long since banished from the definition of that word; let me say, rather, I seek playful and joyous friendships

in which no intimacy is withheld; relationships based
upon a mood which is best set forth in the old mythol-
ogies—the serene indifference of gods and goddesses
and the careless ecstasy of fauns and nymphs; generous comradeships of the moment; inconsiderate of
the dull responsibilities of workaday life, existing for
their own sake, without foolish, elaborate pretenses
and without tremendous consequences, free equally of
the burden of hope and fear.

Through "Moon-Calf" and "The Briary Bush,"
Felix Fay seeks the nymph, the dream-girl. Through
"Janet March" and "This Mad Ideal" Janet and then
Judith seek the faun, the dream-boy. Thus both
the masculine and the feminine sides of the relationship
should receive equal illumination. I gravely doubt
whether they do.

"Janet March" strikes me as a very able attempt
to make a girl out of Felix Fay. She is as like Felix
Fay as two peas, except that her adventures begin in
a modern and comfortable and liberal home, and except
that she appears to have very little artistic talent. She
has no clear purpose other than to be "free," and to
be herself. Mr. Dell, however, does confer upon her
some physiological experiences which are sexually distinctive. And he places her in the various situations
which a contemporary young woman may enter if she
sets out in search of a career and self-realization with
Mr. Dell's ideals in her head. Some aspects of her
rather formless yearnings and some important phases
of her predicaments he discusses with a kind of intimate
sympathy and understanding which are still excessively
rare. "Janet March" seems to me, on the whole, an
informative and valuable history of feminine adventures on the coast of Bohemia.

In "This Mad Ideal," however, I find no advance in the development of the theme, and a marked falling off in the artistic resources. Judith is merely an excessively attenuated sketch of Felix Fay. Her rebellion and the first steps in her adventure are presented with a sophomoric thinness, and with only an occasional glimpse of the "tendrils of imagination" reaching into empty space.

If Mr. Dell is to hold our attention as historian of experiments on the Bohemian coast, it is clear that he should not waste another book in proving to us merely that girls and boys have a pathetic hunger for happiness; that they rebel against a conventional society which objects to their entering where they conceive happiness to be, and that, consequently, they go seeking in Bohemia for "companionships at once light and gracious, irresponsible and sincere, generous and self-respecting."

We know all that well enough. He has communicated to us the shape of his ideal, and we acknowledge that it has a certain attraction on paper. But in order to develop his theme he must proceed to a far more realistic account than he has yet given us of the collision of his dream with reality. In his first three novels there were a good many interesting conclusions presented or implied: for example, the Moon-Calf discovered to his own complete satisfaction that he was merely a silly ass to go looking for *his* kind of intoxication in alcohol, or for *his* species of dream-girls among factory hands and shopgirls and casual neurotic schoolgirls hunting boys by the pheasant cage in the park, and drunken girls in roadhouses, and prostitutes, and hectic maudlin girls in the piggery of drunken Bohemian parties. One by one, the dreaming idealist in "Moon-Calf" eliminated all these impossible partners of a "delicate comradeship," light and gracious, generous and self-respecting. The Moon-Calf began to discover that he had put one or two things into his ideal which could not exist together —that, for example, an ideal comradeship could not in this world be at the same time "irresponsible" and "generous." He was on the brink of *discovering* marriage as Mr. G. K. Chesterton discovered Christianity, as a thing designed to meet his special need.

Mr. Dell's weakness as a writer of fiction and also as a feminist seems at the present moment due to a kind of indolence or apathy or lack of courage in the use of the realistic imagination. I regretfully recognize that he has encountered some dissuasive lions in the way of becoming a thoroughly honest historian of Bohemia. Perhaps being constrained to withdraw the hard truth of "Janet March" has influenced his decline into the soft mush of "This Mad Ideal."

As his readers and his censors gradually accustom themselves to the hard edges of fact, it is to be hoped that they will allow him to broaden the moral basis of his fiction by an adequate disclosure of the relation of his dream world to its environment. I am not sure that Mr. Dell really desired to tell us any more than he did about, for example, the physiology and psychology of the two adolescents sleeping together in the woods; about the psychology of the girls who resort to "criminal operations"; about the future of the two adventurous girls who get drunk in a roadhouse—one of them on the eve of her marriage—or about the psychology of the girl who drowns herself. Perhaps a more realistic development at a number of points where one feels that Mr. Dell simply "isn't there"

[61]

would mar the "light and gracious" air which should surround these delicate, irresponsible comradeships. But so far as the interests of actual Babes in the Wood are concerned—those Babes in whose interest censorship is supposed to be instituted—clearly the danger to be apprehended is not from reality but from the illusion of intoxicating dreams.

V

Ben Hecht and the Supermen

NO ADULT who interests himself in the shapes which the mind of our time is taking can afford to pass by Ben Hecht and his works. They are not appropriate reading for children or unsettled old maids.

To speak briefly of the man: Born in New York City in 1893, son of Joseph Hecht and Sarah Swernofsky Hecht, he was educated in the High School of Racine, Wis., and at the age of seventeen began to be a journalist in Chicago. He has read voraciously in the literature of the nineteenth century. In 1921 he published "Erik Dorn," the most arresting novel of the year by reason of its style and the psychological characteristics of his hero. In the following year he produced "A Thousand and One Afternoons in Chicago," a collection of brilliant sketches contributed to "The Chicago Daily News"; and "Gargoyles," a somewhat Dreiserian piece of fiction dealing in mordant style with the hypocrisies of newspapers, politicians, courts and vice commissions. In the next two years he poured out short stories, a comedy, a detective story, "The Florentine Dagger"; edited and wrote with Mr. Maxwell Bodenheim "The Chicago Literary Times," an explosive pink and green journal of ill-smelling petards; and, in addition to all this by-play, he has produced "Fantazius Mallare," an extraordinarily shocking fantasy, illustrated with rare distinction and sympathy by Wallace Smith, and "withdrawn," Mr. Harry Hansen tells us, "at the request of the Federal government"; the sequel, "The Kingdom of Evil," and "Humpty Dumpty." Succinctly interpreting the facts before us, one may say that here is a high-strung, excitable mind which has got its shape under the pressures of journalism and contemporary civilization and literature in Chicago.

What is the shape of this mind? Mr. Hecht's friends are acquainted with an eager, friendly young "genius," who fascinates and astonishes them. Mr. Henry Justin Smith, of "The Daily News," tells us in his preface to "A Thousand and One Afternoons in Chicago," that there are several genial aspects "which appear rarely, if at all, in his novels; the whimsical Hecht, sailing jocosely on the surface of life; the witty Hecht, flinging out novel word-combinations, slang and snappy endings; Hecht the child-lover and animal-lover, with a special tenderness for dogs; Hecht the sympathetic, betraying his pity for the aged, the forgotten, the forlorn." Mr. Harry Hansen, almost unique among the Chicago "school" in writing always like a man who has at some period of his life tasted the milk of human kindness—Mr. Harry Hansen in his remarkably sympathetic and illuminating study of personalities in the Chicago group, "Midwest Portraits," speaks with enthusiasm of Mr. Hecht's ability as a reporter, his imaginative energy, his "faculty for making a drab world seem gorgeous and full of color," his "infatuation with the primal energies of the American people, and with the material results and symbols of that energy—buildings, streets, houses, fire-escapes, chimneys, bridges, railroad trains." Mr. Hansen corroborates also my intuition that Mr. Hecht is to a notable extent a "product" of his environment by this statement from his author's lips: "I consider myself thoroughly American; my ideas are the result of living in Chicago alone."

But all this is pretty superficial. There are plenty of bright reporters and verbal artists in the world who like big buildings and little children and are kind to dogs and old people. Mr. Hecht interests us because his is a definite type of mind. Mr. Hansen gives us Mr. Hecht's own description of his type, written immediately after the suppression of "Fantazius Mallare," as follows:

Born perversely. Out of this perversity, a sentimental hatred of weakness in others, an energetic amusement for the gods, taboos, vindictiveness and cowardice of my friends, neighbors and relatives; a contempt for the ideas of man, an infatuation with the energies of man, a love for the abstraction of form, a loathing for the protective slave philosophies of the people, government, etc., a determination not to become a part of the mind which the swine worship in their sty. A delirious relief in finding words that express any or all of my perversities. Out of this natal perversity I have written "Erik Dorn," "Gargoyles," "Mallare," some of my "1001 Afternoons," three dozen stories. I have only one ambition: to get away from the future caresses of my friends, from the intimidated malice of their praise, from the grunts of my enemies, and live in a country whose language is foreign to me, whose people are indifferent and where skies are deeper.

I don't undertake to go beyond this in saying to what extent Mr. Hecht's principal books are autobiographical—to a very great extent, I surmise. In dramatic imagination, the imagination which penetrates and lives within other types of personality than one's own, Mr. Hecht is as deficient as Byron. Hitherto he comprehends and sympathizes thoroughly with only one type of mind, and that is the type described by him in the preceding paragraph as his own. The shape of this mind, as I conceive it, is due primarily to three pressures, of which I will describe the operation in a little more detail.

From the age of seventeen to thirty Mr. Hecht has, so to speak, sat at the center of Chicago journalism, a city in which, one would like to hope, journalism is more exclusively concerned with accidents, frauds, and crimes than in any other city in the world. He has sat there for thirteen years, a high-strung, excitable receiving organism, while day after day for 4,745 days there have streamed in upon him from all over the city reports of all the fires and boiler explosions and automobile collisions; all the installment company sharks, and oil promotion companies, and bank defalcations, and City Hall intrigues; and all the raping and lynching and love-nesting and bootlegging and highway robbery committed in one of the great paradises of stick-up men. After excessive subjection to this sort of stimuli one becomes quite incapable of the normal human reaction to it; one ceases to individualize and discriminate; one develops a kind of self-protective callousness and reacts to the moving atrocities as merely good stories or poor stories, "old stuff" or "sob stuff." If in addition to being a journalist one is also a poet, one generalizes all the accidents into one colossal accident, all the frauds into one colossal fraud, all the crimes into one colossal crime;

and one sets these gigantic shapes in motion in a kind
of vast "blurred procession," upon which, pretending
that it is humanity, one looks down with colossal
contempt.

From the age of seventeen to thirty Mr. Hecht has
been gulping modern literature voraciously, with a
sure instinct leading him to the authors who dispense
the strongest vodka. He is himself described as a cool,
sarcastic intelligence; but clearly he loves to stimulate
that cool, sarcastic intelligence by cultivating the society of minds acquainted with strange dreams, de-
lirium, anarchy, nihilism. Mr. Hansen gives an
excellent account of his reading and his successive
literary infatuations. When he first met Mr. Hecht
he was reading Burton's "Arabian Nights," the next
day it was Gautier—in translation, then Dostoievsky,
Huysmans, Anatole France, Arthur Symons, George
Moore, Baudelaire, Poe, Whitman, Andreyev, H. L.
Mencken, Arthur Machen, etc. In his latest novel,
"Humpty Dumpty," there are two or three pages in
which the hero, sorting his library onto the shelves,
gives a summary comment upon modern authors, indicating how swiftly Mr. Hecht runs beyond his old
masters. For example: Nietzsche is now "like an old
Spanish cannon." Pater is "a good teething ring for
embryonic stylists." "Mencken will last as long as
the bookcase at least. He's a noisy guest." D. H.
Lawrence's work is "an amateur blue print of sexual
impulses poorly remembered." "Three psychoanalysis
books are enough for any library. To hell with Sig-
mund. I begin to dislike him anyway. He's corrupted
immorality." "We'll spotlight 'Ulysses' in the center
here. The first herculean effort to disorganize the

[67]

Wells, Walpole, Galsworthy, Hall Caine school of hammock fictioneers."

There appears to be nothing in Mr. Hecht which re-acts to the "dissolving" tendency of his reading with a fresh impulse of organization. Everything in him welcomes dissolution and seconds it. Consequently his reading supplements the effect of his journalistic occu-pation; it intensifies in him his sense that he is a spec-tator of a vast meaningless pageant. He does not find in literature any sobering body of classical experience or any human conclusions, because he does not seek them. He seeks only secrets of stylistic expressiveness, stimulus for his fantasy and assistance in getting his mind beyond good and evil. As soon as he has read an author he tosses him aside like the skin of a sucked orange, like a bottle from which the intoxicant has been drained. James Joyce he reverences still as a master of the moment, merely because James Joyce has pushed on beyond him and beyond almost all other writers of the hour in expressing intellectual chaos.

Finally, in enumerating the pressures which have shaped Mr. Hecht we must remember that from the age of seventeen to thirty he has lived in a city which, though it says nothing to the heart, though it impresses almost every casual visitor as devoid of charm for the finer sensibilities, though its showy pretense of concern for the arts is still vain with the ostentation of mer-chant princes and the pathetic fumblings of amateurs, yet somehow conveys to almost every visitor a stunning sense of enormous brutal, unscrupulous power in its gigantic arms and legs and in the huge, heavy pulsing of animal life through its turgid arteries. Chicago, to the imagination which broods on cities, is a soulless Titan, impressing no civilized being by what she has done; awaking only a dim wonder what she might do if she possessed a mind and a heart. In such a city an impressionable young journalist can easily live for thirteen years and still believe that a Titan is a far more august being than a civilized man. Chicago has imposed her amorphous titanism upon Mr. Hecht; when he tries to think of God he conceives of some amorphous lustful energy about as tall as the Chicago Tribune Building.

In "Fantazius Mallare" and "The Kingdom of Evil," Mr. Hecht paints the logical conclusion of tendencies which he has remorselessly observed in his own mind; he projects upon the screen of his imagination his own type of mind swollen to gigantic proportions by the disease incipient in it; he paints the elephantiasis of evil. Beneath the grandiose phrases and images of an occasionally impressive symbolism, one can trace readily enough the excitable, imaginative journalist, in whom excessive journalism and undigested modern literature have produced an atrophy of the normal emotional faculties, aspiring toward a super-humanity through the repudiation of all normal human sentiments and the untrammeled expansion of curiosity and libidinous desire. Mr. Hecht himself appears to have little sense of the necessity of the laws and conventions which more or less govern human society. The ordinary mortal, tolerably comfortable, moderately law-abiding, appears to his inflamed imagination, haunted by Crucifixion imagery, as a pitiable, contemptible, horribly agonizing wretch, self-nailed on a cross and writhing under a self-imposed crown of thorns. Fantazius Mallare, by selling his soul to the devil, and entering the kingdom of evil, aspires to become a free spirit; and in theory should transcend human limitations and enjoy a god-like expansion of experience. But Mr. Hecht is, I believe, an honest explorer and reporter of this realm of consciousness. As a matter of fact, his Fantazius attains no godlike experience. He attains no freedom. He becomes the beaten and bleeding slave of an amorphous demoniacal deity, which he recognizes as the horrible enlargement of his own lusts. He has left man in his "maggotism," to find the superman only a magnified maggot.

"Humpty Dumpty" is not a fantasy, but a striking psychological novel. It is "Erik Dorn" done over again, and better done. That means, essentially, that Mr. Hecht, with greater mastery of expression, with sharper psychological scrutiny, and with unabated passion for telling the truth, has given us once more a brilliant picture of his own type of mind and of his mind's adventures with other minds, messed up in bodies which interest him only so long as they excite his mind. The hero of this book, Kent Savaron, is a novelist who has read what Mr. Hecht has read and has reacted to his reading as Mr. Hecht has reacted. He conceives himself to be a superior emancipated intellect, belonging to a little group outside their age, who look upon the procession of humanity as a foolish pageant which concerns them only for amusement and derision. Ordinary mortals he regards with ineffable contempt as swine in sties. When he has to deal with them, he loathes them to the point of murderous hatred; he wants to kill them, thinking that is all they are fit for. Whether by love or hate, he is uncertain, he is attracted to Stella. He marries her as a step in an egotistical debate with himself, and partly for the savage pleasure that he feels in cutting

her out of her bourgeois family. Gradually he makes
her over in his own image, till she becomes also a hard
egotistical lust for experience with no end beyond
itself. The men she mingles with, like the women he
mingles with, lose all individuality; become bits of
the mob flesh tossed into the caldron of a libidinous
egotism. Savaron accurately concludes that he has
suffered from "a sort of insanity which concealed itself
in an intellectual honesty toward life." For him, the
end is suicide. It is a very terrible book, brilliantly
written, enriched with poetic vision and original wit,
and psychologically, I believe, perfectly sound.

There are two interesting ways of testing the sound-
ness of Mr. Hecht's horrible psychological realism.
One way is relatively comfortable, and it may even
conduce to smugness. It is to take the report of
"The Amazing Crime and Trial of Leopold and
Loeb,"* and to study the traits of the two brilliant,
well-to-do young college men, who thought they were
supermen and beyond good and evil, particularly Leopold, who was an expert ornithologist and knew half a
dozen difficult languages and was graduated from college with Phi Beta Kappa rank. Study the traits of
these two young supermen who had lost the faculty
of appropriate emotional reaction to experience, who
looked at the human pageant, including their own
trial, as detached intellectual spectators, and who killed
a fourteen-year-old boy "for fun"; and you will find
there, recorded by alienists and psychiatrists, every
prominent feature of the type of mind described by
Mr. Hecht in "Erik Dorn" and "Humpty Dumpty."
The other way of testing Mr. Hecht's psychological
veracity is more painful. It is this: Whenever he tells

* Chicago, 1924.

[71]

you something incredibly atrocious about the mind of
Kent Savaron, remove the rosy glasses with which you
habitually perform your own introspections, and looking with straight, uncolored eye beams into the deeper
recesses of your own "inner consciousness," ask yourself flatly whether you don't find the outlines of that
atrocity there—and tell no man what you find.

VI

Ellen Glasgow: The Fighting Edge of Romance

THE fighting edge of romance is always reality. It is the cut and thrust of an active will amid the material circumstances of present life. Ellen Glasgow is bent on romance with blood in it; therefore she uses the fighting edge. Northern critics haven't known quite how to take her. She disappoints their settled expectations. What they expect of Southern writers is a rapt contemplation of the embossed and beribboned antique sword hilt of romance. She gives them the edge.

By all means read "Barren Ground," if you are interested in American fiction, if you are interested in American life, if you wish the latest development of a great thesis, if you wish ripe comment on the common lot by one of the most intelligent and richly endowed novelists of our time in America.

With "Barren Ground," say the publishers, realism at the last crosses the Potomac. The South, so familiarly pictured in fiction as a land of colonels, old mansions and delicate romances, is here shown to be a hardy country peopled by farmers who live lives as real as any in our great cities or on our wide Western prairies.

Right! There is nothing essentially unreal about the farmer's life anywhere.

Obviously what the writer of that paragraph wishes to have us believe is that Ellen Glasgow is in the strictly contemporaneous larger movement of American fiction. Not the little whirl and eddy of merely fashionable writers who prove their superiority and their "sophistication" by being sick of everything, but that movement which records with stark honesty the adventures of upgirt, courageous young Americans of the middling sort, wrestling with the dark angel of their destiny and murmuring between clenched teeth: "I will not let thee go till thou bless me."

Right again. "Barren Ground" is an expression of the realest thing in American life. It is an expression of the indomitable fighting spirit, the will to live, the desire to be free, the passion for progress and mastery, the determination to bite through to some faint sweetness in the fruit of life, though the fruit be only an osage orange. This is a cluster of fighting virtues which every one fit to speak of the sturdier American stock knows are in hot, eager tumult beneath the cynical and insouciant manners of the hour.

Symbols. In 1920, a writer who immensely accelerated this realistic movement began a well known novel with these words: "On a hill by the Mississippi where Chippewas camped two generations ago, a girl stood in relief against the cornflower blue of Northern sky. . . . She lifted her arms, she leaned back against the wind, her skirt dipped and flared, a lock blew wild. A girl on a hilltop; credulous, plastic, young; drinking the air as she longed to drink life. The eternal aching comedy of expectant youth."

Ellen Glasgow begins "Barren Ground" at almost the same point and on almost the same note. She begins thus: "A girl in an orange-colored shawl stood at the window of Pedlar's store and looked through the falling snow, at the deserted road. Though she watched there without moving, her attitude in its stillness gave an impression of arrested flight, as if she were running toward life."

When I read that paragraph I said: "A cordial and gallant gesture! Ellen Glasgow in Richmond, Virginia, waves a handkerchief to Sinclair Lewis in Sauk Center, Minnesota. These girls, Mr. Lewis's Carol and Miss Glasgow's Dorinda, will not be Northern and Southern much longer. Regret it if you must, they are coming together in a common spirit. They are types of that sincerity and fearlessness which Ellen Glasgow declares mark the American democratic ideal, as grace and radiance marked the ideal of the old Virginian aristocracy."

For the moment, I am conniving at the benignant purpose of the publicity writer who tells us that with "Barren Ground" realism "at the last" crosses the Potomac. Waiving the question, for the moment, whether realism, at this crossing, is going south or going north, I heartily applaud the recognition of Miss Glasgow as a significant leader of contemporary realism. It is absurd to think of her as essentially a writer for the South, wholesomely irritant as she doubtless is to Southern slackness and ancestor-worship. It is high time that novel readers from Maine to California should become aware that she treats provincial life from a national point of view; that is, without sentimentality, without sectional prejudice or softness, with sympathy, understanding, passion and poetic insight, yet critically and with a surgical use of satire—in the spirit of the hour.

But with what a deeply reminiscent smile Miss Glasgow must view the statement that in 1925 realism crossed the Potomac. With what amusement she must regard my apparent derivation of her Dorinda's tune from the tune of Mr. Lewis's Carol. Miss Glasgow is only a young woman of fifty. She has the keenest interest in young people who are "running toward life." But so far as her main literary ideas are concerned, I suppose she has not been influenced by Mr. Lewis much more than General Robert E. Lee was influenced by General Pershing. She was a realist when some of our popular exponents of realism were in the cradle. She preceded into the field Mrs. Wharton, who is twelve years older, and Mr. Dreiser, who is three years older. Her first novel, "The Descendant," was published in 1897, and there have been fifteen since. Her democratic fighting realism is already incarnate in the little red-haired hero of "The Voice of the People," 1900. Realism crossed the Potomac twenty-five years ago, going north!

Presently I hope we shall have a collected edition of Miss Glasgow's work, not monumental, for filling proud, idle, decorative bookshelves, but an edition supple and gracious to the hand, for reading—something in the style, perhaps, of those affable blue leather volumes in which her publishers used to give us Joseph Conrad. For this edition I would humbly petition the author to attempt a revision looking toward a twenty per cent reduction in bulk, out of a tender regard for the brevity of man's life and the artistic satisfaction of going through some passages of it swiftly—indicating rather than exhausting their interest. But, revised or unrevised, I should welcome such an edition, and whenever any Anglomaniac challenged me to name one living American novelist to compare with any one of the first twenty in his English list I should point to this edition and ask him if he had read Ellen Glasgow.

Publishers, booksellers, and readers race along from season to season after the book of the week—so do reviewers. A contemporary novelist soon becomes inaccessible in his entirety. Whether his earlier books are on the way to oblivion or whether he is in purgatory on the way to becoming a standard author and a classic, one can only determine after research in the old bookshops. I have managed to assemble, and read, first editions of seven or eight of Miss Glasgow's sixteen books, including the badly named "The Voice of the People," of which the first half is extraordinarily delicious; "The Deliverance," 1904, a story of rising and falling families with an admirable piece of characterization in Maria; "The Wheel of Life," 1906, a study of several types of men in New York and their ideals, with one flame-like woman; "The Miller of Old Church," 1911, specially rich in humor; "Virginia," 1913, a striking account of the insufficiency of the sweet self-sacrificing Southern wife; "Life and Gabriella," 1916, a study of the woman who finds a fairly satisfactory second-best in business success; "One Man in His Time," 1922, a portrait of a Governor of Virginia who is a self-made man.

Every so often the critics start up a discussion as to what constitutes abiding value in a novel. Mr. Swinnerton, Mr. A. B. Walkley and sundry other controversialists were waging such a discussion last summer. At the point where I looked in upon it opinion tended strongly to the orthodox conclusion that a novel may lack almost all the virtues and yet live by its characters. Some one, I think Mr. Walkley, dissented, maintaining rather that a novel lives by its characteristics—by the sum of all the qualities which the author puts into it.

That amounts, perhaps, to saying that a novel lives by, or on, the character of its author. If that appears true of a single novel, it appears more strikingly true when one reflects upon the entire work of a novelist after one is familiar with it, and his books have run together and made a little world in one's mind. For my part, at any rate, I seldom step into the world of Jane Austen or Charlotte Brontë, of Thackeray or Thomas Hardy or Conrad, looking for any one in particular. I revisit these scenes because I like the weather, sunlit or stormy, because I relish a certain feeling in the air, which I know, when I analyze it, is the pervasive effect of the writer's personality.

For several days now I have been living happily in Ellen Glasgow's world. I attempt to take my satisfaction to pieces, and I find myself cataloging her abundant powers. I like her clear sense of the elemental things in human life and her sense of the profound interdependence of man and nature. She delights by her talent for presenting the wonder and bloom of Virginian gardens and country-side. Go where you will in her Southern world, there is perfume in the sunlit air, hyacinths and the scent of wild grapes and microphylla roses; there are the budding sycamore and the foam of dogwood and red bud; sparrows rustle among the Virginia creepers, thrushes sing, bluebirds and red-winged blackbirds flicker over the pastures; sunsets glow behind dark pines; there is the sound of water flowing.

Of her humor one could write a chapter. Her

humbler characters—negroes and rustic ancient white
folks, religious and irreligious—abound in sage obser-
vations and comparisons, earthy, droll, bitter or wise,
between what the Baptist minister teaches them on
Sunday and what they learn when they go outside the
church door. The rural humorists in "The Miller of
Old Church" could hold their own against any peasant group you may mention in the works of Thomas
Hardy. As for wit of the more intellectual order,
ironical wit, critical wit, epigrammatic wit, brilliantly
serving in characterization and commentary, it plays
incessantly through her books. It is a constant aspect of her thought. She conceives life as a brave
comedy. I incline to think her the wittiest of living
American novelists, and I am not surprised to learn
that her favorite authors are Voltaire and Fielding.

Her range of successful characters is wide. It includes all sorts of colored people, poor whites, middling
whites and old Southern gentry; poor people going up
and rich people coming down; farmers, millers, shopkeepers, artists, poets, lawyers, judges, politicians;
children and octogenarians; sane and insane. She has
a very lively sense of the power of the family, of the
social group and caste, of the community, of the
generation. At the same time she feels with intense
sympathy the elemental needs and hungers and the
ideal motives which animate individual men and women,
and make them, for their hour of crowded life, flame
out against the commonplace.

In all her novels one is aware of an attendant keenly
observant ethical spirit. Her morality is her own,
tolerant of nature, intolerant of cant and humbug, but
her consciousness is as unmistakably ethical as that
of George Eliot. She likes to see the wheel come full

circle. She builds her stories with a view to showing Time bringing in revenges.

Her style is firm, lucid, and if I were not afraid of giving offense, I should add, it has a masculine rhythm. It has wit and beauty. At its best it has a proud and impressive reserve, and goes over depths with the tension and moving stillness of deep rivers.

I have enumerated some of the talents and characteristics of Ellen Glasgow which have impressed me in reading these novels. As I turn away from the "specimens" of her qualities, which I have collected but have not space to exhibit, I ask myself wherein the abiding value of her work lies; what is the nature of the pervasive presence in her world which has rewarded me for entering it. And the reply which comes first to my lips is this: her wisdom, the breadth and justice of her vision.

But I have scarcely uttered that characterization when I recognize that, after all my enumeration of qualities, I have failed to bring out the really distinguishing marks of her individuality. I have said nothing of her daimonic element, her iconoclasm, her affectionate derision of the old South, her tireless satire upon the self-immolating old-fashioned female with faded roses in her cheeks and dying violets in her eyes, her merciless incessant mockery at the ancient egotistical pretensions of the male sex, and, deeper than all, underlying all, the realistic drive of her nature toward the discovery of ends which shall make life for men and women, but especially for women, somehow not wholly unworthy of the brief candle which lights them into the long darkness.

Ellen Glasgow is passionate. With all the passionateness of her soul she hates lies, and she hates

failure. If her realism has not been as popular as
the romances of some of our practising novelists it is
because she is modern with a vengeance. She is a
feminist with a vengeance. If you review her novels
you find that for the last twenty-five years she has
been steadily insisting that the average woman is a
failure, and that the average woman's life is founded
on a lie, a vital illusion, namely, that the sexual attraction which draws her to her man in the mating
season is enough, is her supreme and sufficient affair
with life. With all her humor, with all her wit and
wisdom, and with all her passion, she asserts and re-
asserts that this is not enough. In one form of words
or another, through novel after novel, runs this re-
frain: "There ought to be something more permanent
than love for one to live by." Through novel after
novel, with an insistence most abasing to masculine
conceit, she exhibits the evanescence of sexual passion, exhibits women of all sorts who are quite disillusioned about love, exhibits men in the humiliating
and bewildering attitude of loving without return, and
loving when they are loved no more.

One doesn't get all of Ellen Glasgow's qualities
at their highest in "Barren Ground." It is more
somber than most of the others, less relieved by wit.
It is insistently grim; and it has, I think, needless
longueurs in its last hundred pages. Still it remains
an excellent example of her talent, and it contains
a powerful development of her central thesis.

Dorinda running toward life is embraced by it,
seductively, treacherously. The terror and pathos of
her disillusion are developed in pages of memorable
beauty. Elsewhere Miss Glasgow has mockingly
painted old maids of the Victorian mold who have sat

forty years in an upper chamber pallidly worshiping their penitence and their memory of betrayal. Dorinda has the blood of Scotch-Irish ancestors in her veins. She packs up her wedding clothes. She packs away her dreams. With her young sense unimpaired that life is "precious and indescribably sad and lovely," she stiffens her soft lip and fights for a life which shall be independent of the admiration of men, fights for a successful life, as men rate success, and wins it—incidentally acquiring a husband whom she treats as a superior hired man. As her hands are very full with the management of her three large farms and dairy, he is quite useful to her.

Men who are realistic enough to admit that they could live without their wives but not without their work are likely to see in Dorinda a fine sort of heroine. Others will say: "But what did she get out of it— with her cows and her married hired man?" And I think Miss Glasgow would reply: "Romance! The fighting edge. She saved her soul, as modern women understand the soul. She made herself a character. She learned that in the end 'nothing lasts but courage.' "

VII

Rose Macaulay and Women

ROSE MACAULAY is one of the wittiest writers going. But she makes me as uncomfortable as a patch of nettles, and very anxious about the future of mankind. I sit here uneasily studying her photograph. I conjecture that she herself has described it under the name of Katherine Varick in "Potterism": "frosty blue eyes, a pale square-jawed, slightly cynical face, a first in Natural Science, and a chemical research fellowship." I blench under the rapier points of those eyes, so piercing, so ironically mocking, so candid, so caustic, so pitiless.

Is that the way a woman's eyes should rest upon this wounded, weary world? What did Byron say about soft eyes looking love to eyes that spake again in the same soft dialect? Or is that "old stuff"? Have we had rather too many soft eyes healing the wounds our own folly has made?

At any rate, this face knows too much! It knows everything that I know—which is pardonable; and a great deal besides—which is dangerous and disturbing. In seeing through me and all around me, I suppose she is like every well-informed woman that I have met in the last twenty years. I have never imagined that superior women were dull. But she differs from others in making no concealment of her scathing insight. Ever since I can remember I have adored, under the name of "feminine tact," women's readiness

and ability to lie imperturbably in order to spare other
people's feelings, particularly the feelings of their
husbands and other male dependents. But Rose
Macaulay rejects "tact." Her intelligence has no
reservations. She looks at me without gloves. To
the brutal frankness which is English she adds a hard,
realistic thrust which is feminine—the special characteristic, it seems, of the full-fledged feminine Intellectual.

Once started on logical courses, women, I surmise,
run through them faster than men. Consider the mad
speed with which Rose Macaulay has run through
the bright hopes of the feminist program. Her course
was slowly prepared and her lamp was trimmed by
such poor, old, patient plodders as Samuel Butler, G.
B. Shaw and H. G. Wells. Forty years it took these
fumbling iconoclasts to get the Victorian candelabra
thoroughly junked and the clean cinder path laid
out for the Ann Veronicas of the present age. With
"Potterism," 1920, Rose Macaulay caught up what
for brevity we may call the Wellsian torch, and in
four short years she burned it out and tossed us the
charred wick in "Told By An Idiot."

If she had refrained from the race, who knows?—
perhaps dear old Mr. Wells with his rich resources
of erotic sentiment and his vast social hopefulness
might have kept his beloved young people "forward-
looking" for another ten years. As it is, Mr. Wells
is collecting his works, and closing the great epoch
of social expectation, while Rose Macaulay cynically
explains to the now tittering young people that before
they can get around to reform the world they themselves will be old, and then, of course, it will be useless
to try to do anything about it.

With a presentiment that she has now pretty well exhausted the satirical vein, I have been re-reading "Potterism," 1920. It is a breezy book, and with "Dangerous Ages" contains nearly everything of hers that fans the smoldering ashes of my sanguine years. It is dedicated, a bit pedantically, to *"the unsentimental precisians in thought,* who have, on this confused, inaccurate and emotional planet, no fit habitation." People who hankered to be "unsentimental precisians" were not so few as one feared. In 1921 "Potterism" had run through thirty-five editions.

Just what was it in this first book that cried "come hither" to so many readers? The gospel of Wells, the ideas of Wells, with the rose color rubbed off, the sentiment squeezed out. The Anti-Potterite League for the Investigation of Fact, for the destruction of cant, the slapdash, the second-rate, pomposity, mush, shellacked propriety and every hollow, plausible form of words employed to mask and blur the hard, sharp edges of actuality. Youth was there, shameless, fearless, uncompromising youth, truculently showing up the base compliances of parents. Above all, young women were there, with Cambridge honors, scientifically trained, tempered, edged, going into the world fully prepared to compete with their brothers, and bent on getting some of the important jobs, and demonstrating that "woman's work" is a disgusting Potterism.

"Dangerous Ages," which followed hard upon "Potterism" in 1921, is the only book of Rose Macaulay's which wrings the heart, or, indeed, much recognizes the existence of that organ. It is my impression that no dozen novels of my time have given me so much authentic information about womankind as this one.

[85]

There are girls of twenty here, clean, fine and candid, who have read Freud and Ellis and don't wish to marry, but, open-eyed, to take the risks of a free companionship, in a "keen, jolly, adventuring business, an ardent thing, full of gallant dreams and endeavors." There are women of thirty who write—experienced, brilliant, gay, with a cynical twist, with no religious illusions, yet "with a queer desire, to put it simply, for goodness, for straight living and generous thinking, even, within reason, for usefulness." There are women of forty-three, with satisfactory husbands and promising young children—women turning, at forty-three, to the medical career interrupted twenty years before, turning back to the career, in horror of the threatening vacancy of the rest of life. There are grandmothers and great-grandmothers who have ceased to rebel at their wrinkles, and who stave off the ennui of age by reading Russian fiction and consulting the psychoanalyst.

Pathos broods over them all. For they are all hungry for some more adequate self-expression than they are ever likely to attain. They are bitten with a desire to leave behind in the world some record more permanent, more personal, less undistinguished than—merely children! They are so sick of this self-sacrificial song! They want to live their own lives—for a little while, before they descend into the eternal nothingness. There is a hard core of egotism in them—just as there is in every *man* who sticks to his career. But one likes these girls and these women, so deliberately clean and fine and slim and taut; and one pities them, too. The intellectual life? Not many of them, one fears, want it, as men of their class want it—

as the first indispensable life choice. And a career chosen on any other basis is bitter with relinquishment.

In "Dangerous Ages" as it appears to me, Rose Macaulay let herself go as in none of her other books. She is more or less in love with all these women who are trying to make something satisfactory out of the little interval which is theirs before the swiftly shifting bright dance of the earth shall know them no more. Consequently she has here for once revealed her poignant emotional as well as her pungent intellectual qualities, and she has expressed intensely and adequately the consciousness of existence which her persons feel within themselves—the courage and verve with which they take up life's gauntlet.

If you scrutinize the story, however, you see that she has few illusions about the capacity of her sex to live the "life of reason." Her perception is lucid that the great majority of her sisters, struggling for "emancipation," are inextricably in the grip of the life-force, the passionate admiration of men remains still the secret ultimate object of their heart's desire and at a pinch they will fight for it with the crude ferocity of savages.

She has seen through them.

From the first, therefore, she has been anxious to make known that she is by no means committed to the positions in which her dramatis personæ are found. In "Potterism," for example, she gave us a long epigraph from Evelyn Underhill on that "disinterestedness" of the artist which enables him to see things "for their own sakes." The point of view at which she philosophized upon the pangs of the feminine heart at the ages of twenty, thirty, forty, sixty and eighty is indicated by this epigraph in "Dangerous Ages":

"Reflecting how, at the best, human life on this minute and perishing planet is a mere episode and as brief as a dream."

She has, however, a personal register in one of the characters in "Dangerous Ages." In the final chapter we are told that Pamela has the "key" to the door against which various of the other women bruise their eager hands. The key is not an important job, not a career, nor yet a man, but a philosophic attitude—an attitude of blithe philosophic despair. I will quote a passage which makes a close link between this book and "Told By An Idiot" and "Orphan Island": "Pamela, going about her work, keen, debonair and detached, ironic, cool and quiet, responsive to life and yet a thought disdainful of it, lightly holding and easily renouncing, the world's lover, yet not its servant, her foot at times carelessly on its neck to prove her power over it—Pamela said blandly to grandmama, when the old lady commented one day on her admirable composure, 'Life is so short, you see. Can anything which lasts such a little while be worth making a fuss about?'"

One sees at a glance that Rose Macaulay has flung aside the torch with which Mr. Wells started the Ann Veronicas of 1909 marching toward the earthly kingdom of "God, the Invisible King." She has reverted to a mood nearer the "blithe paganism" of George Moore and Oscar Wilde and old Samuel Butler, with his seductive maxim: "We have all sinned and come short of the glory of making ourselves as comfortable as we easily might have done."

In 1923 she blithely expressed her political disillusion in "A Mystery at Geneva"—not a satire, she assures us in a prefatory note; no, not a satire, but a simple straightforward "mystery story" about an imaginary League of Nations Assembly which somehow dissolves without much result in a subterranean banquet chamber.

In 1924 she chose as epigraphs for "Told By An Idiot" the walking shadow passage from "Macbeth" and a sentence of Paul Morand's to the effect that "history, like an idiot, mechanically repeats itself." If there was to be laughter at the expense of the feminine Intellectuals Rose Macaulay proposed to herself the pleasure of being the first to laugh!

"Told By An Idiot" is saturated with the pitiless, disintegrating, depressing irony of one who conceives that she has seen through "the illusion of progress." "Why so hot, little man, little woman?" she seems to inquire, with a frosty detachment which I find extraordinarily exasperating. "What we are doing and planning and hoping so hotly, with such an elate sense of its novelty, is very old stuff, my children. Come, peep in here at my little puppet show. Here you shall see the generations pass, one by one—Victorian, Fin-de-siècle, Edwardian and Georgian. Mark them well and four times you shall see history mimic the vain spectacle of your anxious progress from the cradle to the grave, with all your empty mouthings and ineffectual gestures. Come, let us amuse ourselves. As the whirligig of dead time spins past us I will mention for you all of the score or so of odd little 'interests' which constituted life and its zest for each of our little marionettes, as, for examples, the untimely death of the Duke of Clarence, the alarming increase of female bicyclists and the prevalent nuisance of that popular song, 'Ta-ra-ra-ra-boomdeay.' "

I should like to call "Told By An Idiot" a heart-breaking tale, but if I did that its author would turn her cool, frosty intelligence in my direction and inquire exactly what physiological change I conceived to take place when I spoke of the rupture of that organ. Let us say nothing of the heart. "Told By An Idiot" is a satire of great wit and even of erudition, but I find it horribly depressing, because it systematically belittles life and denies the possibility of progress.

Fancy becoming so superior to mundane events that in a chronicle of forty years you can tuck such an event as the World War into a couple of pages. On a scale of that sort the individual dwindles to a pin point, and births, marriages and deaths become of infinitesimal consequence. I ask, Whose is this sublime point of view? Where does the observer sit who whiffs all our human affairs into the air like a puff of cigarette smoke? No longer, certainly, at the point of view of the artist, according to Evelyn Underhill's definition, for she no longer is making any effort to see people "for their own sakes." She is no longer expressing the consciousness of existence which her persons feel within themselves.

I search again for Rose Macaulay's "register," and I find it in Miss Garden, a wholly disillusioned feminist—"a little cynical, a little blasé, very well dressed, intensely civilized, exquisitely poised, delicately, cleanly fair. She would soon be thirty-nine, and looked just that, neither more nor less." Miss Garden gambles very intelligently at Monte Carlo; she inquires how the wars are going—"the most noticeable wars at the moment were those between America and Spain and between Great Britain and the Sudanese"; she visits the picture galleries and the theaters; she spends

some hours in the shops buying a clear jade elephant
and a dull jade lump that swings on a platinum chain,
a tortoise shell cigarette case, some Irish lace, ivory
opera glasses and considering the purchase of a Pol-
talloch terrier. She understands that to be a little
in love is fun and adds a zest, but one must be careful
not to be perturbed by it. She philosophizes thus:

"Funny, hustling, strutting, vain, eager little
creatures that we are, so clever and so excited about
the business of living, so absorbed and intent about
it all, so proud of our achievements, so tragically de-
ploring our disasters, so prone to talk about the wreck-
age of civilization, as if it mattered much, as if civilization had not been wrecked and wrecked all down human
history and it all came to the same thing in the end.
Nevertheless, thought Rome, we are really rather wonderful little spurts of life."

In "Orphan Island" I find this yawning bright-
eyed satire far less of an affliction—on the contrary,
decidedly exhilarating, I suppose because it is directed at the Victorians, and I am gradually beginning to see the necessity of proving the Victorians
ridiculous in order to fortify my own sense of progress.

According to the ingenious scheme of this anti-
Utopia, a kind-hearted evangelical lady, Miss Charlotte Smith, undertaking to conduct some fifty miscellaneous orphans from East London to San Francisco,
is wrecked on a coral island, with all the culture of an
early Victorian evangelical spinster safe in her head.
Seventy years later a scientific and sociological party
set out from Cambridge to discover and rescue the
survivors, if any.

It transpires that the survivors of the castaways
number something like a thousand, and they haven't

the faintest desire to be rescued. The island population is divided into two classes, the descendants of the orphans, the working class, and the descendants of Charlotte Smith by the ship's doctor, who are capitalists and land owners. Charlotte herself, aged ninety-eight, and generally tipsy on cocoanut wine, is the recognized source of religion, government and morals. Through the decay of her memory she has almost lost the distinction between herself and Queen Victoria. The society to which she gives the tone is perfectly smug and thoroughly hypocritical. It talks prohibition, chastity, etc., and it does just as it pleases.

For a time I had an awful suspicion that Orphan Island was meant for the United States, but I read an article by Robert L. Duffus in the February "Century" on the progress we have made in the last twenty-five years and decided that my surmise was absurd.

Clearly "Orphan Island" is a picture of Victorian England, and how as intelligent a woman as Rose Macaulay can fail to regain her faith in progress after painting it is past my comprehension. As for myself, I find that my faith and hope and charity are all restored to me when I let my imagination dwell for an hour or so with that tippling, pedantic bigot, Charlotte Smith, and then turn swiftly to the description of Neville's forty-third birthday in "Dangerous Ages."

I see that adorable woman, mother of two grown children, waked from her dream-broken sleep at sunrise of a summer dawn, "roused by the multitudinous silver calling of a world full of birds." She cups her tanned face in her sunburnt hands and, looking out of sleepy violet eyes, she shivers and says, "Another year gone and nothing done yet." She decides to change all that. She hops out of bed, spreads two chunks of bread with marmalade, trots across the lawn in her pajamas and down through the wood to the broad swirling pool in the stream. There she strips, has her swim, eats her bread, "resumes" her pajamas, swarms up the smooth trunk of a beech tree to a limb in the sun and sits there, whistling.

If that doesn't represent progress I give it up.

VIII

H. G. Wells: Dreaming for the World

MR. WELLS now meets his public in a handsome
autographed edition, limited to a thousand and
fifty copies for the United States, on an excellent paper
and in beautiful and legible type.* He is no longer
a journalist.

On the brink of his sixtieth birthday he and I have
been rereading his works. We have found some defects
in them, but we have been charmed by them, and, on
the whole, we have been tremendously impressed by
them. We have felt with fresh force the central drive
and ardor which have been animating his labors these
thirty years. We see the great masses of his work
arranging themselves in intelligible order as the broad
and towering features of an architectural design,
imaginative and splendid. In the illuminating introduction to the Atlantic Edition, he interprets his
works with good humor, with candor and with many
flashes of shrewd critical insight. He establishes
points of view from which one can take in his main
intention and his total effect.

Mr. Wells's main intention developed against the
background of that mid-Victorian England which is
described with extraordinary gusto in one of his best
and most realistic novels, "Tono-Bungay." Mid-
Victorian society, as the young Wells envisaged it,

* *The Works of H. G. Wells,* Atlantic Edition, New York, 1924—.

gazing from somewhere not far from its lower stratum, was a substance in which he seemed to be fixed like a fly at the bottom of a pan of cold mutton tallow. He looked up at Bladesover Hall, where the Olympians sat looking down on the vicarage people, who looked down on the doctor, who looked down on the "vet," who looked down on the tenantry, who looked down on the butler and the housekeeper, and so by immutable degrees one descended from housekeeper to village shopkeeper, to head keeper, to cook, to publican, to second keeper, to blacksmith, to first footman, etc.

After a fist fight with the son of one of the Olympians the low born hero is banished to a stuffy, sniffling religious lower middle class family which on Sundays "met with twenty or thirty other darkened and unclean people, all dressed in dingy colors that would not show the dirt, in a little brick-built chapel equipped with a spavined roarer of a harmonium, and there solaced their minds on the thought that all that was fair and free in life, all that struggled, all that planned and made, all pride and beauty and honor, all fine and enjoyable things, were irrevocably damned to everlasting torments."

If you wish a sympathetic understanding of Mr. Wells's main intention you must first allow the asphyxiating atmosphere of this greasy, malodorous world to enter your lungs. That it may do so, and that you may recognize how easily Mr. Wells might have established a reputation as a "devastating" realist if he had not passionately loathed this reality and deliberately turned away from it, I will quote one other passage descriptive of that beautiful thing which conservatives call "the established order."

[97]

The sounds and then the scene return, those obscure, undignified people, a fat woman with asthma, an old Welsh milkseller with a tumor on his bald head, who was the intellectual leader of the sect, a huge-voiced haberdasher with a big black beard, a white-faced, extraordinarily pregnant woman, his wife; a spectacled rate-collector with a bent back . . . I hear the talk about souls, the strange battered old phrases that were coined ages ago in the seaports of the sun-dry Levant, of balm of Gilead and manna in the desert, of gourds that give shade and water in a thirsty land; I recall again the way in which at the conclusion of the service the talk remained pious in form, but became medical in substance, and how the women got together for obstetric whisperings.

Having passed from the stratified Bladesover Hall world to evangelical hymn-singing society, George Ponderevo then enters the tradesman's world of his uncle, a small English Babbitt, who wishes he were in America, "where things hum," and with him he enters the field of unscrupulous business, which is the main theme of the book.

Now, I am, of course, aware that the short and easy way to describe Mr. Wells's main intention, and at the same stroke to destroy him, is to say that in reaction from this mid-Victorian background he developed "the Messiah complex." But what does that really mean? Elijah III developed a Messiah complex. How does the "complex" of H. G. Wells differ from that of Elijah III? Perhaps we need not go into that. Perhaps we need only characterize briefly any one of Mr. Wells's heroes—for they are all of the same spiritual family. Suppose we stick to George Ponderevo and take his description of the spirit that

was in him when, revolting against the aspects of the
established order in which he had passed his youth, he
came up to London:

I came up to it, young and without advisers, rather
priggish, rather dangerously open-minded and very
open-eyed, and with something—it is, I think, the
common gift of imaginative youth, and I claim it un-
blushingly—fine in me, finer than the world and seeking fine responses. I did not want simply to live or
simply to live happily or well; I wanted to serve and
do and make—with some nobility. It was in me. It
is in half the youth of the world.

Instead, then, of attempting to destroy Mr. Wells
by saying that he developed the "Messiah complex,"
let us say this: He developed a loathing for a society
as fixed and as unappetizing as cold mutton tallow.
He thought it unendurable, and with that thought
came a strong conviction that it is not necessary to
endure it. It could be changed. In this age of astounding industrial and scientific progress the instru-
ments were at hand for producing swiftly enormous
and epoch-making changes in the political, social and
personal life of all mankind. It was undeniable.
What stood in the way? What made the processes
of beneficent change so slow? The vast inertia of
humanity, its vast ignorance, its vast fear, its vast
indolence, the wellnigh impossible task of clearing a
free and open place for adventurous men to go forward
amid the intricate labyrinths of old crooked customary ways. Not the means but the will to use the
means was lacking. It was not that fine ends were
impossible, but that the mass of men had not yet conceived of them. And so in Mr. Wells the vague

adolescent yearning for something finer than cold mutton tallow ripened into his life's main intention, which has been to kindle the imagination, to magnify, glorify and energize the will and reason of man, and to persuade our generation that the human will and reason are the legitimate successors to a creative and governing Providence.

Mr. Wells began his literary career with the publication of a series of fantastic romances, such as "The Time Machine," showing a "chronic" aeroplane in which one could visit the year 2000; "The Island of Doctor Moreau," in which a surgeon with infinitely cruel and protracted operations transforms the lower animals into the shape of men; "The Invisible Man," a study in applied chemistry; "The War of the Worlds," in which the planet Mars bombards Southern England with canisters full of super-scientists who march on London with heat-rays and gas attack, decisively anticipating the Germans; "When the Sleeper Wakes," a new Rip Van Winkle; "The First Men in the Moon," "The Sea Lady," in which a mermaid vamps a most eligible young man, who is already engaged to a suitable young mortal; "The Food of the Gods," more applied chemistry, directed to making people grow forty feet tall.

I am not sure that most of us when these romances first appeared saw anything in them but exciting yarns, "fairy tales of science," the mere exuberance of Mr. Wells's imagination. I notice, for example, that Mr. J. D. Beresford, one of Mr. Wells's innumerable disciples in fiction, classes "The Island of Dr. Moreau" among the "essays in pure fancy," though he notes that some absurd reviewers imagined it to be a defense of vivisection. Mr. Beresford's little book on Wells was published in 1915. In my own recent rereading of the tales I have been much struck by their purposefulness with reference to Mr. Wells's main intention. They are all essays toward a new point of view, essays toward seeing things differently, essays toward liberating the mind and the imagination from the nightmare of our present life and plunging them into another sort of nightmare! They are the religious myths and heroic fables and allegories in the new scriptures which Mr. Wells has been writing for our generation. Boys and girls will read them for their surface meaning as they read Gulliver, but persons of my generation may return to them and find a fresh fascination in regarding them as the meaningful grandiose "poetry" of the leader of the English intelligentsia.

I am supported in this notion by Mr. Wells's prefatory note in the Atlantic Edition on "The Island of Dr. Moreau." It originated, he tells us, as an imaginative response to the pitiful downfall and scandalous trial of a man of genius—presumably Oscar Wilde—which took place in 1895. It was written, he says, "just to give the utmost vividness to that conception of men as hewn and confused and tormented beasts." He calls it a "theological grotesque." Unless one so regards it it is quite too horrible to read. If one thinks of Dr. Moreau as a man cutting up living beasts and reshaping them, it is unendurable. But if one thinks of Dr. Moreau as God cutting up living men and reshaping them, then it is quite what we are accustomed to, and causes no gooseflesh. But if one takes a step further and thinks of Dr. Moreau as Mr. Wells, exploring the plasticity of men and states, attempting to cut up living men and reshape them into something better than the existing race, then one has a really stunning symbol of Mr. Wells's actual life effort as a radical mind of his generation; and in the lapse of Dr. Moreau's semi-human beings back to bestiality—well, consider the time still bleeding in memory when for some years the effort of every patriotic man, woman and child in the greater part of the civilized world was bent on homicide.

"When the reader comes to read the writings upon history in this collection," says Mr. Wells, "he will find the same idea of man as a reshaped animal no longer in flaming caricature, but as a weighed and settled conviction." See "The Outline of History."

One might go through these "fantastic tales" and show how burdened they are with Mr. Wells's moral meanings, now clearly enough legible in the light of his main intention. For example, the attack of the Martians in "The War of the Worlds"—it is really a magnificent fable which ought, if it ever sinks in, to do something to persuade Mark Twain's "damned human race" that they can't afford to risk cutting one another's throats, like a lot of Mexican bandits, but had better get together and concert measures of defense against the invisible, inscrutable, known and unknown foes which threaten the extinction of humanity.

"The Food of the Gods" is an heroic allegory about the world's superior men and women, men and women whose intellectual stature exceeds that of the average man as the height of these forty-foot giants exceeds the human pygmies at their feet. These giants are benevolent creatures of great strength, long vision, creative passion. They would like to do good turns for the little people—make crooked ways straight and rough places plain, but the little people fear them, hedge them, pen them in, forbid their union and finally shoot them—in a sincere conviction that there isn't any place for big people in the world.

In "The Sea Lady" Mr. Wells gives one of his earliest pictures of that dream-woman which all the young men in his social novels go seeking so vainly through the world. She is really quite a lovely and delicious creature, this woman whom Mr. Wells has created out of "infinite yearning." She is free, free and easy. She sings to the heart of man like the Lorelei. And if you desire to know why many people wish that Mr. Wells were Dr. Moreau or the King of the World or God the Invisible King—in his more sanguine moments I think it indubitable that he has identified himself with all three—it is because, if Mr. Wells had Eternal Femininity in his hands to reshape to the heart's desire, he would make it over in some such shape as this:

To go to her is like going out of a house, a very fine and dignified house, I admit, into something larger, something adventurous and incalculable. She is—she has an air of being—*natural*. She is as lax and lawless as the sunset, she is as free and familiar as the wind. She doesn't—if I may put it in this way—she doesn't love and respect him when he is this, and disapprove of him highly when he is that; she takes him altogether. She has the quality of the open sky, of the flight of birds, of deep-tangled places, she has the quality of the high sea. That I think is what she is for him, she is the Great Outside.

And with a flick of her mermaid's tail she slips down into the depths of the sea, leaving the hero to the sort of woman that many of us get on with, well enough, so long as we believe there is no other sort.

I have been describing Mr. Wells's imagination, moving with perfect freedom in the group of his works which he calls "fantastic romances." The relation between the romances and the novels of social life might be suggested by comparing Dr. Moreau with Stratton in "Passionate Friends," with Trafford in "Marriage," with Capes in "Ann Veronica," with the narrator in "The New Machiavelli," with Mr. Britling,—best of all, perhaps, with Benham in "The Research Magnificent."

As a novelist Mr. Wells believes in an adequate "register." He has, I think, endowed each one of his heroes with most of the interests, virtues, and aspirations uppermost in his own mind at the time of composition. They are men of wide embrace, these heroes. Their stream of consciousness customarily includes science, sociology, politics, and education, all subtly implicated with the pursuit of some freer, happier intercourse between the sexes. Each hero has a clear sense that there is something fine in him, "finer than the world and craving fine responses," and he explains this to a heroine, who, being a possessive "female" creature, doesn't more than half understand why he has to cart her off to Labrador or exile himself in Africa in order to understand what she and the world are about. But each hero incarnates what I have described as Mr. Wells's main intention: his desire to glorify, magnify, and energize the will and the reason as rulers and creators of a new world order, a new social order, new forms and qualities of personal relations.

The specific ideas which they have are discussed

at length in "A Modern Utopia," "New Worlds for Old," "First and Last Things," "God the Invisible King," etc. Their proposals for reconstruction have included from time to time most of the forms of social tyranny contemplated by the Socialists. But their spontaneous impulses, like those of Mr. Wells himself, are romantic and egotistic, as he has acknowledged. The instinctive aspiration of each is to be an aristocrat, a prince, an autocrat, or, as Benham in his megalomania puts it, an "uncrowned king of the world," or a kind of mortal God. Benham, as I have said, may be compared with Dr. Moreau because his research is into the plasticity of human nature: he is trying to make himself over in accordance with an ideal, which obliges him to cut out of his nature three of the most elemental and deep-seated passions: fear, desire, and jealousy.

What does Mr. Wells actually think to-day about the possibility of making men like gods by the excision of jealousy, desire, fear? You may find what he thought from week to week throughout 1924 by reading the fifty-five articles in "A Year of Prophesying." If you will turn to the fifty-fourth article, entitled "The Creative Passion," you will come upon this brief statement of his present attitude:

Do men and women generally want a better world than this?

Do they want a world free from war, general economic security, a higher level of general health, long life, freedom and hope for everyone, beauty as the common quality of their daily lives?

The conventional answer to that question, especially if you put it to a public meeting with the appropriate gestures, is "Of course they do."

But the true answer is, "Not much!"

[105]

The French sage who has recently died, Anatole
France, whom, as the head of French letters, Mr.
Wells, as the spokesman of the English-speaking
world, salutes in one of these articles—Anatole France,
after a measurably comprehensive survey of humanity,
turned away smiling, and said:

Yes, evil is immortal. The genius in which the
old theology incarnates it, Satan, will survive the last
man, and will remain alone, seated, his wings folded,
upon the débris of extinct worlds. And we have not
even the right to desire the death of Satan. A high
philosophy will not groan at the eternity of universal
evil. It will recognize, on the contrary, that evil is
necessary and that it ought to endure; for, without it,
man would have nothing to do in this world.

There are always, aren't there, plenty of men who
see the indispensability of Satan and who mock the
heat of those who attempt to dislodge him?

I suppose few men now living have striven more
comprehensively than Mr. Wells to understand the
whole meaning of the world and the world's needs,
and to put fine meanings and purposes into the world
where he saw none. He has grown sage with disillusions, and has relinquished many projects and withdrawn from many experiments. He turns more and
more, as all wise men do, from the expectation of
reforming nations to the hope of educating a few individuals. But to leave Satan sitting "alone" there,
after the death of the last man, upon the débris of
extinct worlds?—no, he can never assent to that! Opposite him Something Else will be sitting, with un-
sheathed sword, breathing for a moment in the pause
of the eternal combat.

You are no realist, Mr. Wells. Unlike Mr. Hardy and Joseph Conrad, you have small respect for Chance, and you minimize Necessity, those great powers in the real world. But you have been a brave myth-maker and a heartening poet to the Intellectuals of your time. You have turned an entire generation of novelists and readers from contemplating the fatal forces of heredity and environment and instinct to considering the god-like power of an intelligent will to control instinct, environment and heredity. And I am going to turn upon you your own fine valediction to Oswald in your "Joan and Peter," for I think it sums up your virtue and your valor and that air of being awake and radiant which you have communicated to the more delightful young people of our day:

There was a light upon his life, and the truth was that he could not discover the source of the light nor define its nature; there was a presence in the world about him that made all life worth while and yet it was Nameless and Incomprehensible. . . . Perhaps some men have meant this when they talked of Love, but he himself had loved because of this, and so he held it must be something greater than Love. Perhaps some men have intended it in their use of the word Beauty, but it seemed to him that rather it made and determined Beauty for him. And others again have known it as the living presence of God, but the name of God was to Oswald a name battered out of all value and meaning. And yet it was by this, by this Nameless, this Incomprehensible, that he lived and was upheld. It did so uphold him that he could go on, he knew, though happiness were denied him; though defeat and death stared him in the face.

SECOND GALLERY

IX

Mr. Brownell on the Quest of Perfection

IT is generally understood, without argument or illustration, that after the late war our morale, using the word in its most comprehensive sense, was "shot to pieces." The task of gathering up the fragments and putting them together again has been undertaken by all sorts of people with various degrees of success or failure. The reconstructors have encountered some opposition from the small group of anarchical minds who really prefer their morale in pieces, and still more opposition from the large body of malcontented minds who would rather have morale remain shattered than see it reconstructed on the antebellum model.

Temperamental reactionaries react and are at peace. Some rest in the capacious old bosoms of Academic Orthodoxy, some in Business as Usual, some in Fundamentalism, some in the Ku-Klux Klan. But among the younger sort who have tasted the uncharted freedom of recent years there is a manifest disposition to say: "Yes, we, too, are a little weary of roaming like homeless winds. We, too, recognize in ourselves what you call the elementary human craving to be formed. But rather than submit to be shaped by such molds as you offer us we will shamelessly incur the reproach of aimlessness, futility and shapelessness."

The problem is to raise a flag from which every

one that you wish to attract—every one with Ram Dass's endowment of "fire in his belly"—does not turn away in disgust. If you mark your flag with "Prohibition," "Inhibition," "Restriction," "Conventions," "*Frein Vital*" or "Inner Check" there is danger that it will rally only, or mainly, those merely gap-filling persons who could not be blasted out of their sterile conventionality with dynamite. From all youths, dear to the gods, in whose blood the spring flames, "wintry negativity," as William James called it, meets with negation. The only point of view to which they can possibly be persuaded to repair is one which promises them some positive object for their expansive and creative energies; some better, more expeditious, route to a felicity of which they have already tasted the sweetness; some glory so unmistakable that the difficulty of compassing it will not seem altogether "not worth while." To the sense of young people, a day passed in positive achievement is better than a thousand years of renunciation, and a small artist who will show them how to paint grasshoppers perfectly is a far more welcome counselor than a great prophet who dissuades them from taking a city.

In recognition of this fact, there emerge, or re-emerge, in France enthusiastic cults, like that of M. Motherlant, for the athletic life; and M. André Beaunier gives eleven pages of the "Revue des Deux Mondes" (August 1, 1924) to extolling a moralist, meet for our times, M. Eugène Marsan, an author whose most significant work is a little manual for the man of fashion *(l'homme élégant)*, entitled "The Walking Sticks of M. Paul Bourget."

What is all this about? Well, the moment you reflect upon your own walking stick you see that in the

W. C. Brownell

click, click, click of that bit of crabtree or malacca there is something which introduces into your form-less slouch the *tension* of art, time in ordered inter-vals, the sweep and seduction of rhythm. Yes, that, perhaps; but morality, too, in a meticulous solicitude about canes and cravats?

The reviver of "elegance" replies:

Oh, to be sure, the existence of God and the frontiers of Poland have importance of another order. We might walk the earth, clad in sackcloth and girdled with a rope. But if man is the only clothes-wearing animal, elegance of costume is commendable. It is moral. It is one of the means of maintaining one's dignity as a civilized white man. So long as a man clings to his clothes he preserves a barrier between himself and barbarism. Let us guard what guards us.

"There are no questions but social questions." It is an utterance of Gambetta's, applauded many years ago by Mr. Brownell, the critic among us who looks most searchingly into every question that he considers. Following this hint, I have been sketching the general social considerations which, I conceive, may have stimulated Mr. Brownell to compose his latest and timely book *—a book savory with wit, of remorse-less penetration, packed with wisdom and informed throughout by that nobility of feeling which is quite the rarest note in contemporary literature. In some respects "The Genius of Style" is Mr. Brownell's most beautiful book—high praise, because each of its major predecessors has been quite the best thing of its kind hitherto produced in America.

* *The Genius of Style*, New York, 1924.

[115]

Looking into the field of literature with eyes instructed by lifelong study of the "principle of beauty" in painting, sculpture, architecture, letters and social life, Mr. Brownell has marked, in common with less instructed observers, the growing tendency of authors to appear *au naturel* "to leave off agony, leave off style"; and he regards this tendency as essentially barbaric. As M. Marsan raises the little pennant of "elegance," so Mr. Brownell raises, on a far loftier standard, the flag of "style" as a positive objective which, clearly explained and persuasively commended, may conceivably enlist the loyalties of an age which acknowledges few. Quoting a Persian poet, he says: "The lion on the flag is but a painted lion, but in the wind it moves and marches." It marches in the chiding wind of current doctrine.

Style, what is it? In "The Nation" of October 8, 1924, you will find, in the resonant and only slightly ungrammatical language of Mr. Maxwell Bodenheim, a sharp, clean-cut answer, which I will cite because it expresses adequately, I believe, the idea of style entertained by a large number of our younger writers —perhaps by most of our "movement" writers who give time to the entertainment of such ideas. According to Mr. Bodenheim, the literary creator is " a dangerous, persuasive and unfair liar." Well, that is candid, at any rate. We see what he means. We know the type. "The literary creator," he continues, "must look upon creation as the egotistic, unscrupulous branding of himself upon human beings and episodes whose essence is a thousand confused faces, neither of them [sic] one whit more plausible than the other. He enters a distraught, elusively vicious and crisscrossed realm—life—and changes it to the world in which, directly or by reference, he would like to live, or to the ruins by means of which his ego brings distinctness to its dream of solitary disdain."

"The egotistic unscrupulous branding of himself" upon his subject matter. We have seen the operation of that passion in the caricatures of Hogarth, in the novels of Laurence Sterne, in the "Sartor" of Carlyle; also, to take only two or three salient recent examples, in the strange "Rahab" of Mr. Waldo Frank, in Mr. Hecht's "Erik Dorn," and in the "Crazy Man" of Mr. Maxwell Bodenheim. It is interesting work—work of undeniable power, of a sort. The author's name is in every line like an obvious cryptogram, "branded" there. Mr. Middleton Murry thinks that this is a questionable stylistic ideal; that, in the long run, this remorseless insistence on one's idiosyncrasy becomes insufferably tedious. But Mr. Brownell, clearing the way for re-definition, tells us that this is not style, properly so called, but manner or mannerism, often violently embraced in the misconception that "style is the man himself"—a misconception largely responsible for the vogue of stylistic nudity and the exploitation of undisciplined impulse.

The celebrated phrase—"style is the man himself," casually dropped by Buffon near the close of his discourse on his admission to the Academy, Mr. Brownell has no difficulty in showing has been wrested from its context—like the "simple, sensuous and passionate," now erroneously but almost universally accepted as Milton's recipe for poetry. It does not represent Buffon's conception of style, but is almost antithetical to it. Style, according to the French Academician, is *not* the man himself, is not a spirit of personal self-assertion. It is rather a kind of human imitation of the celestial order and motion, informing the whole work as the spirit of God informs creation. It is a spirit which pre-establishes harmony in the movement of one's ideas by reference to a thoroughly preconceived design. Indeed, in the body of his discourse, Buffon declares it to be "nothing but the order and movement which one puts into one's thought." In its essence, therefore, it is almost as little personal as the mathematical element in music. A sound style isn't a rigid thing; it isn't a thing to prescribe and impose from without; it isn't a thing to fear as repressive of personality. It is just the order and movement of one's own thoughts *when they are going right.*

Mr. Brownell is susceptible to the charms of perfection. Whenever he contemplates them, in matter or in idea, his own style takes wings; and this, he declares with contagious ardor, is the high reward of those who, in letters, seek not their own idiosyncrasy but that moving order which is "art's and heaven's first law."

For the effect of the spirit of style in a work of art is precisely to add wings to it. The effect of following any objective ideal is elevation. Uplift means first of all getting out of one's self. It appeals in this way to the imagination as adventure does. But it also involves what adventure does not, definite aspiration rather than vague enthusiasm. And this aspiration to achieve rather than to experience, to reach a goal rather than to explore the unknown, to attain the normal rather than invent the novel, springs from perceiving the existence in the ideal sphere of a quality for which we have no other word so apt as perfection.

When we depart from the "great tradition," when we abandon in our own souls the arduous pursuit of the ideal perfection, when we seek only in a "dream of solitary disdain" to affirm and "brand" upon our work the uniqueness of our own essence, then we are likely to flatter ourselves that we are becoming "original" and are manifesting "genius." Mr. Brownell, after some comparison of current specimens of "originality" with the classifications of recent scientific investigators, warns us that this unique disdainful ego, in which we exhibit such overweening pride, is likely to slip rather ignominiously into some large category of psychopathology, group complexes, or mob-psychology. It isn't so terribly difficult to be queer. We are born that way.

The difficult thing is to be normal. We have to achieve normality. It is quite a different thing from "normalcy," which is merely some one's old coat. Normality bears to normalcy about the same relation that the living and perfect body of an athlete bears to an old coat. The way to be the most original man is to seek to be the most normal man; it is the most difficult path, and therefore the path least followed, least likely to be hit upon by chance. It is the path demanding the upgirt loin, the unsleeping heart, and eyes fixed upon the beauty which dwells among the rocks, high above the reek and stench of our self-seeking oblations. Self-denial as an end in itself? No. Self-denial as a means to begin the ascent of those heights "where Orpheus and where Homer are"; self-denial as the first step toward the level of workmanship that resists time and toward the level of feeling which rewards the work:

[119]

Nothing melts us like nobility of thought caught up into style. Nobility stirs us more exquisitely than exquisiteness. Imagination, however sympathetic, warms us but superficially compared with the high disinterestedness of personal detachment exhibited in impersonal exaltation. This moves us like music that strings the sensibility taut and affirms its capacity for forgetfulness of self. Style, in fine, has a play of interrelations and a sustained rhythm, when in combination with adequate substance, that stanch the personal preoccupation of self-pity and stimulate the generous fervor of self-abandonment to the ideal.

In an effort to convey, or at least to suggest, the singular fire and potency of Mr. Brownell's special virtue, his enkindling passion for the ideal in art, letters and life, I have left no space to comment upon his fruitful, many-sided development of his theme, which he has enriched from an extensive field under perfect cultivation. I particularly regret the necessity of abridgment, because Mr. Brownell has here given full and most stimulating development to that aspect of his subject which the high intellectuality of his talent has hitherto led him to postpone, or to underemphasize, in behalf of the more abstract, structural elements of style. I refer to his illuminating discussion of "poetic prose," to his finely eloquent justification of emotion and, above all, to his plea for the cultivation by our own writers of the too long neglected poetic resources of prose speech. Those who are familiar with Mr. Brownell's previous books—as every one who cares for our distinguished criticism is—will doubtless regard this salient as the point at which he has most signally advanced his flag of leadership. It gives a curious relief to a reviewer to know

that all Mr. Brownell's admirers will understand why
no review can give any adequate notion of the artistic
tension and fullness of his treatment: "No man ever
spake more neatly, more weightily or suffered less
emptiness, less idleness in what he uttered."

When a man of letters of Mr. Brownell's eminent
talent spends a lifetime in an inflexible pursuit of perfection, it is not strange, yet it is singularly inspiring,
to consider how fittingly the fine things which have
been said of other men may be applied to him. As,
for instance, with reference to his social consciousness,
this tribute of Pater's to the Greek master of all those
who seek to think straight and feel nobly: "It is life
itself, action and character, he professes to color; to
get something of that irrepressible conscience of art,
that spirit of control, into the general course of life,
above all, into its energetic or impassioned acts." And
this tribute of Joubert's to the same master:

Somehow or other the habit of reading him aug-
ments in us the capacity for discerning and entertaining whatever fine truths may afterward present themselves. Like mountain air it sharpens our organs and
gives us an appetite for wholesome food.

Yes, Mr. Brownell belongs to the Academy, to the
true sons of that Academy which met under the plane
trees outside the city wall and asked the gods that
haunted the spot, not in vain, for "beauty in the inner
man."

X

Chekhov, Chekhovians, Chekhovism.

IN his stories and plays, to which I shall merely
allude, Chekhov presents the Russian people drunk
and sober, mad and sane, in squalor and in wealth;
and one may like them or not, these Russian people,
according to one's national affinities. In his letters,
on the other hand, Chekhov presents himself with his
family and friends, and, in the second volume, with the
talented actress who for his last three years became his
wife. He presents freely and abundantly the rich
spontaneous personality which it was a matter of principle with him to exclude from his works. And I defy
any intelligent reader to resist the fascination of his
high spirits, his delicious humor, his artistic alertness,
his critical penetration, his steady good sense, and his
sensitiveness to the ideas of his time. Popularization
of the letters* should create for him a much better
informed public than he has yet had in this country.
He is worth wide attention, and, in a sense, he deserves
the sort of attention given to a contemporary writer
who is still unfolding himself, and who has, therefore,
still fresh sources of stimulation in store for us.

Had not God put a bacillus in Chekhov which termi-
nated the career of his body in 1904 he might be alive
to-day and, according to Metchnikovian standards, yet

* *The Life and Letters of Anton Tchekhov.* Translated by S. S.
Koteliansky and Philip Tomlinson, New York, n.d.
   The Letters of Tchekhov to Olga Knipper. Translated by Con-
stance Garnett, New York, 1924.

in the prime of life—only sixty-five last January.
Even with the handicap of bodily death he is much
in the literary movement as an example, as an influence, as a theorist. Yet he adequately arrived on
the scene only within the last ten years. Except for
a few stories and two or three plays—"The Sea-Gull"
was translated by Isabel Hapgood in 1905, and "The
Cherry Orchard" by Mr. Mandell, 1908, in the "Yale
Courant"—his main circulation here begins sharply in
1915 and 1916, with the revived interest in the Russians occasioned by the World War.

Behind the Chekhov revival in England—from
which our own is obviously imported—one sees, beside
those experienced "Russians" R. E. C. Long and the
Garnetts, the influence of S. S. Koteliansky and a
series of significant literary collaborators of the
younger set: Gilbert Cannan, Leonard and Virginia
Woolf and Katherine Mansfield and her husband, Mr.
Middleton Murry. The Russian seed has fallen on
fertile English ground.

Gilbert Cannan assisted Mr. Koteliansky in trans-
lating "The House with the Mezzanine and Other
Stories," 1917; and I seem to scent Chekhov in Mr.
Cannan's own "Stucco House," 1918. Virginia Woolf
goes into ecstasies of admiration over Chekhov and
"the Russian point of view" in her collection of essays,
"The Common Reader." And the lecturer in Russian
literature at King's College, University of London,
Prince Mirsky, in his admirably lucid brief survey,
"Modern Russian Literature," 1925, declares that "the
late Katherine Mansfield was probably the most faithful and at the same times the most original of his (Chekhov's) disciples."

To the group of English Chekhovians one must add

William Gerhardi, who has lately fluttered our dove-cotes with "Futility" and "Polyglots," novels touched with Chekhovian humor in the presence of big wigs and embroidered uniforms. As a critic Mr. Gerhardi has linked himself with the group by declaring his discipleship to Middleton Murry. And in 1923 he published an extensive and intelligent study of Chekhov's art and his character, inspired, I suppose, by the letters and enriched certainly by many pertinent extracts from them. By no means incidentally he shoves Chekhov into the critical arena and eagerly backs him for genuine artistic modernity against Henry James and his militant champion, Mr. Ford Maddox Ford, on the one hand, and, on the other, against Dostoievsky and his alleged successor in psychological profundity, Mr. James Joyce.

I have no intention of thrusting myself among these glittering blades. In general I think Chekhov's English friends have taken hold of him and presented him wisely as a fine, conscientious artist whose realism is far more subtle, suggestive and truly profound than that of more flamboyant novelists who have invaded us since the Japanese War, Andreyev and Gorky, for example. Perhaps in the excess of appreciation they push his claims a little harder than he himself would have approved against the looming figures of Gogol, Tolstoy, Turgenev and Dostoievsky.

Chekhov did a marvelous thing: he carried fine art into the newspaper and kept it there as long as he was alive. He picked up the newspaper reporter's "human interest story" and treated it with the fine scrupulosity of a great artist working on the perfection of a sonnet. He wrote innumerable little stories with a touch which made them classical, and the cumulative

[126]

effect of them is large. Chekhov is a Russian classic, yet doubtless, as Prince Mirsky says, a classic of the Silver Age.

He is not to be described as an imposing elemental force. He is not a huge, originating, crushing and dominating mind. He hardly cared to be that. Between 1885 and 1904—a relatively languid generation, spiritually, between the liberalism of the '60s and the incipient Bolshevism that followed the Japanese War —Chekhov made for himself a personal ideal of sensible, sensitive civility. As an artist he sought to reflect Russian life from the point of view of a sensible, sensitive intellectual. His purpose, one may say, was to make readers see and feel the contemporary spectacle as such a man sees and feels it. He stands, then, for culture as contrasted with passion, ethical urgency, and yeasty fermentation. In respect to mood and temper, he stands in relation to Tolstoy as Matthew Arnold stands in relation to Carlyle, or Renan in relation to Victor Hugo, or, say, Mr. Santayana in relation to Royce and James.

Now the fact that Chekhov is coming into English-speaking lands twenty years after his death and is finding sympathetic and intelligent friends among the disenchanted writers of the post-war period, may greatly help us not only to see where *his* force lies, but also to enter more sympathetically into the minds of contemporary writers of our own time whom ruddy purposeful persons are prone to dismiss as unprofitable pessimists, dilettantes, futilitarians, belittlers of all that is venerable and august. I am thinking now of the vogue enjoyed by the Stracheyan biography, the Beerbohmian caricature, the fiction of Rose Macaulay, the Aldous Huxleyan "novel" and tale, and our inelegant and somewhat brutalized American version of the same Zeitgeist, which we may perhaps summarily designate as Menckenism.

Prince Mirsky, to whom I must refer once more, underscores Chekhov's "pessimism," his "realistic gloom," his gentle melancholy, his pity and sympathy, his consummate artistry. He links him with Turgenev in the "cult of inefficiency," and there is his dominant emphasis. Chekhov, he declares, with more than a touch of paradox,

hated the man who deserves success quite as much as the man who commands it undeservingly. Ineffi- ciency is for him the cardinal virtue, and defeat the only halo. This attitude has been believed by some to be essentially Russian, but in its extreme expression it is certainly quite personal to Chekhov. The tendency of English literature has been the other way, but latterly, and *parallel with the great vogue of Chekhov, the cult of inefficiency and the hate of Vulgar Success has spread in this country.* There is nothing more Chekhovian, outside Chekhov, than Mr. Lytton Stra- chey's life of Cardinal Manning, with the pointed con- trast between the active and obviously detestable Arch- bishop of Westminster and the gentle dreamer, New- man. [Newman, by the way, was less "gentle" than he is made out.]

Of Chekhov as an artist, Prince Mirsky speaks, to be sure, in the highest terms. But "Chekhovism" as an historical mood of Russia—a mood for which he ap- pears to hold Chekhov in some measure responsible— he condemns unsparingly as "a stage of the past we have no grounds to be proud of, of a past which is largely responsible for the greatest shame of Russian history, the inglorious bankruptcy of the middle classes (intelligentsia) in 1917."

An American who does not read Russian, while at liberty to take exceptions to almost any American interpretation of Chekhov, should, I think, dissent warily from an obviously well informed and acute Russian critic. All the same, I am constrained by the full force of my own personal reaction to my author to protest against accepting pessimism, negativity or defeatism as the keynotes of Chekhov's character, and, therefore, as the logical essence of Chekhovism. The center of the man is positive. The force of his character is positive. The letters prove it.

Chekhovism is always defeated in war, but in the long run Chekhovism undermines war and returns generation after generation to its task of defeating the passions which make war possible. Negativity can perform no such stupendous work. To declare that Chekhov made "a cult of inefficiency" is a partisan's disparaging way of saying that Chekhov had an exalted, inalterable faith in humane culture, which you, for one, can't quite bring yourself to share. You probably believe that humane culture, like Christianity, is too rare, too slow. It doesn't get "results." It is too fragile for this world. It is too easily trampled under and made naught of by any uprush or inrush of vigorous barbarism.

Poor Chekhov! I take it that he is out of date in this respect only: He thought he was standing for "European culture" as against "Asiatic barbarism"! If his life had been spared ten years longer he would have seen the European frock coats cast aside just as hastily as the Asiatic smocks. And if he had stood fast by his own ideals he would have withdrawn to some place "above the clouds" to laugh and weep with scorn and with compassion.

I am afraid that he was not a "joiner." He was not easily enlisted in Great Causes. He even shrank back suspiciously from membership in a literary "union." It reminded him, he said, of a German who had taught a cat, a mouse and a merlin to eat from one plate. He wrote for a conservative paper; and when some one, scenting popular sympathies in his stories, asked him if he were not slipping over toward liberalism, he replied that the question constrained him to consult his "innards." After consultation he reported that he was neither liberal nor conservative, but against pedants, nincompoops, madmen of all stripes. I think our new generation is beginning to turn toward that unnamed party which originates in negations, yet after all does come to stand for something quite definite.

Open the volume called "The Life and Letters" and you will find out quickly enough what Chekhov stood for, what serious purpose he had, in what sort of "practical" activities he was willing to be enlisted.

Descended from a peasant ancestry, familiar through his impecunious and hardworking boyhood with the Russian village, Chekhov knew intimately and revolted from the repulsive side of the Russian peasant: his ignorance, his boorishness, his inebriety, his gluttony, his dishonesty, his unbridled passionateness, his brutality, his chronic habit of slapping children in the face and clouting menials over the head with a shoemaker's last. All that aspect of "Asiatic" manners he observed and painted with merciless fidelity in scores of stories, for which he is credited with being the first unsentimental realist to deal with Russian village life.

But Chekhov quite ceased to be a peasant. He had enjoyed immense advantages: a decent and intelligent family life, full of kindly and affectionate feeling; a university training followed by a medical education; and early and lifelong association with cultivated men. He knew modern science and modern literature. He read Darwin, Spencer, Buckle; Goethe, Schiller, Hauptmann, Nordau, Nietzsche; Zola, Bourget, Daudet, Maupassant; H. B. Stowe and Thoreau; Cervantes; Ibsen; Gogol, Turgenev, Tolstoy, Grigorovich. He emerged from the peasant class into the intelligentsia. He emerged from Russia into Western civilization. And very keenly at an early age he felt responsible for conducting both his life and his art like a European gentleman who was also an intellectual.

You can see him applying that standard effectively to his own friends, to the actors in the theater, and, very significantly, to such authors as Tolstoy and Gorky. The sincerity and elevation of Tolstoy's spirit he profoundly revered: he recognized the man's essential nobility, and for that reason loved him above all other Russian writers. But Tolstoy's asceticism and his glorification of the peasant he regarded as wide aberrations from common sense. Chekhov hadn't the faintest desire to return to the peasantry. He knew it too well. He admired the talent of Gorky, befriended and helped him. At first meeting with him he was pleased with Gorky's intellectual outlook, pleased with everything about him except his peasant smock. Later he reacted against something raw, overstrained and violent in him—Maxim had a tedious tendency to "scream" under excitement and roar a man down. Chekhov had a well bred hatred of domination and could never have been duped into exchanging one tyrant for another. Chekhovism eludes tyrants.

Whether the fine spirit of a gentleman is inside a man is tested less conclusively in drawing room and club than in family life. Chekhov's relations with his parents were beautifully tender and regardful. When his future wife visited in his home she found its atmosphere delightful. His family letters, especially to his brothers, are charming. They are alive with affectionate interest. They are spontaneous, spirited, sympathetic, candid, stimulating and rich in excellent advice on the handling of artistic problems, on the payment of debts, and on the way to behave and to feel if one insists upon living with a woman to whom one is not legally married.

To one of his brothers, who is trying to write stories, he makes himself a literary coach and gives away all the little secrets of his craft. To another brother, Nicolay, the painter, he administers needed moral tonics—the poor fellow was ill and also, it seems, a little unkempt. There is a remarkable letter to this brother, dated 1886, written in response to Nicolay's complaint that he is not "understood." Anton thinks just a touch of the Dutch uncle is "indicated" by the symptoms. "The trouble with you," he says, in effect, "is that you are in a false position. You really wish to associate with cultured people and you are still dreadfully half-baked and amazingly uneducated." Then follows Anton's analysis of the responsibilities of an educated man. I wish there were space for more than a condensation of it:

Educated people, in my opinion, must satisfy the following conditions:

(1) They respect a man's personality, and therefore they are always tolerant, gentle, polite, yielding. . . . (2) They are compassionate, and not only with beggars and cats, for they grieve in their soul for what the naked eye does not see. (3) They respect other people's property, and therefore they pay their debts. (4) . . . They do not show off, they behave in public as they behave at home, they do not throw dust in the eyes of humbler people, they do not chatter, and do not make up soul-to-soul conversations when they are not asked. . . . (5) They do not belittle themselves to arouse the compassion of others. They do not play on the strings of other people's souls so that they shall sigh over and fondle them. . . . (6) . . . They do not care about such false diamonds as acquaintance with celebrities, shaking hands with the drunken P—— . . . Doing a farthing's worth, they do not walk about with attaché cases as if they had done a hundred rubles' worth. . . . (7) If they possess talent, they respect it. For it they sacrifice rest, women, wine, vanity . . . They are proud of their talent. . . . And also they are fastidious. (8) They foster the æsthetic feeling in themselves. . . . From woman they require, not a bed. . . . They, especially if they are artists, need freshness, elegance, humanity, the capacity for being not a . . . but a mother.

A notable program that, coming extempore from a young fellow of twenty-six, desperately busy, up to his neck in medicine, up to his neck in short-story writing for the newspapers, and already attacked by the disease which eventually carried him off. I call attention to it because it contains a good part of the ethical code of Chekhov. It is perfectly genuine. There is no windy inflation in the man—nothing to

[133]

puncture. The ideas and spirit of that letter—its good sense and its sensitiveness—pervade all the family letters and all the relations of his life pretty consistently straight through to the end. And these rules for decent behavior by no means constitute his entire conception of the obligations devolved upon a man by accepting membership in the intellectual class. Courage, gayety, vivacity and the "light touch" are clearly elements in his ideal, as they are also constant elements in his practice.

The letters to Olga Knipper I read with mixed feelings. They are a batch of ante-and-post-nuptial love letters almost too intimate for publication. An intellectual in love and in the intimacy of marriage. Piquant themes. Rather curiously, as it seemed to me, their substance is far inferior to that of the other collection. Many of them are little more than flights of caresses and salutations of the author bowing down at the "little feet" of the lady, till his forehead knocks on the floor. Nevertheless, I should defer to Chekhov's unquestionably superior knowledge of the right thing in this connection and assume that he knew what the recipient wanted, except that she herself frequently complains of his brevity and his triviality—to which he often replies with announcement that he has had his hair cut and has brushed his teeth but could not bathe.

His playful epithets are amusing: "My sweet actress," "popsey," "sweet dog," "ginger-haired dog," "my fiery dog," "my splendid spouse," "my little crocodile," "my little whale," etc. So is much of his incessant banter amusing, especially when he plays at being a brutal peasant, threatens to "smash" her if she doesn't write, reminds her that he is her "lawful

[134]

husband" and has a "perfect right to beat her"—when she lets a single day go by without a letter. But all this sustained to the very end and involved, these caresses, with the distressing medical details of the progress of his disease becomes a little ghastly.

And yet I am not sure that the correspondence is not a model of what a dying gentleman's letters ought to be when he is married to a wife of whom he has grown very fond, but whom he is obliged by his principles and by his magnanimity to leave quite at liberty to absent herself all winter, following her own profession on the stage in Moscow. This much is clear: only a highly civilized man could have played Chekhov's part in that marriage with unfailing gayety and unfailing generosity.

Chekhov was tremendously industrious at all periods of his life. While he was dying he undertook the writing of his best play, "The Cherry Orchard." He put it through. "Ineffective" is a word that does not apply to the Chekhovism that one finds in the letters. With the ineffective "Russian Hamlet" of Turgenev, with the really unpractical and impotent members of the intelligentsia—idle, chattering, vodka-drinking triflers—he has personally as little in common as he has with the Asiatic manners of his peasants or with the stolidity of his bureaucrats, or with the self-satisfaction of his new bourgeoisie.

Oh, once upon a time, doubtless, he felt in himself something of the melancholy impotence of Ivanoff in the play of that name; something of the automatism expressed by the author Trigorin in "The Sea Gull"; much, perhaps, of the vague unrest expressed by the idealistic student Trophimof in "The Cherry Orchard." But Chekhov himself, as revealed in the letters, is a man who early took himself in hand, organized his aims and efforts and drove with incessant energy toward a perfectly definite goal.

But I haven't finished my account of genuine Chekhovism till I say that when Chekhov had emerged from the peasantry and had become an intellectual he proceeded then to emerge from the intelligentsia in order to become an individual and a "free artist."

The artist, too, has his ethics and his honor. "Respect yourself, for the love of Christ; don't give your hands liberty when your brain is lazy." That is pure ethics. The first principle of honor is that the artist must preserve his integrity as a spectator, letting nothing interfere with the pure objectivity of his vision. We know, of course, that "pure objectivity" is an illusion, and doubtless Chekhov did also; but there is a relative objectivity which may furnish a working principle:

It seems to me that it is not the business of novelists to solve such questions as those of God, pessimism and the like. The novelist's business is only to describe who has been speaking or thinking about God or pessimism, how and in what circumstances. . . . For writing fellows, particularly for artists, it is time to confess that one can't make anything out in this world, as once Socrates confessed and Voltaire, too. The mob thinks it knows and understands everything; and the stupider it is the wider it fancies its outlook to be. If an artist in whom the mob believes will make up his mind to declare that he understands nothing of what he sees, that in itself will be a great gain in the sphere of thought and a great step forward.

To this should be added his more intimate avowal of skepticism and positive faith in a letter of 1889:

I am not a liberal, nor a conservative, nor a meliorist, nor a monk, nor an indifferentist. I should like to be a free artist and nothing more. . . . I hate falsehood and violence in all their aspects . . . Pharisaism, stupidity and arbitrariness reign not in shopkeepers' houses and prisons alone. . . . I detect them in science, in literature and in the younger generations. . . . For these reasons I nurse no particular partiality for gendarmes, or butchers, or savants, or writers, or the younger generation.

There is his skepticism.

"My Holy of Holies is the human body, health, mind, talent, inspiration, love and the most absolute freedom—freedom from violence and falsehood in whatever they may be manifested. This is the program I would follow if I were a great artist."

There is his faith.

If that is Chekhovism, I, for one, hope we are in for a long season of it.

XI

Llewelyn Powys: A Sick Man's Vision or the Naked Truth?

LLEWELYN POWYS, like R. L. Stevenson, entered upon his literary career with a sinister experience which I have heard the witty euphemists in a sanatorium describe in jeweled phrase as "spitting rubies." This experience subsequently gave a fine edge to his appreciation of the Masai curse: "May you never spit white again!"—the noble savage as observed in East Africa does not overflow with brotherly love. It also contributed—this experience—toward edging his appreciation of many other things, and, again, as in the case of R. L. Stevenson, it already bids fair to get him into serious trouble with the critics.

Mr. Powys emerges for us out of a background reekingly British. He emerges by virtue of his talent for bringing into high and often into startling relief the universal interest in whatever theme he touches.

He has, for a minor example, the habit of talking in print about the members of his own family, and the habit of dedicating his books to them. What with affection, derision, humor and cutting irony he has, within the limits of "Skin for Skin" given a distinct flavor and a memorable word to both his parents and to nearly all his numerous brothers and sisters. Yet they but flicker across the pages. They are but notes of the background from which he himself emerges with

(Lewelyn Powys)

a figure—not reekingly British—the figure of an uncompromising post-war pessimist with a marvelous faculty for expressing a vision which will encounter quick sympathies in disenchanted people all over the world.

He was born in 1883, eighth of eleven children, at Dorchester, famous town in the domain of the "Wessex" pessimist, whose somber intuitions of long ago we feel as so prescient and so refreshing. He was born in a very English home, apparently fixed in English traditions of what used to be considered the best sort: upper middle class; Church of England; Cambridge University for generations; addiction to country life in the southern countries; William Cowper somewhere in the family tree; the sword of an East India uncle hanging in the library of the rectory; family prayers; maids bringing in cakes and tea.

As for the immediate family, a mother with the gift of sorrow; a white-headed *pater*, a fine leonine figure of the Victorian divine; a sister with the gift of ecstatically identifying herself with nature; brothers—three or four of them writers, notably Theodore and John, and the lot of them men of enterprise and talent, unconventional thinkers, talkers, suitable persons to sharpen one's wits upon, suitable fellows to assist one in breaking out of the paternal sheepfold—goatish sharp-horned young pagans in their youth, butting their way out of the "bourgeoisie," butting their way to intellectual freedom.

We got our first sharp impression that Llewelyn Powys was arriving with something of more than parish lane concern when, in 1923, he published an arresting little volume called "Ebony and Ivory," containing sketches and stories of East Africa and southern

England—containing also a personality with a pungently bitter tang. In 1924, ostensibly eschewing "æsthetic effects," seeking only the beauty of a merciless veracity, he returned in imagination to the swart continent, and plucked at its mystery with even starker grip, with even more potent effect, in "Black Laughter." Now, in "Skin for Skin," with only occasional allusions to the profound and shattering adventure of his soul as a stockman in Uganda, he reverts to the origins of his vision and his point of view, giving us, in the same almost incredibly poignant style, his experience as an invalid in an Alpine sanatorium and as a convalescent in Southern England, during the period between his twenty-fifth year and his five years' sojourn in Africa.

I read these three books with a quickening of consciousness which I regard as one of the chief rewards for reading anything. I read them with intense excitement, exclaiming over page after page: "Upon my soul, what a writer! How the man can write!"—or words with an even higher accent but to the same effect. Among imaginative modern interpreters of nature and the soul of alien peoples, he belongs with men of the first mark—with Pierre Loti, Charles M. Doughty, D. H. Lawrence.

But already I hear a dissentient murmur rising, which sounds something like this: "Yes, a very striking writer, to be sure. Impressive books—in a way. But unpleasant . . . morbid . . . a taint in them. Clearly a man of abnormal sensibilities. Really, unhealthy books, you know . . . cruel and of a most dubious morality. A sick man's vision of life—after 'Skin for Skin' transparently so."

A sick man's vision of life. My first impulse is to

parody Lincoln on Grant's whisky-drinking; you remember, when critics informed him that his commander was habitually soaked in whisky he inquired: "What brand? I want to send some to my other generals." My first impulse is brutally to ejaculate: "Would that more of our authors were ill!" But one must be serious and sober, and one must admit that here is a subject that asks a little threshing-out. What is the relation of disease, particularly tuberculosis, to the development of literary talent? Does it affect one's vision of life in such fashion as to invalidate the vision?

A night or so ago I was sitting before a fire with a robust and sanguine friend who, like myself, restricts a physical strength adequate for a lumberjack, adequate for driving logs through the rocks of a foaming river, to driving a little fountain pen over sheets of smooth white paper. We were full of the summer, full of the delight of not even trying to think, full of remembered pleasure in making something with our hands and in going somewhere with our feet—the sweet, heavy thoughtless monotony of building stone walls all day long in a country garden, the joyous, thoughtless effectiveness of swinging an ax in the woods and such entirely satisfying activities as swimming, canoeing and tennis.

"The ideal human life," I said, "is in some physical action which one has just brains enough to perform." "Yes," agreed my literary friend, and he began to brag of the beauty of his garden tools and of the glorious workmanship and singing rhythm of a scythe. "I am convinced," he concluded, "that no one takes to writing who hasn't something physically or mentally the matter with him." We were in precisely the mood, you see, to be impressed by recollection that Powys and

[143]

Stevenson and Symonds and Hood and Keats and
Sterne were "TB's" and that there must have been
something abnormal about Chaucer and Shakespeare
—*must* have been! Thank heaven, there was.

Now, in the case of Stevenson, evidently it was a
point of pride and honor to play the part of a well
man in life and in letters. So far as possible he suppressed in his public thinking and feeling, and even
in his private consciousness, the fact that on his body
a "damned defeat" had been made. Latter-day critics
ridicule his point of honor; declare him unsuccessful
in his gallant pretense; "explain" him by tracing
everything to his illness; and—quite absurdly, in my
opinion—attempt the destruction of his literary reputation by the same stroke. I doubt whether Stevenson
himself was fully aware in how many ways and how
deeply his art was affected by his disease. But that
is another question. Our point now is that he based his
honor and his philosophy and his art upon the assumption that he possessed a normal *mind*, equal to all
hazards, and also competent to furnish sound entertainment to healthy people.

Mr. Powys is of another generation, which attacks
the "problems of life" from a different angle. I fancy
he is consciously somewhat anti-Stevensonian. He
speaks, at any rate, superciliously of the "courtly collect," "Virginibus Puerisque," which Stevenson wrote
at the Davos Platz sanatorium. I can even imagine
his swearing, with a round Elizabethan oath, that he
will have none of this "gallant pretense." As for him,
his honor, *his* philosophy, *his* art, are to be fashioned
in absolutely open recognition of this stunning fundamental fact of his bodily circumstance: that he, a
young fellow to whom life has just feigned to wish the

top of the morning, he, strolling through flowers of a sunlit garden, rejoicing in his youth, discovers of a sudden that myriads of cane-like micro-organisms have taken lodgings in his lungs, and that the struggle for possession of them is "on" between him and invaders more ruthless than Vandals and Huns.

It was rather a shock. It did not come to him gradually, but abruptly, in a mouthful of blood—knowledge of the sort of infested tenement he had leased, consciousness that his spirit now, at any time, might be evicted without notice and turned adrift on the chill air. It was a shock, but it did not floor him.

On the contrary, it startled him upright, it stabbed him broad awake. He began to think and to feel with unwonted vividness. And in a world which had become singularly bright and sweet to his senses, a vision dawned for him and abided with him and widened till it made a background for all our banqueting and revelry. Should he veil it? Not he. The first sentence of "Skin for Skin" flaunts his theme: "I first discovered that I had consumption during the small hours of a November night in the year 1909"—and it is 1925 now. In the entire period of his literary production, then, Mr. Powys has had a lively awareness that his house was on fire and that he was his house; that to Alpine snows and African heats he must flee from what he must carry with him.

A vision of life reported by a sick man under menace of death—may we dismiss that as "interesting, in a way," but not significant for the rest of us? Evidently Mr. Powys thinks not. His contention is that he, by a slight excess in the malignity of nature toward him, has attained an intenser sense than most men of the conditions which nevertheless confront and encompass us all. We—the rest of us—dance before a pictured curtain masking a bottomless abyss. For him, the veil has been rent—that is all; he dances with a wilder elation because he sees where the last figure ends.

The men of science and the physicians, in their confidential hours, are in agreement with Mr. Powys. They tell us that the difference between a well man and a sick one is so small that we should brag about it in whispers, for fear of the overhearing gods. We are all infected, and it is merely a question of how long we can "keep up." We are all hosts of invisible enemies waiting only for some favorable coincidence of falling temperature, tainted food and wet sidewalks to make an insurrection and dispossess us. We are all swimming in seas of noxious micro-organisms; the stronger swimmers manage to keep their noses above the surface a little more steadily and a little longer than the others; but sooner or later they too grow weary, throw up their arms, gasp, get a mouthful and go under, go down, forever and ever. That is the normal thing.

The abnormal thing—no, let us not say that—the queer, inexplicable thing, is that, though we have a proverb "as sure as death and taxes" most of us think and feel and act as if we should live forever, not in our Father's mansion, but right here in our five-room apartment at the corner of Riverside Drive and Seventy-second Street. We never get up to see the rising sun nor watch to see the going down of the planets nor walk to the house where Washington Irving lived, six blocks east of us; but, half asleep, we go mooning along in the strange hallucination of health and longevity till cold hands take us by the throat and remind us, when it is time to die, that we have not yet begun to live.

It does seem to stand to reason that the soundest views of life should be expressed by men who refuse opiates and briskly manage their affairs and husband their moments in a shrewd wide-eyed awareness that they are under sentence of death.

But this bottom-of-the-cup realism, this straight unblinking look at The End—doesn't it freeze the heart, palsy enterprise, overcast heaven's blue and the verdure of earth and, in short, destroy both the illusion of seriousness and the reality of mirth in the play of the *petites marionettes* who make their *trois petits tours* and then go away? The traditional portion of his family, friends, and neighbors thought that it *should*.

When Llewelyn Powys was stricken—so he remembers it—they dealt with him in the manner established by Job's comforters for dealing with a man who has "got his." They engloomed his bedside with orthodox prayer and bungling condolence and mute bewilderment and the general lack of imaginative sympathy customary on such occasions. His father supplicated divine intervention. His mother, "who ever loved sorrow rather than joy," resented his purposed migration to Switzerland, wishing him to return to the family home—"to die there peacefully clinging to the Christian hope." One brother nervously betrayed his fear of infection. The old stonemason assured him that he had "a churchyard cough." And, amid these ministrations, he had transient moods—so he tells us with a devastating stroke of his irony—he had transient moods when, taking the sacrament in the parish church, he thought he might "become as a little child and go to heaven along with the Master of Corpus."

[147]

"To become as a little child—along with the Master of Corpus." Obviously that is one of the points at which one exclaims: "Upon my soul, what a writer!" One aspect of the genius of Llewelyn Powys, the Voltairean aspect, is lit by the blinding flash which issues from that astounding juxtaposition. I have murmured the phrase over and over to myself—"Along with the Master of Corpus, along with the Master of Corpus"— and each time that I have murmured it I have seemed to hear all the stained-glass windows of fashionable Christendom rattle as in an earthquake. It is necromantic—no less.

Mr. Powys revolted from the ministrations at his sickbed. He did not wish to die—still less did he wish to spend the residue of his days, long or short, in preparing his genial spirit for the shroud. Life clamored within him that it is better to be anything alive—a midget, a mud-eating lobworm, a white-bellied beetle— than a "dead" stone. At first he was stung into sharp rebellion by what he mistook for the exceptional character of his fate. He felt an extraordinary mental activity. "I became," he declares, "like one drunken with wine. A torrent of words issued from my mouth." He dramatized his situation and railed at God. But he didn't expect to be heard. He didn't even believe with any "realizing sense" in the reality of his fate. "My head became completely turned, and I chittered at Death like a little gray squirrel who is up in a fir tree out of harm's way."

It was in a high-class sanatorium in Switzerland that coolness returned to Mr. Powys and self-collection became possible, and he began to shake off the mortuary consolations of English parish Christianity, and to reconstruct his personal philosophy on a realistic basis.

I admire enormously the little delicate strokes with which he produces just enough of the sanatorium life and atmosphere to suggest how and where it impinged upon his consciousness, modifying it steadily, insensibly, in the direction of the creed held, perhaps, by most experienced inmates of such institutions—a creed which might be described as a mild and cautious form of Epicureanism, with intervals of great philosophic quietude following the excessive "spitting of rubies."

These young people draw the covers over their heads when the rumor runs that a clergyman or a pious "good woman" is coming through the corridors. And yet nothing interests them, among themselves, like exchanging free views, in absolutely free language, upon religion and metaphysics and the wider implications of science.

Nothing interests them like religion, unless it be love—playing at love, delicately, with girls of an ivory pallor, not averse to a caress in their "zero hour," or when they are lying in mortal stillness after a return from an "engagement" in the front line trenches. After one has chatted for a little with a Hungarian pessimist who gives one an aphorism on the necessity of working in order to forget one's destiny, one taps at the door of Daphne, and sits with her for a while: "I could not endure that you should be wicked with any one but me."

No, nothing interests them like love, unless it be bawdry. Their first inquiry of a newcomer is: "Have you any naughty books?" For these and their scribbled verses and their epigrams and their picturesque imprecations on the food and service of the sanatorium —imprecations to the excogitation, elaboration and artistic polishing of which they devote a morning's

[149]

careful meditation or long hours of the midnight watch
—all these circulate, along with their Victrola records, from room to room, as the chief media of social
exchange. And when any remark particularly "good"
or particularly "naughty" is devised by any of them
it floats through the halls, swift as a whiff of ether,
bringing relief and a quickened sense of life to liers-in-
bed, a little bored by watching the rise and fall of their
temperatures and by wondering what progress or re-
gress has been made since the last time they looked,
with the aid of the X-ray, into the operations beneath
their own breastbones of those swarming micro-
organisms, so zealously obeying the Almighty's behest
to "increase and multiply."

In a sanatorium "enlightened selfishness" may be
described as the official philosophy, and it is deliberately prescribed to patients as the only philosophy
fit for them to embrace. The two positive watchwords
which Mr. Powys recalls from that period are "good
manners" and "expedience." On the negative side:
"Insensitiveness is the one cardinal sin." In the depths
of consciousness, however, one places as the grand
consolation, the foundation stone upon which rise
courtesy and gaiety and vivacity and all other
amenities—in the bottom of consciousness one rests
ultimately upon this grand consolation: "Nothing
matters." The maxim is not incompatible with a great
deal of eagerness in all the chief concerns of life and
punctilious care in the little ones. Often it seems con-
ducive to just the proper degree of internal coolness
for the best external functioning of hot little men.

When Mr. Powys emerged from the philosophical
school of the sanatorium he found that he did not relish
"the smell of the inside of churches," but that the

inside of an English tavern seemed savory and right and all in consonance with his new realism: "Here, at any rate, no spiritual treachery is tolerated; here, at any rate, no deceitful idealism stretches tendrils white and sickly. He who sits down on a tavern settle must even take the world as he finds it. He must know what birth means, and that we come into the world in no very cleanly manner; he must know what love means, and wrath, and lust, and, above all, death. In a tavern, come winter, come summer, the truth will out."

Now in "Ebony and Ivory" and in "Black Laughter" Mr. Powys carried his personal philosophy far from the sanatorium, where he first encountered it in general practice, and tested it for its universal values among the brutalized English stockmen and big game hunters, the Indian traders, the black "boys" and the animals, wild and domesticated, of a ranch in Africa of 30,000 acres, grazing 2,000 cattle and 14,000 sheep.

But before he entered on his career as ranch manager he had subjected his sensibilities, acutely sharpened to the sweetness of life by the prospect of death— to the loveliness of southern England, where he tasted the delight of a stately Elizabethan garden and brushed the dew from bluebells and pink campions while the cuckoos called, and roamed on Egdon moor, "in the meadows by the river Yeo," and between "musk-laden Wiltshire hedges," trying his brother John's advice to the convalescent, to divert his mind "from what is mean and sordid, so that large, luminous thoughts may roll in upon it like amber-colored waves."

The effect upon him of passing from the most exquisitely cultivated beauty of the English scene to the raw savagery of an African wilderness vibrates in all three of his books. The contrast is an obvious principle of composition in "Ebony and Ivory." It is an even more intimate and pervasive element of his consciousness throughout "Black Laughter." Perhaps the reader will feel its potency most amazingly if he turns from reading "Skin for Skin" to "Black Laughter."

"Skin for Skin" ends, I ascertained by reference, with another attack of "spitting rubies," and with a picture of an invalid who, after having recklessly courted disaster, lies on his back, "perfectly motionless, like a rabbit that 'freezes' in a thicket of thorns, in the hope that he will not be seen, in the hope that the danger will pass him by." But what I remember, *without* reference, in this book is a fragrant gorse bush at the top of an English lane and a young man there, intent on the "murmuring rapture" of a honey-bee buzzing among the golden bloom.

From that one turns, in "Black Laughter," to darkness and wind and flying sparks from a little Uganda train which at midnight dumps this lonely fugitive at a station on a plateau of East Africa. He crawls exhausted into a rusty bed in a match-board shanty roofed with sheets of corrugated iron, leaving the door open so that he may look through its ebony-black aperture into the cavernous blackness of Africa. He is too much excited for slumber, visioning no longer the honeysuckle lanes and dreaming orchards of his childhood, but dark immensities of wilderness peopled by "naked black men, asleep at the moment by the white ashes of myriads of campfires with their tall spears ready to hand." When at length he dozes off, uneasily, filled with "ancestral misgivings," it is to

open startled eyes and find himself sitting bolt upright
on his creaking bed, roused by the long reverberation
of a lion's roar. Before Mr. Powys is done with that
astounding welcome, the reader himself is ready to yell
with the excitement of it.

Doubtless the invalid's nerves were a little "jumpy"
at first, overwrought and subject to "uncanny" sugges-
tion. You and I might be startled by a lion's roar or
rendered uneasy under "the flat equatorial moon" by
the moaning of hyenas "as they slunk along the darkened banks of forest streams nosing for death with
heavy, obtuse jowls." But who that was not a sick
man would have been troubled at the tropical noontide
by a sudden awareness that he was *"being looked at,*
that from behind the trellis or from behind the bloom
of a mammoth nasturtium, a haggard and very old
chameleon was peering at me, intelligently, cynically."
Who but a sick man would have been troubled by the
excited eyes of rabbits—eyes "black as ivy berries"—
eyes peering from a fissure of a rock as if in query as
to what purpose "could have brought this pale, deliberate gorilla to invade their lofty isolated retreats."

But Mr. Powys's nerves steadied down as he went
about his wholesome human business of managing
black labor and tarring, dosing and castrating 2,000
cattle and 14,000 sheep, so that his brother, the former
manager, might with an easy conscience be off to fight
the Germans. The invalid's nerves, in the course of
five years of farming, so far approached normality
that he was able to slaughter and butcher a bullock,
knock down a black boy, shoot a caged leopard, fight
fire, trap lions, get a sulky native witch doctor out of a
hut by touching a match to it, and, I should say, carry
most parts of the white man's burden among subject

peoples. He made, it appears, for a sick man, no bad deputy among the savages during that period when, as he muses, his "own race"—the abler, "healthier" portion of it—"his own race, along with the others, was causing the very crust of the planet to tremble with its barbaric and malignant onslaughts."

Yet, going with steadier nerves about his business on an African ranch, he did, nevertheless, continue to observe things which bore on his personal philosophy and developed the fundamental pessimism which had originated in his primary philosophic intuition and upon which rests his superstructure of mild, cautious and sensitive hedonism.

He observed the hideous cruelty of white men from "Christian" countries toward their black servants and laborers. He observed the hideous cruelty of the blacks toward one another—poor, pitiful, abject devils in whom obviously was neither hope nor prospect of a "blessed resurrection." He pursued his observation down the scale of animal life, watched the rancher baiting the lion's trap with the headless corpse of a native, the leopard rending the cattle, the ticks clinging to the sleek body of the cheetah, ticks and maggots and tapeworms and smallpox struggling to reduce all life to carrion, while foul-beaked vultures hovered over all. Cruelty, rapacity and lust were at the heart of the plot, and with a strange shudder of exaltation he recognized all those hideous passions in himself, squarely faced the fact that he was one of the plotters.

I think critics rather misinterpret Mr. Powys's thrill at the discovery of his own cruelty. His exultation is due to his progress in self-knowledge. He is thrilled by seeing through himself and recognizing that he is cruel, like a lion, like a savage, like a bandit, like a prime minister, like a little child.

I will quote you now a philosophic summary from the first of the books, "Ebony and Ivory":

Africa, like one of her own black-maned lions, laps up the life-blood of all the delicate illusions that have so long danced before the eyes of men and made them happy. Truth alone is left alive. What was suspected in Europe is made plain here: *At the bottom of the well of life there is no hope.* Under Scorpio, under the Southern Cross and in the clear light of this passionless, tropical sunshine, the hollow emptiness of the world's soul is made certain—*the surface is everything, below is nothing.*

But we have said all this, haven't we? some of us— among ourselves—privately, and then dismissed it as morbid, as a sick man's vision of life, as inconvenient, as not a respectable way of conceiving things and not respectful to the universe. We have said these things. We have half way known them. Something—merely beginning with the introspection of an invalid—has made Llewelyn Powys flamingly aware of them. And the curious fact is that, in consequence of a general increase in self-knowledge and, still more, in self-acknowledgment, among "civilized" people since the World War, there is hardly any one to be found, no matter how sound his lung cavity happens to be, who will stand up and dispute the truth of them. Unless neomysticism has more for us than yet meets the eye it looks as if the reconstruction of our personal philosophies would have to *begin* there—about where Mr. Powys stands.

XII

R. L. S. Encounters the "Modern" Writers on Their Own Ground

THE publication of a popular and complete edition gives me a desired occasion to inquire a little into the relations between Stevenson and the "modern" school of novelists and essayists. At the present moment those relations are decidedly strained. My own notion, briefly stated, is that spokesmen of "the modern school" are, as Hamlet remarked of the little eyases, exclaiming "against their own succession." They ought, I think, to be saluting Stevenson as a valiant forerunner in their own movement toward that sharper self-knowledge and that more candid self-acknowledgment which animate the important writers of all periods.

But the "moderns" seem to miss this vital link between their efforts and the effort of Stevenson. They are rather bent on drawing a line than upon establishing a connection. For example, that delightful cockney novelist and shrewd disciple of Gissing, Mr. Frank Swinnerton, strains the relation between Stevenson and his heirs to the breaking point. He expresses the asperity and the condescension of the heirs in a critical study of the testator, bristling with such distinctions as these:

The modern school of novelists . . . provides little enough material for loving hearts. The modern school

Robert Louis Stevenson

says to its readers: "You are wicked, selfish, diseased, but horribly fascinating, and I'm going to set you right by diagnosis"; and the reader feels a sting in the fascination. Stevenson says, "We are all mighty fine fellows; and life is a field of battle; but it is better to be a fool than to be dead; and the true success is to labor"; and the reader feels that Stevenson is One of Us! He is not austere; he does not ask uncomfortable questions; he makes no claims upon his readers' judgment, but only upon their self-esteem and their gratified assent.*

I think that this distinction between Stevenson and the modern school is false.

Stevenson *begins*, just as the moderns do, just as Llewelyn Powys, for example, does: he begins with austere diagnosis. He makes all the fundamental admissions which they make: he admits the wickedness, selfishness, disease, and horrible fascination at the heart of life. But he recognizes also that mere diagnosis does *not* "set you right." A diagnosis such as that of Llewelyn Powys, which I have just discussed, is not the end, but only the starting point, of a personal philosophy which is to be truly realistic.

The real distinction between Stevenson and the moderns is that, while they devote themselves to elaborating diagnosis, he devoted himself to the elaboration of therapy. Or, to shift from Mr. Swinnerton's clinical images, let us say: At the age of twenty-five, Stevenson had definitely ascertained what was the matter with him and with life. He had looked into all the abysses which Mr. Powys is astonishingly fathoming at forty-

* *R. L. Stevenson, A Critical Study*, New York, 1923.

two. And then, never oblivious of his darker vision, he turned to the task of fashioning, on the verge of the abyss, a dance and a music as heartening as the sound of bagpipes.

The grimmer members of the modern school say, in effect: "We are going to exclude from the audience of significant modern art the following classes: children, nice young girls and boys, old maids, old fogies, the entire ruck of the *bourgeoisie*, and all people who insanely insist that they are happy and contented. We shall address only stern, unblinking adults, such as are at least theoretically pessimists and we intend to give them their first full realizing sense of the abyss."

To that I reply, "Bring on your abyss!" That is one perfectly legitimate object of letters. I like to think of myself as an "unblinking adult"—not dizzy at precipices. I am ready to hear whatever honest report the moderns may bring in concerning their soundings in the abyss. But, surely, for an adequate literary movement, the exclusions of "the modern school," as Mr. Swinnerton describes it, are too wide, its remorseless intention is too narrow. Ultimately it will be forced to expand and make room for the dancing and music of children and for all the other folk to whom Stevenson showed, with so much grace and charm in the showing, how to be happy in "playing the game."

The game of which we are speaking is not optional— is not so regarded by my crowd. It *must* be played. Therefore, it is not a whit more the business of a realistic personal philosophy to acknowledge where it ends than to devise good ways of playing it with some spirit and with some style to the end. But I definitely exclude here discussion of Stevenson's great rôle as instructor in the game, contributor to its rules and keyer-up of the sporting spirit on the grounds.

That is not our theme. What I wish to inquire is whether this graceful fellow is alive yet or whether he has succumbed to the only thing which really threatened him—the danger of being too much at his ease in Bohemia, too much a play-boy.

A quarter of a century ago I had read everything of Stevenson's then accessible, and in every year since I have reread some portions of his work. In all that time I have not exhausted him, and the violence of reaction against him by the "movement" writers puzzles me. Probably I shall have to be classified as an incorrigible Stevensonian.

Inevitably the long crusade of the anti-Stevensonians against him, his character and his art, and against us—the Stevensonians—our character and our taste, infuriates me. All of them, from the atrabilious W. E. Henley to Messrs. Swinnerton, Steuart* and Hellman†—all of them say such nasty things about us: about our author and his readers. In general, they are consistent in their very curious line of attack. First, demonstrating that he was an invalid and an immoral man, they contend that his work is invalidated by the fact that it expresses too much of his invalidism and too little of his immorality!

It is true that when last fall Mr. Steuart discharged his double-barreled blunderbuss in Stevenson's direction Mr. Swinnerton took him roundly to task for his bad shooting. (I had taken him to task for his superfluous and exultant repeppering of the straw man set up for his own peppering by the ingenious Henley.)

---

* *Robert Louis Stevenson,* Boston, 1924, two vols.
† *The True Stevenson, A Study in Clarification,* Boston, 1925.

[161]

But no one has dealt more drastically with Stevenson than Mr. Swinnerton himself, and no one has said nastier things about him and about those who persist in admiring him. Doubtless he knows what he is about. He calls it criticism, but he means war. Stevenson persists in enchanting readers generation after generation. He fails to "senesce" as a writer should do who has been before us so long. Mr. Swinnerton desires to give him a knock-out blow and to drag him out of the circle of his glamour, so that there will be elbow room and attention for "the modern school of novelists." But let the Stevensonians consider the mortal nature of such thrusts as these—if they really reach home, if they really touch the man we know:

The teaching of the essays is one of compromise, not of enlarged ideals; it is the doctrine of that "state of life" which finally ends in a good-natured passivity not unlike the happy innocence of the domesticated cat. . . . With all his writing he took the road of least resistance, the road of limited horizons; because, with all his desire for romance, his desire for the splendor of the great life of action, he was by physical delicacy made intellectually timid and spiritually cautious. He was obliged to take care of himself, to be home at night, to allow himself to be looked after. . . . His plays, his poems, his essays, his romances— all are seen nowadays to be consumptive.

In short, this R. L. S., it seems, was a swathed, coddled, and timorous weakling of a tedious virtuosity, consciously fashioning toys and polishing truisms "fit to be culled and calendared for suburban households."

Now, I confess that I enjoy the clash of school with school in a struggle for survival, and I like encounter with a critic who drives a thesis hard against the ribs of an adversary. A stiff fight over the body of a wounded or assaulted leader animates the scene, recruits fresh combatants and jolts the sleepy-eyed to partisanship. But I like, too, a nice regard for truth in these collisions—the blade of the swordsman entering a joint in the armor and not shattered on impenetrable steel, or coarsely used as a bludgeon. And to lapse a little into the Elizabethan style of my youth, most of these things which Mr. Swinnerton says about Stevenson seem to me "as false as hell," and for saying them I could "eat his heart in the marketplace."

It should perhaps be explained that the Stevenson controversy has been waged in great part over the heads of the public. Poems, letters, essays, unfinished novels, commentaries by Mrs. Stevenson and Lloyd Osbourne, and all sorts of supplementary evidence, which even old readers had not seen, constantly entered into the debate. Much of the material employed by disputants on both sides has remained till recently in manuscript or in semi-private publication or in separate collections of the letters or in stately subscription editions of the collective works which, for many of us, were too expensive to ink and thumb in the familiarity of private ownership. As for previous popular and unauthorized "dry goods" editions, they contain, relatively speaking, but an expurgation and abridgment of the man, upon which no argument can now rest.

The material in the new South Seas Edition* described as "not previously published in any popular edition" includes more than a dozen introductions to

* New York, 1925, 32 vols.

[163]

the individual volumes, by Lloyd Osbourne, vividly sketching his stepfather at various ages of his life from twenty-six to his death; five "ethical" papers; twenty-two pages from the Silverado diary, first published in the Vailima edition; some eighty pages of critical reviews; a play, "The Hanging Judge," first published in the Vailima edition; a story called "When the Devil Was Well"; an autobiographical fragment of twenty pages containing an important statement of his relations to Mrs. Sitwell and Sidney Colvin; "Moral Emblems"; nearly two hundred pages of new poems; half a dozen unfinished stories in "The Ebb Tide" volume; the juvenile "History of Moses," with sundry sketches; a "Protest on Behalf of Boer Independence"; Stevenson's "Companion to the Cook Book," and, above all, the letters, all of them, four volumes of them, of which more than a hundred "appear here for the first time in a popular edition."

I say this is the best possible counterblast to the undermining operations of the anti-Stevensonians. None of them, from Messrs. Hellman, Steuart and Swinnerton back to the atrabilious Henley—none of them, I firmly believe, will be able permanently to impose his destructive views upon a public which has, as now, easy access to the complete works.

I have emerged from my explorations brimming with fresh wonder as to where the anti-Stevensonians collect their impressions. What wild and savage life have these London and Edinburgh critics lived which enables them to speak of Stevenson as a physical weakling, barred from a romantic life of action because, forsooth, "he was obliged to take care of himself, to be home at night, to allow himself to be looked after"!

What lions have these critical fellows shot with a

bow and arrow, that they turn up superior noses at Stevenson, who merely consorted with thieves and harlots in the slums of Edinburgh and London, ran through the professions of engineering and law before he was twenty-five, explored the Scotch coast in a sailboat, canoed the Sambre and Oise, slept in a lonely bivouac *à la belle étoile* in the Cévennes, fled to San Francisco by emigrant train, ran away with a wife and family, camped on Mount St. Helena, chartered his own schooner, sailed the South Seas for three years, feasted with cannibal chiefs, refused to sleep with their wives, conspired with Kanaka kings, was threatened with deportation, planted a wilderness, governed a small tribe of savages and died in his boots?

If these lofty critical fellows hold that Stevenson's sheltered and coddled life starved and devitalized his romance, come, let us bring them to confession and require them to tell us what sort of dare-devil existence a really "modern" writer must live.

The field of battle to which he likened marriage as well as life was a field in which there was no headstrong conflict of ideal and practise, but a mere accommodation which a phrase could embody.

This is Mr. Swinnerton again. But where did he pick up that impression? Not, surely, from considering with any attention Stevenson's long heart-breaking fight for his own morality, his own religion, his own love choice, and his own profession, against the stubborn opposition of his parents and all the embattled forces of time, place and circumstances. Can't they see, these superior critics, that what they call a "toy," this romance of "Kidnapped," for example, with its

[165]

desperate flight of David and Alan Breck Stewart through the heather is a vital poetic symbol for the whole course of Stevenson's running fight for life both physical and spiritual?

"The teaching of the essays is one of compromise, not of enlarged ideals."

Well, now, who was it before Stevenson that compounded the French artist with the shorter catechist and was in dead earnest about both? Was it Wilde or Pater or Ruskin or Carlyle? Who, for the behoof of us all, cured himself of all reverence for the stereotyped mid-Victorian Calvinist, and for "the common banker," and for all types whatever of smug, prudential, conforming "respectability"? Who taught us that if a sour morality was all we had, for pity's sake to keep it, but to keep it to ourselves? Who took his favorite authors—Montaigne and Shakespeare and Bunyan and Dumas and Hazlitt and Thoreau and Whitman— and derived from them, and tested to the hilt in his own experience, a modern gospel, realistic, based on self-knowledge and self-acknowledgment, boldly individualistic, with independent standards of honor and loyalty, with a quite fresh assortment and proportioning of virtues, gleaming among them courage and charm and gaiety and passionate kindness and fidelity inflexible to one's calling?

If Stevenson did not enlarge ideals, who was it between 1870 and 1893 that clear-cut, brightly colored and popularized just his type of Bohemianism throughout the English-speaking world, and in particular infatuated with it starved, stodgy, stiff, frockcoated America? Did it change the tune here, or didn't it?

Yes. But some of the iconoclasts tell us, with an

immense deal of scorn, that this picturesque Bohemian
pleased the clergy!—never stopping to inquire whether
that fact was creditable to the clergy or discreditable
to him; whether it indicated that he had been won to
their view or they to his. The iconoclasts noticed that
he "preached," without noticing what he was preaching; and that he wrote "Lay Morals," without noticing
what virtues he commended; and that he composed
prayers, without noticing the objects of his suppli-
cations or the nature of the deity that he addressed.
And so, one must assume, they reached the conclusion
that his vision of life was essentially conventional, his
beliefs spiritually timid, and his maxims acquiescent
and compromising.

Assuming that his moral ideas were purely conventional, others of the iconoclasts argue that he was
a hypocrite, with obvious reference to the field of sexual morality. They produce evidence for believing
that in early life, at any rate, his conduct partook
more of the French artist than of the shorter catechist.
Mr. Osbourne, indeed, tells us that he was involved in
several tempestuous affairs with women, and that he
never heard him regret the experience. Mr. Steuart,
of course, made this the outstanding feature of a two-
volume life. Several of the "new poems" are corrobo-
rative. Why did not Stevenson speak out frankly all
that he thought and felt about these matters, as
"modern" writers do?

Well, now, in the first place, modern writers *don't.*
The most "outrageous" of them is still so far from his
own ideal of self-acknowledgment that it is indecent of
him to twit Stevenson with compromise in that field.
Living in an environment, as he declared, of realism
à l'outrance in the South Seas, he ventured in "The

[167]

Beach of Falesà" to introduce an illicit relation under a fictitious marriage. You may read in the introduction and in the letters how he strove against editors and publishers in order to present to English and American readers of thirty-five years ago that mild overture to modern realism. After this attempt he concluded that he knew "nothing—except that men are fools and hypocrites."

As all observant readers know, Stevenson did deliberately shun the treatment of "modern love." Was that because he really desired to suppress that side of life? No, it was because he was unwilling to write falsely about it. It was because, as he said, "You *can't* tell any of the facts; the only chance is to paint in the atmosphere." He shunned it because he knew that he could not treat "modern love" in English in accordance with his increasing bent toward a biting realism and the sharp noting of physical sensation. He could not treat it in accordance with his own experience, and therefore he preferred not to treat it at all; for, as he said, "I can't mean one thing and write another."

But, *Messieurs et Mesdames*, if you believe that Stevenson's opinions in this matter reposed upon an orthodox, conventional or clerical conception of human passions, if you think that he looked timorously into the abysses of nature and shrank from the full implications of his vision—or even really concealed his vision from readers, then, I pray you, open again that "courtly collect," as Mr. Llewelyn Powys calls it, "Virginibus Puerisque," and read again with unsealed eyes, weighing phrase by phrase, those two bits of stark realism regarding life and death, which you passed lightly over twenty-five years ago, because they were entitled, with a kind of classical elegance then in vogue, "Pan's Pipes" and "Aes Triplex."

Read what he says about "tearing divines reducing life to the dimensions of a funeral procession" and about "melancholy unbelievers yearning for the tomb as if it were a world too far away." Consider his glowing young pagan preference of those dwellers on the sides of the volcano who give themselves to life as to a bride—give themselves "to the appetites, to honor, to the hungry curiosity of the mind, to the pleasure of the eyes in nature and the pride of our nimble bodies." Read again his contempt of the "tooth-chattering ones who flee from Nature because they fear the hand of Nature's God," and his contempt of "respectable citizens" who, in order to keep their hats on in the midway of custom, flee life's pleasures and its responsibilities, its ecstasies and its agonies. Consider again his stunning characterization of this fertile earth—"sunshiny, lewd and cruel!" Through all the "winning music" of the world he heard a "threat," yet that music, that Panic music, "is itself the charm and terror of things." These are, he declares, at the very heart of all true romance—the charm and the terror, one and inseparable.

Where one is not the other is not. Do you understand? And is that, I ask you, the way the matter is set forth in Sabbath school?

If you wish a brief and candid expression of Stevenson's response from his early years till his death—his response to the Panic music—I commend to your attention one of the "new poems," called "Stormy Nights." He had a way, you remember, of writing poems and then of fulfilling them with his life. The famous "Requiem," for example, he wrote on a sickbed in France, and then fulfilled it "under the wide and starry sky" of Samoa. But what asks your attention in "Stormy Nights" is the stark realism in his account of his passage from the fierce, stifling, suppressed lewdness of adolescence through a period of savage Indian revolt to "Greek" serenity, from the midst of which he contemplates the possibility, as the seasons pass, of entering his "Saint" Louis period. All in due season, he tells us, he will be ready to embrace the whole of life. But,

Why would you hurry me, O evangelist,
You with the bands and the shilling packet of tracts
Greatly reduced when taken for distribution?

Now, I am a Greek,
White-robed among the sunshine and the statues
And the fair porticos of carven marble—
Fond of olives and dry sherry,
Good tobacco and clever talks with my fellows,
Free from inordinate cravings.

Isn't he all there in that little poem, in *esse* and in *posse*, the "R. L. S." that real Stevensonians have always known and have always loved? Isn't he all there? —the "R. L. S." who *did* touch the quick of life; know the sting of sex, the taste of blood; get his feet wet— wet to the waist, man; foot the open road; test sleep in lonely hills under "a clear night of stars"; fare on through blossoms—drunk with the scent of them; up rocky pitches, putting his back into it—eh, what! on to the place where the fog began, and the swift bright stream of his life went down—as he had prophesied the day before that it would—"foaming over a precipice."

[170]

Look up the poem, I pray you, Stevensonians, and ask yourself if he isn't all there.

And I say it is not a man of no character, and it is not a man of no genius for vital characterization neither, that can stamp, clear-cut, a figure like that of "R. L. S." into the consciousness of three generations. Try it, O superior "modern" young men! We are waiting for you.

I ask you if you can find a single one of these thirty-two volumes in which "R. L. S." is not effectively present. In running through his letters and his essays on the art of fiction I came repeatedly upon a certain ideal for the writer of romance: namely, that each chapter should (1) advance the story, (2) develop the character, and (3) embody the theme.

Now Stevenson wrote out the romance of life in many chapters, with astonishing technical versatility. There are poems, essays, criticism, descriptive sketches, travel books, plays, biography, history, short stories, novels and letters; and within most of these forms there is as much variety of form, mood, and substance as appears when one contemplates the large divisions of the complete works. Yet in each main division and in each subdivision, I, for one, feel that he advances his story, develops his character and embodies his theme. Compare him with any author of his bulk that you choose, where will you find such unity in variety, such centrality and emphasis with so little of repetition?

What is the controlling informing spirit throughout the mass? Style, of course. Not style, as his critics allege, conceived as a mere foppishness in words. Style for him is not mainly in the words but in the "web" or "pattern" which the synthetic stylist weaves in order to hold fast "a far more deep and stimulating view of life and a far keener sense of the *generation and affinity of events*" than the styleless writer can convey.

In one of his letters Stevenson suggests what is indubitably true, that he looked in prose for a *texture* to which many of his fellows were indifferent and that he listened for a music to which their ears were deaf: "The little artificial popularity of style in England tends, I think, to die out; the British pig returns to his true love, the love of the styleless, of the shapeless, of the slapdash and the disorderly."

But, for all that, it is absurd to say, as his critics do, that style took him by the ear and led him away from life. It is even, in my opinion, absurd to deny that he was driving as hard as he could toward the goal of "modern" writing. He had no technique for the immense penumbral suggestiveness of some modern masters. He is nearer Meissonier than Monet. He worked with sharp form and clear color. "I have," he declared, "in nearly all my works been trying one racket, to get out the facts of life as clean and naked and sharp as I could manage it."

But every new thing that he wrote was for him a fresh problem in style, because every new thing palpitated to his sense with its own unique individual thrill. And the throb of life in the individual thing—that is what he was after. He felt along the sharp edges of "the fact," only half content with his method, groping for something beyond, fully conscious that there is no great art which shows "no blot of heart's blood and the Old Night," tormented by the desire of all "modern" writers to express "a touch, a sense within sense, a sound outside the sound, the shadow of the inscrutable, eloquent beyond all definition."*

* To Charles Baxter, 18th July, 1892, in *The Letters of Robert Louis Stevenson*, Vol. IV, page 74, South Seas Edition.

XIII

Anatole France: A Secretary and His "Immortal"

A FIRST-RATE book of its class is Brousson's account of Anatole France "in slippers"—acceptable as a basket of choice assorted nuts and fruits. Whether for consecutive reading—I profess myself a consecutive reader—or for random sticking in of thumbs, the repast is excellent. To the plum hunter one may exhibit, for instance, this comforting prescription for the overworked man of letters harassed by a heavy correspondence: Let letters, books, papers, pamphlets, telegrams accumulate in a spare bathtub till the tub is full. So advises the great French master of letters. Then sell them to the second-hand dealer at fifty francs the tub; or to the fireplace with them—without regret, without malice, opening none, with equal justice to all! Nearly four hundred pages of that quality, and better, constitute a precious contribution to what we, journalistically, call the "human" side of Anatole France's life.

I find only the title of M. Brousson's book in the translation slightly irritating. "Anatole France *Himself!*" We live in the age of Einstein. A quarter of a century ago we had an outburst of "true" biographies: "The True Benjamin Franklin," "The True George Washington," "The True Ananias," etc. But that arrogance of affirmation in the title is quaint to-day and outmoded. What does M. Brousson's translator mean by "Himself"? Am I a whit more myself in dressing gown and slippers than in khaki and leggins or in the most formal apparel that I can master for the most public of performances? More comfortable, more happy, in one than in the other, but not a whit more myself. Indirectly this title perhaps protests against James Lewis May's "Anatole France," published in the autumn of 1924. Mr. May, coming to the master with Anglo-Saxon reverence for the "greatest living man of letters," saw in him a gracious old gentleman, with a strain of Virgilian sadness in him, who approached his disciple with a flower. Mr. May placed the flower opposite a tender passage in his Virgil, called into his mind all the expressions in the works of Anatole France which reveal his gentle and sad lucidity of soul, and declared that, for him, poetry was the master's precious and immortal part.

Now, this M. Brousson formed his impressions, took his pictures, at altogether different points of view. Moreover, M. Brousson is a different sort of artist. His Anatole France is not in the least respect a Virgilian personality. He is not, in any careful sense of the phrase, a "gracious old gentleman." He is an elderly Gallic antiquarian and voluptuary, tart, malicious, salty, a studious flatterer, an egotist, a cynic, a libertine, with a senile vanity concerning his prowess with "God's creatures."

M. Brousson has a sharp eye for the traits which attract him. He has a sharp pencil. He has a clear coherent conception of his subject as a most interesting and distinguished literary animal. His scores of brilliant distinct little pictures of him all "hang together." They produce a unified effect, which is not

Anatole France

cafés on the way and heats up his courage with cups
of coffee and thimblefuls of cognac. In vain!

Introduced into the reception room, stuffed with
books, pictures, reliquaries, saints and cases of curios,
he finds it already filled with callers, attending the
Master's leisure. The Great Man sits at his desk,
formidable in dressing gown, felt slippers and silk
skull cap.

In his hand are a drawing and a reading glass.
He makes a little collective bow to the newcomers,
who arrange themselves around the room. . . . "You
come at the right moment, gentlemen," Anatole
France goes on, "you shall decide the question. We
are in need of your judgment. Should a painter of
religious subjects have faith? The other day I bought
this lovely face from my friend Prouté: it is a Virgin
by Boucher. This Virgin, it is clear, is not a model
of virtue. Perhaps the artist painted it from his own
wife and baby."

The young man from the country, aghast at the
discussion of matters so much beyond the depth of
provincial scholarship, takes refuge behind the library
ladder and at the first opportunity retreats, without
presenting his letter of introduction or making himself
known. One sees at a glance that the young man understands the artistic value of innocence!

A private meeting is arranged. Anatole France
explains to his new secretary that his business is to
hunt up learned references for "Joan," in order to shut
the mouths of critics who contend that he is only a
novelist. Then he examines a little the innocence
of M. Brousson. He wishes to know first whether the
young man has been religiously emancipated. His own

notion is that religion is a kind of congenital infirmity. He pulls down a fine edition of La Bruyère and reads classical authority for his position: "He who is in perfect health doubts the existence of God, but, when he gets a dropsy, leaves his mistress and sends for the priest." On another occasion when Huysmans sends by the secretary some pious exhortations to the disciple of Renan, France replies that Huysmans had better have an inquiry made into the condition of his kidneys. When the downward turn in a man's physical state comes, "he gives himself to drugs and the Deity."

It is refreshing to hear that Père Anatole did not wish for himself the reverence which he himself denied to the Deity. When his secretary addressed him as "Master" he was gently reproved:

I, too, in my youth, said "Master" to academicians. I know what it means. It does not really signify "My good sir, you are worth thrice what I or any simple man is worth." It means: "You poor, old pedant, your chatter is sheer drivel! Mere head-wagging! Tedious redundancy! You think you're the equal of the gods. Then don't delay in this low world. You have lasted long enough. It's high time to make place for the young." Yes, that is what little rascals think while they are busy incensing old idols. Don't protest! I was the same as you.

He seems to have felt about being called "Master" as Matthew Arnold used to feel about being called "Professor."

The real solid advantage in being famous and a member of the Academy, he assures his disciple, is that he can wear his old gray felt hat and snap his fingers at statutes and magistrates. There follows an illustrative incident. A gendarme takes him to task for unconventional behavior with a "tender soul" in the Bois de Boulogne. He presents a visiting card which shows him to be a member of the Académie Française. Result: profuse apologies.

As a young man he had entertained grand and austere notions of the scholar's calling, derived from seeing members of the Academy of Inscriptions on dress parade or, after a meeting, turning over some edition of the classics in his father's bookshop by the Seine. His youthful ideal was something like this: "To live with a hobby apart from one's own century in another age, to know hardly anything about one's contemporaries, but to be intimate and familiar with Cicero, Corneille or Mme. de Sévigné. That was what fame seemed to me."

"And to-day, *Master?*" That discreet young man repeats the offensive title. You see that he knows the old man is a bit insincere—really enjoys well enough what he pretends to despise.

"To-day, my son, fame lies in being able to do what I like. I receive ministers and publishers in my dressing gown and slippers. I give audience, and often I refuse it, to them. It's my turn to make them wait, as they often did me."

This is but negative counsel for a young man from the country bent on a career. What advice has our modern sage equivalent to that painstaking and conscientious thought which the great lexicographer gave to young Boswell's reading? Well, Père Anatole appears to believe that the young man may follow his own instincts, so far as his reading goes. "I know," he declares, "the vanity of all human learning. What useless reading, what crushing knowledge, for a life so brief and passed in the midst of dunces! Why take all this tiresome luggage for so short a journey? People praise my learning. I no longer want other learning than in the realm of love. Love is now my unique, my particular study. It is to that I devote the flickering remains of passion. If only I could write all that the little god inspires in me! Dismal prudery reigns in literature, prudery more silly, cruel and criminal than the Holy Inquisition."

Day after day the indulgent and salacious "old dog"—this is Mr. Pollock's word for "the greatest man of letters" in his time—recounts to his disciple his amorous adventures, usually with a humorous twist —adventures with all sorts of heroines, concerning whom the master seems not to have been more fastidious than Sainte-Beuve, the grossness of whose tastes was offensive, it may be remembered, to George Sand, whose own tastes were, from some points of view, catholic. Again and again, the "old dog" gives to the young one the advice which Robert Herrick addressed to the Virgins. He tempers this, however, with a theory that the men who have done great things in the world have not been happy in love. He discourses at length on Napoleon Bonaparte, and is quite sure that the Little Corporal's conquests in the tented field were a kind of noisy demonstration to draw the attention of the world away from his thorny defeats under love's banner. "If Lætitia Ramolino's son overturned the world and made blood run like rain water, it was because he was impotent."

The only branch of morality to which the master gives much careful thought is the morality of writing well. His method of composition he had from Renan.

The author of the "Vie de Jésus" scribbled whatever it might be and sent it to the printer. The proofs came back. He corrected them—once, twice, thrice. At the fifth time it began to be like Renan. In my case it is the sixth and often the seventh time. I insist on as many as eight proofs. What can I do? I have no imagination, but I am not without patience. My most valuable working tools are the paste pot and the scissors. . . . My pen has no lyric powers. It does not leap, but goes plodding along its way. Nor have I ever felt the intoxication of work. I write with difficulty.

In the course of correction he cuts out the "too finely spacious and melodious phrases." He cuts out the "dog grass," which has sprung up; the "which's," "who's" and "whose's" and "whereof's." He shortens sentences wherever possible. But, above all—this, I think, is the great secret of his limpidity—he cuts out the "dog grass," declaring that it gives the best style "a crick in the neck."

Plagiarism, asserts this liberal counselor, is nothing, provided only that you steal to advantage. What stealing to advantage means is prettily illustrated. From a biographical dictionary he copies, without changing a word, this sentence: "The lady Théroulde was rich and of good fame."

He remarks: "It's as flat and insipid as a pancake."

"But," exclaims the young man from the country, "you will see; we shall trim the good lady to the taste of the day." Anatole France, revising, writes:

"Since the lady Théroulde was rich, men said she was of good fame." It now has some character, though the lady has none. That is stealing to advantage. And Anatole France, his best friends will admit, became "a man of great possessions," largely by such forms of theft.

M. Brousson points out that his habit of defamation was rather a consequence of his humor than of his spleen. He deprived people of their reputations, quite without bitterness or malice. Normal and conventional people did not interest him.

When he feels drawn to any one, be it man or woman, he hastens to discover vices in him. He seeks for defects, failings and eccentricities and even monstrosities. . . . The oldest of his friends is announced, and he shouts to Josephine in presence of a dozen people: "Don't leave him downstairs for a moment! Keep a sharp eye on my precious objects!" The oldest friend appears and, to the stupefaction of the visitors, Anatole France falls on his neck. He embraces him with frantic delight. He kisses him on both cheeks and sharpens his long nose on them by way of compliment. He seems unable to unlock his arms. Then in a suave voice and with a sweet smile he will say: "My dearest So-and-So, I was just talking about you to these gentlemen. I can't say how charmed I am to see you."

There is much of this enthusiastic show of affection in the record, coupled with calling downstairs, after the guest has closed the door, "Never let that man into the house again!" M. Brousson's most gorgeous anecdote is of that sort. It describes a formal call paid to Anatole France by a provincial bishop "candidating," according to the French custom, for a vacancy in the Academy. As the season was Lenten, Monsignor appeared in black. "In his poor cassock and shiny cope with worn velvet collar you would

made to perform, he was expected to show off, and
he much preferred to get off in a dark corner and talk
with a nonentity about a piece of Majolica, or with a
pretty woman about something else. He had his public
conversation by heart—all his good stories about Hugo
and Renan and Maupassant—even to the tone of his
voice, even to the exact point at which he pulled out
his handkerchief and wiped a histrionic tear from his
eye. His public conversation he performed as a matter
of duty, and he performed a little as one plays old
records for new friends. He was bored, too, by nature,
by landscape—except when it was framed and hung
inside four walls.

The things which frightened and dismayed him
were illness and death. On one occasion M. Brousson
was so indiscreet as to swoon in the Master's presence.
He took that up seriously and sharply. He wished
to know at once whether the young man did that sort
of thing often. He explained that he should not like
him so well—not nearly so well—if he did. He really
did not care for sick people in his neighborhood. Then,
again, on another occasion, the young man from the
country, thinking to gratify the Master's love of glory,
spoiled a visit to the Pantheon by intimating that Anatole France would be the next great man of letters
to repose there.

This joyous paganism of Anatole France is, of
course, an attractive religion for people who are well
and happy and prosperous. If one is poor or wretched
or ill, it is less consolatory. But, as M. Brousson
exhibits him, this great gambler who staked all he
had on the turns of this world enjoyed an almost un-
interrupted run of good luck. He was one of those
thoroughly prosperous worldlings who almost per-

suaded the author of Ecclesiastes that righteousness
is "vanity and vexation of spirit," and that all that
profiteth a man is to enjoy the work of his hands
and the delight of his eyes and the pride of life, for
the wicked get on in this life just as well as the pious,
and all go together into the dust and rest in one common grave. So we see him to the end, the gay old
graybeard, enjoying his meals, with a grand appetite
for his dinner; eating, like a god or a drayman at a
humble wine shop, a full repast of boiled beef with
coarse salt and gherkins, sheep's feet in a white sauce,
beans, Brie and custard tart; sniffing out a fine old
Quintilian from the booths by the Seine, or chaffering
with an old woman in an antique shop or chattering
with a demi-mondaine in the park; then turning home-
ward, creeping into his canopied four-poster, and
reading Casanova by tall church candles till he falls
asleep.

XIV

Oscar Wilde: A Dandy of Letters and Acquainted with Grief

OSCAR WILDE would have enjoyed his appearance in this large paper edition of 575 numbered copies in dull blue boards with white paper labels, chaste as a set of Wedgwood china.* "I must try to live up," he might have said, "to my wide margins." He would have liked the note of ducal luxury in his personal marks on the binding: the small gold sunflower under his name in the upper left-hand corner and the seal at the center, symbolic of his literary conquests, bearing the lion rampant, the fleur-de-lis, and the harp of Erin. He would have been gratified, too, by the company of friends and critics who bring their tribute of roses and thorns to this edition of his works.

The esthetic movement which Wilde was ultimately to mislead into unseemly places was, in its earlier pre-Raphaelite phase, conspicuous for its chivalric Arthurian reminiscences and for "the white feet of angels coming down the golden stair." (Oscar Wilde subsequently gilded the feet.) And so the general introduction is appropriately by Richard Le Gallienne, whose head and halo-like hair pleased Wilde by reminding him of the angel in Rossetti's "Annuncia-

* *The Writings of Oscar Wilde*, New York: Gabriel Wells, 12 vols, 1924.

[188]

tion." Sir Johnston Forbes-Robertson, who, I believe, posed for Rossetti's Dante, contributes a prefatory page to "The Duchess of Padua," which Wilde read to him from a lectern, over which he draped himself in the esthetic attitudes immortalized by Gilbert and Sullivan in "Patience." William Butler Yeats, who gave the green carnation new life by transplanting it in Irish soil, introduces the fairy tales, and he speculates in his moon-stricken prose on the joy it would have given Wilde to know that his works are widely read in the land of jade and powdered lacquer and in Arabia: "In the midst of my meditation it was as though I heard him saying with that slow, precise, rhythmical elocution of his, 'I have a vast public in Samarkand.'" Coulson Kernahan expresses his pained distaste for "Dorian Gray," and Walter Pater's appreciative but suavely condemnatory review of it is also included.

One misses many minor figures whom one might expect to see in this procession. One misses the major figures of G. K. Chesterton and G. B. Shaw, who certainly learned from Wilde much about the uses of paradox as a form of wit and as an implement of intellectual exploration. One misses also the belligerent championship of Frank Harris. But all three of these warriors have defined their attitude toward Wilde and his movement elsewhere. The other contributors are Edgar Saltus, Richard Butler Glaenzer, A. B. Walkley, John Drinkwater, John Cowper Powys, Michael Monahan, W. F. Morse and Padraic Colum. Since Wilde in his glory regarded himself as peerless "king" of his world, he would have denied the possibility of a trial by his peers; but I think every one else will acknowledge that the publisher has assembled a jury as competent and as sympathetic as a problematic man of letters could hope for.

In those years when Wilde spent his golden hours scrubbing his cell in prison, washing his tin dishes and, in the evening, reading a few chapters of the New Testament in Greek, he wrote in "De Profundis": "If life be, as it surely is, a problem to me, I am no less a problem to life. People must adopt some attitude toward me, and so pass judgment both on themselves and me."

One aspect of the problem which Wilde presents to us is suggested by George Bernard Shaw as follows: "Oscar seems to have said: 'I will love nobody; I will be utterly selfish, and I will be not merely a rascal but a monster, and you shall forgive me everything. In other words, I will reduce your standards to absurdity not by writing them down, though I could do that so well—in fact, *have* done it—but by actually living them down and dying them down.' "

So far as his moral character is concerned, our jury is in substantial agreement. Wilde's own intimates cheerfully concede nearly everything which a moralistic critic cares to allege against it. They concede that he was indolent, colossally egotistical, selfish, weak, flabby, incomparably vain, insolent to tradesmen and inferiors, a flatterer of wealth and titles, a thoroughgoing snob in the English sense, extravagant and untrustworthy in money matters, intemperate in eating and drinking, incapable of genuine friendship, and a sexual pervert.

And yet we forgive him everything; and yet in his earlier years he was welcomed by every hostess in London; and yet Mr. Frank Harris declares that "he would rather spend an evening with him than with Renan or Carlyle, or Verlaine or Dick Burton or Davidson. . . . I have known no more charming, no more quickening, no more delightful spirit. . . . It may be that I prize humor and good-humor and eloquence of poetic speech, the artist qualities, more than goodness or loyalty or manliness, and so over-estimate things amiable. But the lovable and joyous things are to me the priceless things, and the most charming man I ever met was assuredly Oscar Wilde."

The solution of Mr. Shaw's "problem" is simple. Whenever we become infatuated with what we have conventionally called "a thoroughly bad man" we find on consideration that he possesses a string of virtues, sometimes rare virtues, which are not listed as such in the catalogue of the austere moralist. It was, for example, Wilde's central virtue that he enjoyed his life, enjoyed it immensely, enjoyed it in obviously felicitous circumstances, and enjoyed it keenly even in circumstances of misery and shame. That is one of the rarest of human virtues, and Wilde possessed it to an extraordinary degree. There is nothing whatever which human beings covet more, when they are honest, than a capacity for enjoyment.

Wilde possessed also an extraordinary faculty for communicating his pleasure. The "vice" of his vanity, if we choose to call it so, operated to social profit, spurring him incessantly to give pleasure in exchange for the pleasure of being conspicuous. Like all the famous dandies from whom he is descended—Beau Nash, Beau Brummel, Byron, Disraeli, D'Orsay, Bulwer-Lytton—he courted the public like a player; he dressed, posed, talked and sinned for the public, and he won the public because he kept it incessantly in a state of wonder, delight, amusement and horror. Like the world's famous courtesans, bandits and assassins, he contributed by his vices no less than by his virtues to the precious sum of life's interests. Digest this "unedifying" truth as we may, all mankind loves a villain, and it is a commonplace of experience that the most atrocious criminal, if he keeps a stiff upper lip and steps out with appropriate bravado, may go to his execution amid the roses and love letters and tears and adulation of admiring thousands.

Certain of Wilde's friends who admit the numerous and gross defects in his character attempt to make a sharp distinction between his life and his works. Mr. Frank Harris, for instance, says: "If his life was given overmuch to self-indulgence, it must be remembered that his writings and conversation were singularly kindly, singularly amiable, singularly pure. No harsh or coarse or bitter word ever passed those eloquent laughing lips. If he served beauty in her myriad forms he only showed in his works the beauty that was amiable and of good report."

This line of defense is, I think, absolutely untenable. It is as untenable as the contention that his "downfall" was due to a temporary aberration or a progressive disease of the brain. There was nothing fortuitous in Wilde's downfall, except the discovery of his state of mind by the law-enforcing portion of the British public. His downfall was the logical conclusion of his career in a country which disciplines his state of mind in the criminal court. Spiritually he was no more "down" in prison than he was while he scintillated in the drawing-room. His conversation and his writings are just as "abnormal" as his career. In his poems, in his comedies, in "Dorian Gray," in his critical discourses, he paints his portrait, he displays his own sentiments and opinions, again and again, with remarkable fidelity and completeness. And his ideals and his philosophy as presented in his works are entirely consistent with the conduct for which he was sent to prison.

Wilde was of the smart set, and he wrote for the smart set about the smart set. Now, the smart set has many superbly attractive traits and aspects. It does not, as Mr. Harris observes, habitually employ the coarse and obscene language of guttersnipes. Its hair does not fall over its collar, its heels are not run down, its nails are in order. It bathes frequently, dresses modishly, dines daintily, drinks exhilaratingly, lives easily, conforms with many courteous and agreeable social usages, occupies good seats at the theater, buys pictures, hunts in season, attends races, gives house parties, exchanges amenities, talks of beautiful and diverting objects, cultivates conversation and seeks in a multitude of ways to impart to the ordinary slack intercourse of life the tension of style and, for its own members, to raise the entire depressing and disgusting business of being born, married and buried to the level of a fine art.

In compensation for the arduous task of keeping up a beautiful appearance and conforming to its own code, the smart set demands certain privileges, and it takes them. When Lord Henry Wotton (or Lord Arthur Savile or Lord Goring or Algernon Moncrieff or Lord Darlington or Lord Illingworth) has seen the midday sun breaking through his ivory silk curtains, has had his cup of chocolate served by a flawless valet, has drawn his portière of peach-colored plush, bathed his fair limbs in the moonstone waters of his onyx tub, thrown himself upon his divan of

Persian saddlebags and lighted a perfumed cigarette from his jeweled case, he must be allowed to begin the pleasures of the day by tearing up his tradesman's bills, pointing a half-dozen epigrams at the bourgeoisie, making a few assignations, and ruminating on some new and strange and "fiery-colored" sin.

The hero of the smart set, as Wilde conceives him, must be allowed to turn over all responsibility for truth and goodness to the middle class. What is the use of being a hero unless one can be relieved from "the sordid necessity of living for others"? "Unselfishness is letting other people's lives alone." "Industry is the refuge of those who have nothing to do." "Vulgarity is simply the conduct of other people." "Life is too important to be taken seriously." "There is nothing in the world like the devotion of a married woman. It's a thing no married man knows anything about." "The world is perfectly packed with good women. To know them is a middle-class education." "Sin is the only real color-element left in modern life." "One could never pay too high a price for any sensation." "The only way to get rid of a temptation is to yield to it." "Every impulse that we strive to strangle broods in the mind, and poisons us." "Nothing can cure the soul but the senses."

There is just enough of sharp and piercing truth in these epigrams to carry their maddening poison into the veins of foolish and humorless young men. If one can take the point without the poison, they are worth collecting.

It is absurd to pretend that Wilde's heroes are right-thinking young men. These gilded youths are adored by adolescents, as Byron was adored, for the brilliance and daring of their wickedness. As for

"Dorian Gray," our æsthetic jury deals with it as harshly as any moralist could desire. Says Mr. Kernahan: "I found the atmosphere stifling and tainted, and was repelled by the sneers, the cynicism, in a word, by what seemed to me the wickedness by which Lord Henry sought to remove the landmarks of good and evil." Says Walter Pater: "To lose the moral sense therefore, for instance, the sense of sin and righteousness, as Mr. Wilde's heroes are bent on doing as speedily, as completely, as they can, is to lose, or lower, organization, to become less complex, to pass from a higher to a lower degree of development." Says that eminent authority on the lives and deaths of the heroes of the Yellow Nineties, Mr. Arthur Symons: "Wilde was an extremely typical figure. . . . If he might be supposed for a moment to represent anything for himself he would be the perfect representative of all that is evidently meant by us in our modern use of the word 'Decadence.' "

It is interesting to observe that critics of Wilde's own school of art for art's sake are beginning to pull his literary accomplishments to pieces, to praise "Intentions" and "De Profundis" and "The Ballad of Reading Gaol" with reservations, and to grant him but one flawless masterpiece, "The Importance of Being Earnest," which, however, Mr. Shaw says, is "heartless." The line of attack is this: They declare that he originates little or nothing, that his convictions are all second-hand, that his taste and judgment are defective and his knowledge superficial, that he has no assured personal style in either poetry or prose, that his purple passages are full of echoes and mimicry of Ruskin, Whistler, Arnold, Pater, Rossetti, Gautier, Baudelaire. Whistler, who of course was a fountain of malice, charged him outright with plagiarism, and, more venomously, asserted that he was as poor a judge of a coat as of a picture! But that—*c'était la guerre.* Much more damaging are these cold verdicts of Mr. Arthur Symons who cannot be accused of defective sympathies towards diabolists.

Wilde, certainly from what I knew of him as a man and as a writer, was almost utterly devoïd of artistic judgment, and it is no wonder that Whistler had to drop his acquaintance. . . .

Wilde said nothing which had not been said before him. In his devotion to beauty he seemed to have given up the whole world, and yet what was most tragic in the tragedy was that he never recognized the true face of beauty. He followed beauty, and beauty fled from him, for his devotion was that of the lover proud of many conquests. He was eager to proclaim the conquest, and too hasty to distinguish between beauty and beauty's handmaid. His praise of beauty is always a boast, never a homage. When he attempted to create beauty in words he described beautiful things.

That reaffirms in other words what Pater said about him thirty-five years ago. Oscar Wilde is properly and accurately called a decadent because he degrades the æsthetic movement, lowers its level. The æsthetic movement in its highest phases was the successor of a moribund religious explanation of the world. Along toward the middle of the last century it undertook the task which was falling from the palsied hands of the church: it undertook a fresh, sincere, adequate expression of man's feeling toward the mystery and beauty and terror of life—the whole of it. So Ruskin conceived of it, so Arnold, so Pater, so, somewhat less austerely, did William Morris.

Oscar Wilde will always be of great historical interest because he was the heir of all that the æsthetic movement had achieved up to 1880, and because, attempting to improve his inheritance, he wasted and well-nigh ruined it. He began by throwing out nature, which Ruskin had brought into fresh relationship with art; by throwing out religion, which Arnold had brought into fresh relationship with poetry; by throwing out moral conduct, which Pater had associated with music; by throwing out the social and altruistic feelings and the welfare of the laboring masses, which all the great leaders from Ruskin to Morris had associated with the possibility of an artistically productive epoch.

Wilde was proud of his "improvements." He plumed himself on the divorce which he had effected between art and life. He asked applause for his invention of an art which was a pure protest against life and the strenuous passions of life, an art which was as beautiful and was intended to be as sterile as a collection of blown birds' eggs. He thought his improvements would make the æsthetic movement popular—with the smart set; and they did. But, of course, we shall have nothing but smart-set art as long as the æsthetic movement is conducted by the smart set.

I wish to say a word about what sentimental biographers call "the tragedy of Oscar Wilde." By that phrase sentimental biographers refer to his spending some years in prison and ending his life in disgrace. But surely a man's real tragedy is to fail in what he attempts to perform, and Wilde never attempted, never seriously attempted, to keep out of prison. On the contrary, he applied his brilliant intellect to getting in; so that his imprisonment must be counted among his successes.

Wilde's major life effort was directed to the task of separating art from morality; in that he failed deplorably. That is his tragedy. Far from being an artist pure and undefiled by ethical intention, as he declared that an artist should be, he is himself incessantly a moralist, often a very bad moralist, sometimes unconsciously a very stern and sound moralist, but always his art is inseparable from his morality. In other writers, the story, as we say, carries a moral. In his case the morality carries the story, carries the dazzling critical dialogue, carries the bright flimsy structure of his dining-room comedies. And it is as a moralist that the exponent of art for art's sake has been most influential.

Oscar Wilde's works are in English literature, and they are likely to remain there. He will be revisited by successive generations of pilgrims, chiefly young pilgrims, as the affable, indulgent, sparkling host of a famous and infamous house on the æsthetic turnpike. There are better houses—and worse—farther along the road, but many pilgrims will never ask anything better than Wilde can give them. He has good wine, white and red; he will chant you poetry, not as good as Shelley or Keats but almost as good as FitzGerald and Housman; he will show you lovely pastorals which won't remind you of nature but will recall "Thyrsis" and "The Scholar Gipsy"; and he will show you charming "Hellenic" things which won't feel quite Greek but will remind you of the pictures of Albert Moore and Sir Frederick Leighton.

Didn't some one say truly enough that he is a man

with only a third-class ticket, yet with so much appearance of style that he always manages to ride in a first-class compartment? He is, he will remain, the Goethe of undergraduates who can't read German, the Ruskin of art lovers who are bored by nature and great masters, the Arnold of moralists who dislike morality, and the Pater of those who seek culture without cultivation. He will always be "in" when scent and rouge and dyed hair and tinted finger-nails are "in"; for Wilde, if he had not been an author, would have been a dealer in perfumes and cosmetics.

XV

Pierre Loti and Exotic Love

THERE are two sorts of people in this world: those who enjoy, above everything else, getting home, and those who enjoy, above everything else, getting away from home. One may push the distinction a little further: among those who would enjoy getting home if they could, some have a clear notion what and where home is, but there are others whose sense that somewhere there must be such a haven is engendered only by a vague homesickness, which keeps them wandering and homeless all their lives. And so, since the days of the much-experienced Odysseus, there have been two kinds of sailors on the sea: those who listen to the sirens' song and go ashore on Calypso's isle and, drinking the magic potion, take what shapes the enchantress wills; and those who stop their ears with wax and, lashed to the mast, sail by. This banality may serve as a primary distinction between the two most eloquent sailors of our time: Pierre Loti and Joseph Conrad.

The English sea captain finds the essence of romance in the testing of the hero's resistance to the elemental powers which surround and inhabit him—the power of the storm and the seduction of alien and savage manners, or some cowardice of the flesh, some insidious treachery to his own caste or calling, lurking in his own breast. Whether or not Conrad ever learned

to write English—a point about which George Moore
and others have raised doubts—certainly he learned to
feel like an Englishman the burden of those self-imposed obligations which one carries in order to retain
one's own respect. In his austere scrutiny of the point
of honor, the ethical scruple, there is something almost
"puritan," something that links him with Hawthorne,
Henry James and Mrs. Wharton, writers who get
their "fun" out of refining and multiplying the more
or less artificial problems of life, like the proverbial
Englishman who preserves the integrity of the blond
Nordic by donning evening clothes and dining in solitary state in the Indian jungle.

Pierre Loti is not in that gallery. Though an
officer himself, as a man of letters he has shown little
interest in what men do under the stress of code and
convention. As an author he is incurious about Occidental society. He wishes to forget all that. His
friends and his heroes, for literary purposes, are men
of the people, peasants, common sailors, whose un-
governable propensity for drink, brawling, and deser-
tion prevents their ever winning more than a woolen
stripe to their sleeves. The crises in their experience
are not crises of the will but crises of the emotions.
For Loti all the possibilities of romance depend upon
the hero's susceptibility to seduction, depend upon his
surrendering himself utterly to the deep inebriation
of strange loves and lands. "This price the gods exact
for song: to *become* what we sing." Before Loti interprets Tahiti he wishes a Tahitian baptism; before
he speaks of Japan he must have a Japanese marriage.
Transient unions, but while they last he craves the
deepest possible impregnation of his spirit by the spirit
which he woos, the utmost expatriation and self-dis-

[201]

solution. Romance for Loti means an escape from the classical circle of humanity and an adventure outside its law.

How foolishly we say that the French, conceiving Paris as the end of every man's desire, are no travelers. True, they seldom visit us except on business; to the Parisian sense New York is more of the same but not so good. But tell the French of something rich and strange, talk to them of lands where "the cypress and myrtle are emblems of deeds that are done in their clime," and none are so attentive as they. Consider the reflection of Algiers, Morocco, Egypt, Turkey, Syria, China, Japan and the two Indies in their imaginative literature and in their art and you conclude it is near the mark to call the French the discoverers of travel. I speak of travel not as an aspect of commerce but as an aspect of culture. The American visits Paris to confirm his Americanism. The English poet visits Italy to recover his cultural inheritance. The French poet visits Senegambia to get rid of his. They cross the sea to change their minds. They travel precisely because Paris contains everything that a civilized heart desires—except an escape from civility. For a hundred years the French have been contriving fascinating tours and detours for those tired hearts in which the Parisian paradise palls and desire is a burden, and the century moves forward with an ever more listless and monotonous hum.

Pierre Loti is not the first but only the most proficient of the long line of French prose masters who offer travel as something better than hashish or absinthe as an exit from the cul-de-sac of civilization. The man savors contrasts, and on his admission to the Academy he declared that Loti was no reader. But

we know well enough what masters turned his steps
toward the sea and the desert and the wilderness,
taught him the luxury of grief and the exile's accents
of anguish, the consolations of nature and the pleasures
of a quivering sensibility. As a small boy he declares
that he had already a clear prescience that he was to
have a life of voyages and adventures, with hours of
fabulous splendor and hours of infinite misery. Yes,
the Arabian Nights, of course. And then Bernardin
de St. Pierre, wafting his chaste lovers to an idyllic
West Indian isle. Chateaubriand following his dusky
maid into the American forest. Mérimée pursuing his
brigands among the rocks of Corsica. Gautier inviting
to Spain, Greece, and the Mediterranean. Flaubert
plucking his melancholy harp above the ruins of Carthage. George Sand and her swarthy peasants among
the menhirs of Celtic Brittany. The Goncourts plum-
ing themselves on their exploitation of the acrid savors
of dark-skinned races and upon their assimilation of
Japan. These are the magicians who presented travel
to his lips as one of the higher forms of intoxication.
He inherits their taste for the exotic as Yves, in "A
Tale of Brittany," inherits dipsomania.

A totally flippant person might summarize his work
as thirty-five volumes about the good fortunes of a
French Academician who was a larking midshipman
before he was a captain, and had a sweetheart in every
port. And I suppose that Loti, if asked to speak of
love, might have replied like Socrates, "I certainly
cannot refuse to speak on the only subject of which
I profess to have any knowledge." But Loti, it should
be said emphatically, is something infinitely more
complex than a mere sailor-lover. His vague rich passion invades and envelops him with a ravishing melan-

choly, like the music of Chopin and the poetry of Musset, in which his adolescence reveled. It has overtones of almost mystical rapture and undertones of philosophical despair. It is begotten of life poignantly conscious of itself and shuddering wide-eyed before the black gulf of annihilation. The fourteen-year-old islander Rarahu, with the red hibiscus flowers behind her ears, can neither fathom it nor reciprocate it. These little sweethearts, brown and yellow and black, fierce and real as their own passions may be, serve him but as pathetic go-betweens in his affair with "the soul of the land." When dark blood burns hot in the swift tropical spring, when tomtoms beat in the village and mad shouts rise, kinky-haired Fatou-Gaye may fancy it is she that he comes to meet under the baobab tree by the edge of the swamp at the red moonrise; but the mind of the lover wanders in that strange embrace—he has a rendezvous with Africa.

Loti is no simple-hearted sensualist. The specific "carnal sting" is sharply indicated where it is patently present, as in the vernal orgies of the "Roman d'un Spahi"; but it is the least of his preoccupations. Loti is a romanticist and an imperfect lover. He doesn't keep his mind on the object or the subject; it wanders into the moonlight and among flowers and plays with the amulets and the ancestors and the gods of his mistress. The merely fleshly relation between him and Mme. Chrysanthème he does not present as even interesting. That relation, he declares outright, was detestable. He tolerates her only when he regards her as a bit of art in amber-colored flesh, as a translation from a painted fan or a piece of porcelain. Emotionally, they have less in common than a child and a doll. She has not even the heart to be heartbroken when, having paid her wages, he departs for his ship. Returning unexpectedly, he finds her busy with a little hammer testing the lapful of coins he has left.

"An impious hymen," says Anatole France, and suggests that the sadness of Loti is due to his perpetual quest of little thrills and to the impassable racial and cultural abyss which yawns between the Parisian and the Japanese. Yes, Père Anatole, perhaps. A more or less flattering unction to the Occidental soul. But is this spectacle quite so inhuman after all? What about the unfathomable abyss between any two wedded mortals, surveying each other across the coffee cups—between Mr. and Mrs. Jones, who have washed their faces and brushed their hair in considerable intimacy these many years? Have Mr. and Mrs. Jones many more words than Loti and Mme. Chrysanthème, which really pass from heart to heart and make their spirits one? Suppose Jones departs for *his* ship —dies—to-morrow, as he may, easily enough. Won't there be three good days of mixed grief and mourning show—till Jones is safely out of sight? And then, even in this Western world, won't they pretty calmly go over the will, with the relict, and open the lockbox and tap the securities with their "little hammer" to see if they are sound, and say cheerfully enough, if all is as it should be: "Well, Jones didn't do badly by her." And life will go on much as before, and all the more tolerably because Jones and Mrs. Jones were never so close together as they pretended to be. Loti is sad because he knows that human life is like that, and he can't forget it, even in Nagasaki.

He can't forget it, but by intensifying and varying his sensations he can make almost a rapture out of his consciousness of it. In "The Iceland Fisherman" and

"A Tale of Brittany" one is besieged by sensations from the first paragraph to the last; gray clouds, freezing rain, granite rocks, the smell of tar and salt air and steaming woolen and clay pipes, church bells for baptisms and weddings and deaths, the wayside *calvaire*, the summer flowers, the processions of girls in their white head-dresses, the lovers walking in the deep lanes, then the farewells, the mist and the rain again, the scream of gulls, hot liquor in the throat, cordage slipping through bleeding palms, the fishing, the voyage into the bleak north. And out of this saturation with raw sensations rises a sense of profound sympathy and intimate communion with the "soul" of Brittany and with the spirit of all sailors and of all wives and mothers and sweethearts who wait for ships that will never return from the immense and mournful monotony of the sea.

If I were to select from Loti's collection the six books which have impregnated my memory most indelibly with their color and fragrance I should probably choose "The Iceland Fisherman," "A Tale of Brittany," "A Tale of the Pyrenees," "Le Mariage de Loti," "Le Roman d'un Spahi" and "Madame Chrysanthème." Each of these is equipped with a sweetheart or so—poor little thing, and a sweetheart does unquestionably assist one's impressions and sensations to focus and compose themselves. But the enchantment of most of these tales is only very moderately dependent upon the erotic interest, unless one extends the term to include the sentiment that sailors feel for their mothers and mothers for their sons, and the bond of brotherhood, and the affection which greets the changing loveliness of the seasons, and piety toward the customs of one's ancestors and reverence for all

forms of religious faith in all regions of our mother
earth. What the reader falls in love with is in each
case a *milieu*, to which he finds himself bound in a
kind of sacramental relation—so much of its natural
beauty, and so much of its elemental humanity have
entered, with such an exquisitely melancholy commentary, into his heart through his thrilled senses.

Let us have one illustration of Loti's white magic,
aspersing his pages with the odors of a delicious spring
in the Pyrenees, on the soft nights when young Basque
smugglers run their contraband over the Spanish bor-
der and return in time for early mass:

For Ramuntcho, it is the time when smuggling becomes a calling almost without fatigue, with hours of
positive delight: climbing towards the mountain-tops
through springtime clouds; crossing ravines, wandering in the regions of the springs and wild fig-trees;
sleeping, while waiting for the hour agreed upon by
the complacent carbineers, on beds of mint and ragged
robin. . . . The wholesome fragrance of the plants
impregnated his clothes, and his jacket, which he never
wore, but used only as a pillow or a coverlet—and
Gracieuse would sometimes say to him in the evening:
"I know whither your smuggling took you last night,
for you smell of the mint of the mountain above
Mendiazpi."

There certainly is one of Loti's extraordinary
achievements: to make each one of nearly two score
volumes of which the scenes are wherever a French
cruiser calls or the colonial empire has extended—
to make each volume stir all the senses and reek of
its proper scene as pungently as the jacket of Ramuntcho reeked of the mint of the mountain above
Mendiazpi.

Sensation as Loti employs it becomes romantic; it lifts horizons, it stirs racial memories, it stimulates wide-sweeping reveries, it wakens a consciousness of impersonal powers and of unshunnable destiny; and these things are bitter rivals to the affections of a young girl. There is not a love-tryst in the works of Loti to which he goes with any such breathless fullness and expectancy of soul as he takes to Gethsemane in his yearning midnight vigil in "Jerusalem." No honeyed phrase from any of the sailors' sweethearts moves him so deeply as one musical sentence which he chants to himself, standing alone by his window at night, in "Un Pèlerin d'Angkor": "In the depths of the forests of Siam, I have seen the evening star rising above the great ruins of Angkor." And how can one hold by feminine coquetries a philanderer with all nations and all cultures and all gods, who cries out at one moment that Christ is his beloved lost brother, in the next that his soul is half Arab, and Mahomet is his prophet, and lo! a little while, and this homeless pilgrim is lying prostrate at the feet of Buddha?

XVI

Don Marquis, Poet

"DON MARQUIS, you know," Brander Matthews remarked to me the other day, "is essentially a poet." I didn't know it! I doubted it, on general principles. I regretted it, thinking the country over-populated with essential poets on part-time, Apollos in the pressroom and that sort of thing. Instantly my imagination linked him with the melancholy company of Charles Lamb, Thomas Hood and Mark Twain, three gloomy men who, it is now suspected, secretly yearned to add to the world's woe, yet were hopelessly condemned by chance and circumstance and fatally unwise marriages and the economic theory of history and the depraved state of public taste—were hopelessly condemned to contribute to the sum of human happiness.

Tragic maladjustment!

I don't know—nobody knows—just how it came to be accepted as axiomatic that it is better to be even the worst kind of a poet than even the best kind of a humorist. Probably it is connected in some way with our deep-seated northern European conviction that there is no virtue where there is no suffering. And, confidentially, I think it is nonsense. All the same, when I was told that Don Marquis is essentially a poet I elevated my eyebrows in the conventional way and said, "Alas!"—meaning what a pity that a

[209]

man who is essentially one thing should be devoting himself, however successfully, to something else.

My curiosity, however, was aroused, for I had sat once within eyeshot of Don Marquis for an hour or so; and having in surreptitious sidelong glances studied his bulk—I like to see letters represented by men and women whom the wind won't blow away—the silvery grizzle of his solid head, his tawny temperamental skin, and a certain gravity of the *ensemble*—a gravity illumined by occasional lambencies of smoldering eyes—I had wondered then what *else* he was besides the creator of the aspiring Hermione, the Red-Haired Lady and such Falstaffian poetry as the Old Soak. Something else, I was sure; for he was a visible reminder of George Meredith's discovery that all the great wits have been grave men. Several feet away one could feel that there was some one there. If I had possessed the *sang-froid* of the representative of the press who interviewed the sanguinary Cleopatra, in "Famous Love Affairs," idly flicking a slave, from time to time, from her roof garden to the crocodiles below as she chatted with the journalist, I might then and there have boldly accosted the daimonic mask and have plucked at the heart of his mystery, saying, "What are you, *essentially?*"

That sort of pike and cutlass boarding of a personality might have been attempted by Mme. de Staël or by the late Amy Lowell; and, of course, if they had attempted it they would have got away with it. But I was deterred by two considerations. In the first place, the natural savage intrepidity of my character has been mollified by contact with *belles-lettres*: I have read "Hermione," and know what arrows its author has in his quiver for persons who go about

Don Marquis

inquiring with earnest frivolity into the mysteries of art and into the natures which "we best give the clouds to keep." In the second place, I doubted whether Don Marquis could have answered my question if I had ventured to put it to him, and if he had cared to try.

He interested me, indeed, because he is, I suspect, like most modernized and well sophisticated men, a good bit puzzled himself by what he is. In several of the most striking of his personal poems he exhibits a kind of desperate amusement and bewilderment over the classical task of self-knowledge. Something—what is it?—has knocked our tight, snug little personalities to pieces. We see our fragments strewn all about us; but where is our core? In "Heir and Serf" Don Marquis speaks of his Self as "a chance loose knot in the skein of life where myriad selves combine"; he feels a heart quivering "with hatred not mine own"; he thinks of his Self as a house haunted by old doubts, old faiths, old lusts of the blood, unreconciled, and he ends his rummaging from basement to garret of that ancestral dwelling of spirit and flesh which he inhabits with a blank question—"What is this Self of mine?"

If the occupant of the tenement doesn't know, what should I learn by knocking at his door? Shall I turn to another poem called "The Struggle"? It describes a terrific combat with a spirit in a Dantean "dark valley" under frowning cliffs, a combat terminating in the death of the fell adversary, but—"He that lay upon the ground was—I!" That suggests much. So does the poem called "The Jesters," which speaks of disillusions and acrid tears and numb moments of despair, drowned in "an incorrigible mirth." So does the poem called "A Gentleman of Fifty Soliloquizes," which bids affection stand a little farther off:

Give me your mind, and I will give you mine.
　Then, should it change, no heart will bleed or burn.
Give me your wits. I want no heart of thine.
　You'll ask too much of life-blood in return.

We foiled self-seekers, we shattered fragments of personality, have devised ways to conceal our frustration and to keep impertinent curiosity from ascertaining whether the inner chamber of our lives contains a shrine or a tomb, or whether it is merely vacant. As for Don Marquis, he walks habitually in a defensive cloud of the humorous butterflies that his brain gives birth to; behind his whimsy moods and his satirical laughter he is, you will find if you pry into the matter, reticent—for a lyric poet, very reticent— about himself.

The only legitimate way to get at these reticent authors is to sit down before their complete works and read them straight through. It is infinitely better sport than cross-word puzzles, I conjecture, never having tried the latter. It is like big game hunting, when you get a soul at bay. When you have done that, you are in a position to tell the author all sorts of things about himself which he doesn't know—some of which may be true. I have tried this method with Don Marquis, and shall report my discoveries presently. But first let us consider the immediate occasion for subjecting a humorist to treatment so cruel and so unusual.

The occasion is this: Don Marquis has just proved by the severest of tests that he is a poet of very nearly the rarest sort—a dramatic poet. He has published a drama of poignant beauty and memorable reality on the betrayal, trial and crucifixion of Jesus, "The Dark Hours." Whether any other poet in America could have approached his achievement on this theme, I do not know. No one has. He has accomplished what I had thought was impossible: He has thoroughly dramatized the chief narrative of the New Testament, developing with marked originality several of the principal characters, notably Judas, and freely inventing incidents and speeches for subordinate figures, yet—to my sense, which is reasonably sensitive—without striking a note which is not in harmony with the tone and atmosphere of the Gospels. In the case of the central figure, he attempts no interpretation that deviates a hair's breadth from the Christian tradition. The character and personality of the Son of Man, the Son of God, are left quite inviolate; and this makes the more marvelous the congruity of his own developments. His feeling about the delicate ethical and artistic questions involved in handling this material he discusses with admirable taste and insight.

I have almost nothing strictly parallel to compare with the effect of "The Dark Hours" except a Passion Play which I saw a few years ago solemnly presented in a canyon of southern California, with the Crucifixion dim on the hilltop above it. With its elaborate reproduction of Palestinian dwellings, costumes and scenery, it was pictorially correct, like the colored illustrations in a modern Bible, of which it constantly reminded me, and the lines were gravely and eloquently recited, yet somehow it seemed remote and it left me cold—as cold as a colored picture in a Bible.

"The Dark Hours," on the other hand, even silently read, is of a seizing and transporting reality. Its tremendous dramatic stress is intensely felt. It puts one there—in ancient not modern Palestine. I am there—with Judas, with Peter, with Lazarus. I feel within myself the suspicious spleen of the high priest, the impotent deprecation of Pilate, the anguish of Procla, the nonchalance of the Roman soldiers gambling for the seamless garment, all the troubled confusion of blind men, lepers, and possessed men healed, the mocking scoffs and panic blood-lust of the rabble—and the stark solitude of one crying: "It is finished." As for the question whether this was indeed the Son of God who was crucified, at the end of the play one is facing it again with freshly astonished mind and senses, like the centurion standing there aghast at the foot of the cross. I believe this to be a great tragedy, greatly conceived and written with austere sincerity. When it is adequately produced, as I hope it may be, it should affect us as the tragedies of Æschylus and Sophocles affected the Greeks—religiously.

Socrates argued all night on one occasion to prove that the type of mind best adapted for tragedy is also the type of mind best adapted for comedy. If you reflect just a little about "The Dark Hours" you recover from your first surprise at the thought of its coming out of a mind which had just produced "The Old Soak's History of the World." In a sense which Charles Lamb understood when he shocked Carlyle by expressing regret that the Royalists didn't hang Milton, the Crucifixion, the execution of Socrates—all such incidents in history may be conceived of as tragic and stupendous jokes. In order fully to appreciate them one must be endowed with a comic poet's comprehension of the immensity of human folly, which is the prime source of all tragedy. To put the matter

[216]

in more familiar terms, no one can adequately know how dreadful the World War was who does not at the same time adequately know how absurd it was, how ridiculous, what an inexhaustible subject for the laughter of gods and men. In Don Marquis the tragi-comic spirit is very strong. He respects gods because he knows fools so well, so intimately; indeed, he knows them so affectionately that, as he suggests somewhere, he will be found fighting on their side "*against* the millennium" till the Judgment Day.

But it is time we had a little more definite information about the author of this notable religious drama.

Don Marquis is a typical New Yorker—that is to say, he was born in Walnut, Bureau County, Ill.—some sixty miles southwest of F. P. A., and three years earlier. Where and when he was educated I do not know. The book with which he seems to be most familiar is the Bible. Next to that, I should say the most obvious influences traceable in his prose and poetical styles and in the form of his humor are Mark Twain's "Huckleberry Finn" and "Tom Sawyer," the various yarns of Frank Stockton, O. Henry, perhaps H. C. Bunner, the poems of Swinburne, Kipling and Arnold, and an extensive study of prosody.

His first published book, "Danny's Own Story," 1912, is a picturesque narrative with an earthy Mid-Western flavor, Illinoisian, and much in the vein of Huck Finn, whose domain lies in the same rich humor belt, to the south. This is the soft drawling tune of it:

Old Hank mostly was truthful when lickered up, for that matter, and she knowed it, fur he couldn't think up no lies excepting a gineral denial when intoxicated up to the gills. . . . A man has jest naturally got to have something to cuss around and boss, so's to keep himself from finding out he don't amount to nothing. Leastways, most men is like that. And Hank, he didn't amount to much, and he kind of knowed it, way down deep in his inmost gizzards, and it were a comfort to him to have me around.

In 1915 Don Marquis made the first collection of his serious poems, under the title "Dreams and Dust." In 1916 he uttered a farcical Stocktonian yarn, "The Cruise of the Jasper B.," which relates the adventures of a romantic journalist attempting to sail his schooner, scow or canal boat—it isn't quite clear which —from her moorings *on* a brick pier *in* Long Island. In the same year appeared "Hermione and her Little Group of Serious Thinkers," asking themselves at bedtime many heart-searching questions. In 1919 a volume of "Prefaces"—thirty-two of them, introducing A Check Book, A Cook Book, The Works of Billy Sunday, etc. In 1921 appeared the first records of "The Old Soak"; also a notable collection of short stories, "Carter and Other People," and a volume of humorous verse, "Noah an' Jonah an' Cap'n John Smith." Next year, 1922, a second collection of serious verse, "Poems and Portraits," in which Don Marquis takes the war seriously, and adds thirty-three satires with teeth. In 1922, "The Revolt of the Oyster," containing some capital stories of dogs and boys and the ripe tale of "The Saddest Man"; also "Sonnets to a Red-Haired Lady." In 1924, "The Old Soak's History of the World," "The Dark Hours," and, with Christopher Morley, "Pandora Lifts the Lid."

There are some things among these fourteen volumes

of a sort which I never read except in the line of duty. With me, a very little Stocktonian extravaganza goes a long way. So does a very little of the ordinary run of humorous verse. Practically all the rest goes very well, including the satires in "Savage Portraits," which are as neat and sharp as those of the Roman masters. But I enjoy Don Marquis most when he is enjoying himself most, and that is obviously when his imagination is at work and he is creating something, if it is only a prolific cat, a loquacious cockroach, or a special kind of thoroughbred dog: "*Any* dog can be full of just *one* kind of thoroughbred blood. That's nothing! But Spot here has got more different kinds of thoroughbred blood in him than any dog you ever saw." I admire the creative energy with which Don Marquis steers his elderly inebriate through his bar-room reminiscences; I prefer the Old Soak's gorgeous, glowing historical style in his account of Ancient History to that of Gibbon, Wells or Van Loon, and I admire immensely the masterly poetizing stroke in the invention of "that damn little athyiss, Hennery Withers." That is Shakespearean—no less.

But previous to "The Dark Hours" I suspect the most memorable writing that Don Marquis has done is in eight or ten short stories: "Old Man Murtrie," "Never Say Die," "McDermott," "Looney, the Mutt" and "The Locked Box"—in "Carter and Other People"; and "The Saddest Man" and the dog and boy stories in "The Revolt of the Oyster." In reading this group of stories I have no compunctious feeling that I am enjoying humor by the sacrifice of a poet; for in the wider sense of the word these stories *are* poetry. Several of them are, I think, the kind of poetry in which Don Marquis expresses himself most adequately, that is, tragi-comic poetry.

Take Old Man Murtrie dying behind his prescription counter in a Brooklyn drug store, with God and the Devil disputing as to which of them has got to take in his miserable soul; first neither of them wants him; then both of them want him, and Death peevishly urges them to settle it somehow—pure poetry! Take the story of the man who, when he has killed his wife out of jealousy set in motion by the Locked Box, finds that it contains only a tender letter to him, marked "Not to be opened till after my death," confessing that now, after five years of marriage, she has begun to love him passionately; she has sealed the confession only because she does not wish him to know there was ever a time when she did not love him. Take the story of "Looney the Mutt": a half-witted tramp who has lost his pal seeks him, seeks him, following false clews, scoffed at, mocked at, fondly, eagerly, hungrily —seeks him as a man seeks a God who forever eludes him.

We are, I think, on the main trail that runs from "The Dark Hours" back to "Dreams and Dust." In 1915, when this volume was published, Don Marquis was both technically and essentially a poet. I am struck by the sort of poet he was then. There is in this first collection little indication of historical passions, little indication of locality, no very particular or specific attachment to "Nature," and no significant love-interest. The dominant note is an almost Arnoldian concern about God and the soul and their relations in a world which has lost faith in supernatural guidance.

Whenever he turns from polishing a rondeau or a

triolet, which he does very nicely, to grappling with a theme, he is idealistic and religious. He sounds the silver trumpet to "paladins, paladins, youth, noble-hearted." He scornfully bids farewell to the "lost leader." He sees that man has "at his noblest an air of something more than man." He is the receiver of mystical intimations. He speculates on the mystery of the Self. Disillusioned, he yet sees man as the god-seeker, the god-maker, and he respects man's aspiration, in the face of "the hissing hate of fools, thorns, and the ingrate's scoff"—

For all of the creeds are false, and all of the creeds
    are true;
And low at the shrine where my brothers bow,
There will I bow too;
For no form of a god, and no fashion
Man has made in his desperate passion
But is worthy some worship of mine;
Not too hot with gross belief,
Nor yet too cold with pride,
I will bow me down where my brothers bow,
Humble—but open-eyed!

The only trouble about bowing down "open-eyed" is that presently you notice every one else has his eyes open, too; and you see such funny things going on around you, that the first thing you know you are conducting a Column. And if you *will* insist upon giving people a choice between Jesus and the Old Soak —well, you know what people are.

XVII

William Osler: The High Calling of Medicine

IN the house of letters there are many delightful mansions; but, according to my own taste and judgment, the first competent, comprehensive biography of a great contemporary is the most important and the most stimulating form of current literature. It presents what our society needs above everything else: an objective made visible, an ideal made contagious by realization. If wishing could do it, I would wish "The Life of Sir William Osler" into the hands of every man, woman and child who reads the six best-selling novels.

When one comes to think of it, there are excellent reasons for bringing the layman in at this point. The lay public often fears the lawyers, sometimes shuns the clergy, but, through thick and thin, it clings to the physicians. Year after year we laymen furnish them "laboratory material." We are intensely interested in the outcome of their experiments. In the long run from the cradle to the grave we are certain to have been many times in debt, and indebted, to them.

Furthermore, Dr. Osler, though a most resolute and devoted physician, was much else that interests the laity. In his earlier years he was a passionate student of the fundamental sciences, and as an Oxford professor he was a propagandist for scientific studies

Wm Osler

in the last refuge of the classics. He was a great teacher and a persuasive speaker on the regimen of the student and on the arts of instruction. He was a medical publicist and statesman with messages of the highest importance to mayors, town meetings and that miscellaneous rabble out of which that noble force known as Public Opinion proceeds. He was a book-man, an enamored bibliographer, a curator of the Bod-leian, a director of the Oxford Press, a founder, pa-tron and promoter of libraries in England, Canada and the United States. Besides all this, he was a beau-tiful and lovable character, completely possessing several great and simple virtues which drew men to him and held them.

As for the medical profession, I fancy not much inviting will be required to bring it to this sumptuous feast. The head of the Johns Hopkins Hospital, the author of "The Principles and Practice of Medicine" and "Æquanimitas," touched it at all points. Wher-ever he touched it, he glorified it. He loved every honest medical man from Galen, Hippocrates and Avicenna to his Alabama student, and if he had en-joyed the leisure of Methuselah he would have delivered an address or have erected a monument in honor of every one. Fearful of specialism, he loved the whole range of pathology, and in the laboratory or the clinic or in strategic counsels with his colleagues, he had a hand in the fighting against all the major plagues of mankind. The story of his life must appeal to his old comrades as Grant's "Memoirs" appealed to the veterans of the Civil War. Nor can one conceive of any intelligent and aspiring young physician, sur-geon, nurse, trustee of a hospital, or any one earnestly concerned with public health or medical education and research who will not desire to own the book—no owner would lend it long enough to read it through—and repeatedly to make his way through its fourteen hundred inspiring and richly informative pages.

The author, whose name appears on the title-page without any professional identification or display of learned letters, has a record rather strikingly like that of Osler: nine years on the Johns Hopkins staff as associate surgeon, three years of the period with Osler in charge; professor of surgery at Harvard since 1911; in charge of a base hospital and consultant in France during the war, with a colonelcy in the Medical Corps of the U. S. A.; many foreign honors, membership in British and French medical associations, and enormous acquaintance with the history, bibliography and personnel of his profession.

Without using the first personal pronoun, Dr. Cushing keeps his eye on the object from first to last. He has made his imagination work to realize every step of Osler's career from the Canadian backwoods to the Regius professorship.

The prime question about a distinguished man is how he got his start. Introducing Osler in 1909 at a session of the London School of Tropical Medicine, the American Ambassador, Whitelaw Reid, presented the speaker as "a very excellent example of what the States could do with a Canadian when caught young." That was a fair ambassadorial crack, but Dr. Cushing's admirable opening chapters on the birth and upbringing of our physician do not justify it. The States were more indebted to Osler than Osler to the States. What the Johns Hopkins got when it called this Canadian was a physician who had supplemented his training in the best Edinburgh traditions by ac-

[226]

quaintance with the latest developments on the Continent.

Osler was a good Canadian, a good American, a good Englishman, but of nationality he made little, and he was never an American citizen. His parents were English people out of Cornwall—the father a Saxon, the mother a "black Celt" who, in 1837, crossed the Atlantic to propagate the Gospel in the upper Canadian wilderness. William was born in 1849. You see the sturdy father, a Cambridge University man and a fine mathematical scholar, by the way, riding through the woods on horseback with the baptismal register in his saddlebags, hunting out his youngest parishioners, helping them spiritually into the world. You see the mother of nine children conducting a large Sunday school class and also a big sewing class twice a week, to second her husband's efforts for the civilization of the Canadian backwoods. She is an educated woman and writes charming, affectionate, humorous letters to her boys, when they are at school, which you may be sure they are, and under the best masters, men, English university graduates. This good woman lived to be three months more than a hundred years old. The family reckoned twenty members in the World War. It is English-Canadian, and it is magnificent. William Osler got his start from his parents: black hair and black eyes from his mother, and good blood, brains, character and indomitable energy from both.

As a schoolboy William was at or near the head of his class, he was the best athlete in school and he was a ringleader in mischief—with an inherited leaning toward the ministry. The decisive turn in his career was made at school in Weston, conducted on the Eton plan, including the top hats. Opposite page 33 you

[227]

may see William Osler, aged sixteen, in his top hat, as head prefect. At Weston he became the favorite pupil of a master with a passion for collecting, labeling and microscopically examining every conceivable specimen of "natural history." The passion was contagious. William caught it, became an infatuated microscopist and soon was so deeply absorbed in fresh-water polyzoa that he neglected his letters to his family. The influence of the master was reinforced by the medical director of the school, James Bovell. In 1868 William bought his first edition of Sir Thomas Browne's works, and began his life-long collecting of the "Religio Medici." Theology waned and medicine waxed. He went to McGill, where he received the best medical education to be had in Canada, and graduated with a special prize for a thesis "greatly distinguished for originality and research."

Perhaps the most significant thing that Osler did immediately after he was graduated was *not to get married*. Marriage he postponed till his forty-third year, in accordance with his advice to young medical students, that they should put their affections "on ice." Instead of getting married he went abroad for two years and studied with the masters in Europe and England, including seventeen months with John Burton Sanderson, whom thirty-four years later he succeeded as Regius Professor of Medicine at Oxford. At the age of twenty-four he returned to McGill as Professor of the Institutes of Medicine, which position he held from 1874 to 1884. He was called to the Professorship of Clinical Medicine at the University of Pennsylvania in 1884 and remained there till 1889. Then he accepted his post at the Johns Hopkins, and held it, in spite of all temptations, till 1905, when Oxford called him. "Stick to your last" was a maxim that he preached and practised.

Dr. Cushing disclaims any attempt at a systematic "appraisal of his professional accomplishments." Osler's name is not identified with any of the great epoch-making discoveries of his period. He cannot be ranked with men like Virchow, Koch, Lister, and Pasteur. He was never, says Dr. Cushing, an "adept in bacteriological technique," and this defect in his training rather precluded his participating in the most important way in the main line of the scientific advance. In his farewell to his American colleagues he himself declared that he had had but two ambitions in his professions: first, to make of himself a good clinical physician, and, second, "to build up a great clinic on Teutonic lines, not on those previously followed here and in England, but on lines which have proved so successful on the Continent and which have placed the scientific medicine of Germany in the forefront of the world." His biographer, who makes some reference to his studies of a third element in the blood, "Osler's disease," etc., inclines to believe that his greatest services were performed as an inseminator of other minds and as a propagandist for public health, perhaps with special reference to his participation in the anti-tuberculosis and antityphoid crusades. To this should be added the fact that the Rockefeller Foundation for Medical Research seems to have been directly inspired by the reading of his "Principles and Practice of Medicine."

Osler himself repeatedly denied that he had attained the objects of his ambition by any extraordinary faculty, and I don't think Dr. Cushing brings any extraordinary faculty to light. What one sees is a young fellow of energetic mind and body who at the age of sixteen or seventeen discovered what he wanted to do with his life and stuck by that with a most consummate doggedness. From his medical student days onward he was a hard, regular and systematic worker. "Work" he gave as the master-word of success in the profession. He had performed more than a thousand autopsies before he left McGill, and that was but an incident in his labors. In another of his addresses, he offered students three master keys: the Art of Detachment, the Virtue of Method and the Quality of Thoroughness. The Art of Detachment he explains as "the faculty of isolating yourselves from the pursuits and pleasures incident to youth." Perhaps he was jesting a little, but so far as the record shows he was master of the Art of Detachment. Till he went to Oxford and let himself out in his bibliographical passions and in society he seems to have sought all his pleasure in his work, in the hospital, in scientific publications, in association meetings, in professional dinners.

There is no indication that getting rich was one of his ambitions. His "Principles and Practice of Medicine," of which he presented the hundred thousandth copy to his son, made him so independent that when fire devastated Baltimore he could offer to turn his salary for a period of five years back to the Johns Hopkins. Checks for a hundred dollars to needy students or struggling libraries slipped from him easily. But when he took to purchasing first editions, incunabula, and manuscripts, he appreciated a gift of £1,000 from a prosperous brother. Always he looked on medicine as "a calling, not a trade." He refused to become involved in a general practise; he wanted to keep his hands free for science and for clinical instruction.

The highest praise that he could find for one of his masters at McGill was to say that he resembled Thomas Arnold, of Rugby. The molding of the Arnoldian tradition is plainly visible in Osler. It is easy, furthermore, to trace in his writing the influence of Matthew Arnold as a powerful formative influence. Under a photograph of himself with his little son on his back he has written jocosely: "And on his shoulders, not a lamb, a kid"—which is the last line of Arnold's sonnet "The Good Shepherd with the Kid." He praises Locke for the "sweet reasonableness," which is Arnold's phrase for the master quality of Jesus. When he leaves the United States he applies to himself the lines of Arnold's Empedocles:

> I have loved no darkness,
> Sophisticated no truth,
> Nursed no delusion,
> Allowed no fear.

He is like Arnold in his love for the Bible and for the classical moralists, and like him in this: Externally gay, affable, full of quips and drolleries, eminently companionable as he was, one recognizes that the groundwork of his character was stoical. Self-mastery, the performance of duty, unmurmuring acceptance of destiny were lessons that he learned early and never forgot.

Shortly before he left this country—to return only for "week-ends," as his friends put it—he made what the newspaper men distorted into his most notorious public utterance: his remarks on the uselessness of men over forty, whence the verb "to Oslerize." As a matter of fact, Osler had not a particle of malice toward old men; he had always, on the contrary, a special fondness for them. Significantly, he praised the French lecturer's habit of constant reference to "my distinguished Master." His remarks about old men had come out of his humility and his quizzical kindness. What he had meant to suggest was that he himself was on the verge of "senility," and that consequently his colleagues would not lose much by his migration to Oxford. He was tenderly trying to temper the wind of his departure to his shorn lambs. He had long been an advocate, however, of a "quinquennial braindusting," and he believed in the "peripatetic" life as a preventative of premature old age. I think it is clear that his growth in the years of his English residence was rather social, historical, and literary than scientific.

He had to take his part as a medical officer in the war, but I find no evidence that his heart was in it. He simply bowed to the inevitable as silently as possible. The entire vast madness lay entirely outside his scheme and philosophy of life. The Stoics whom he loved, Marcus Aurelius and Epictetus, and his adored Sir Thomas Browne, had taught him early to denationalize himself, to think of the human race fraternally, and to cultivate charity toward all men. As a man of science, he knew that he must be a cosmopolitan: there are no national boundaries to the commonwealth of science. And so he went about with tight lips and a stricken heart visiting the hospitals and preparing himself to surrender all that makes life of much account to a man who has done his work. In the second volume Dr. Cushing gives us some captivating glimpses of Osler's notable wife and of his only son, an affectionate boy after his father's own heart, and with his own

[232]

tastes, a pacific book lover and angler of Izaak Walton's school, soon to be employed in stopping German shrapnel with chest, abdomen and thigh.

Dr. Cushing's conception of his many-sided subject is broad and humane. He is reticent about Osler's intimate personal life during the first forty years, but one suspects that there was not much intimate personal life before his forty-third year. In his English period the sweetness and gentleness of his nature come more and more to the surface, through the rush of professional and social duties, all the way to his own deathbed, on which he jests and takes notes and reads the "Religio Medici." They tell him that he will get well, but he smiles and says to his nurse: "Ah, Sister, we know, don't we?" His chief regret is that he will not be able to see the post-mortem.

The great length of the narrative is partly due to a lax application of the principle of selection among abundant materials, and in so far as that is true it results in a lack of perspective. But the urgent fullness of the work is partly attributable also to Dr. Cushing's brimfulness of every sort of information relevant to the entire life-course of the subject. He knows, for example, for any year you please, the condition of the medical faculty at McGill, Pennsylvania, the Johns Hopkins, Harvard, London, Edinburgh, Paris, Berlin and Vienna. He seems to know who read the important papers at every meeting of every important medical association. He knows the steps in all the great discoveries: the germ theory of disease, the place of aniline dyes in the detection of the tubercle bacillus, the differentiation of fevers, the development of serum therapy and the conquest of malaria, diphtheria and typhoid, the discovery of the Roentgen ray, the ex-

ploitation of the ductless glands, etc. As a consequence, he has almost inevitably made the life of Osler
also a history of the revolutionary progress of medical
science during his time.

In justice to his performance of this immense "labor
of love" one other point should be made. In his modest
one-page preface he disclaims having attempted a
"final portrait." He calls these records *mémoires pour
servir.* They are extraordinarily substantial and purposeful *mémoires.* But, on the whole, that characterization of them is just, and more accurate than a description of the book as a brilliant biographical portrait. It is a marvelously thorough piece of spade
work. Osler was an artesian well, and Dr. Cushing
has dug up the well. All the materials are here and
in order, and the huge gusto of a like-minded colleague will find every scrap of them precious.

It is an immense and wonderful book, and it should
be made prescribed reading for all those grim, sad-
eyed conservative killjoys who go about denying "the
dogma of progress."

XVIII

H. L. Mencken as Liberator

IN keeping house with from two to seven bickering personalities treading on one another's toes within the castle of his bones Mr. Mencken resembles the rest of humankind. For the outside observer, as well as for the beleaguered spirits, the most interesting question about the housekeeping is which one of the inmates is finally going to rule the roost. In this case attention may well center on the long contention between a reckless, callous, two-fisted grobianism and a being with "immortal longings" remotely akin to Heinrich Heine, who enjoined his heirs and assigns to lay on his coffin a sword—"for I was a brave soldier in the Liberation War of humanity."

I am grateful to Mr. Mencken whenever he reminds me of Heine, and, as a matter of fact, he has done that more than once. If he did not, like Heine, live in mortal terror of betraying his "immortal longings," he would reveal them more frequently. Heine, my dog-eared copy of his lyrics, my underscored copy of his travel books, his delicious book, "The Romantic School," his gay war on the professors, the preachers, the princelings of provincial Germany, his intoxicating sentiment, his tenderness toward the old traditions that he mocked—the grandmother sitting by the hearth; his infinite malice, his irony, his heart-breaking wit— Heine, the Jewish nightingale of Düsseldorf, the only

[235]

German writer who ever thoroughly bewitched and enchanted me, curiously came back into my mind, from the intermittent exile of a quarter of a century, at the bidding of a gesture of Mr. Mencken to his flock and at the penny whistle piping of two or three pages at the end of his fourth series of "Prejudices," headed "Bilder aus schöner Zeit," jottings, merely, of things sweet to his memory, as thus:

The little pile of stones on the beach of Watling's Island, marking the place where Columbus landed. . . . The moon of the Caribbees, seen from a 1,000-ton British tramp. . . . A dull night in a Buffalo hotel, reading the American Revised Version of the New Testament. . . . The day I received the proofs of my first book. . . . A good-by on a Hoboken pier. . . . The Palace Hotel in Madrid.

When I read these pages I was touched, and I fell to thinking about Heine.

Was it because I too was brought up on the literature of Israel that I never had any difficulty in understanding Heine's humor, was never offended by it, even in its most irreverent sallies, and sympathized in the main heartily with his neo-paganism—his attempt to rediscover the goodness of this earthly life, and with all his efforts to free the Children of Light from Philistia's yoke, from the stodginess of missionary society culture and from the straitjacket of small-town theology?

Heine told me that the Quaker who bought up the loveliest mythological paintings of Giulio Romano in order to burn them deserved to be sent to heaven and whipped there every day for his pains. Heine wakened my apprehension of professors when he told me that

the three greatest adversaries of Napoleon had "ended
miserably: Castlereagh cut his own throat, Louis
XVIII rotted upon his throne and Professor Saalfeld
is *still a professor at Göttingen*." Heine told me that
"to Goethe the Cross was as hateful as bugs, tobacco
and garlic," and I understand why. Heine had spoken
of the Virgin Mary as "the fair *dame du comptoir* of
the Catholic Church, whose customers, especially the
barbarians of the North, were attracted and spellbound
by her heavenly smile." Heine told me that religion,
by inculcating a houndlike humility, the rejection of
all earthly goods and the renunciation of innocent
pleasures, had "really brought sin and hypocrisy into
the world." And I was not wounded by any of these
things, because I felt myself to be, in my ethical and
religious inheritance and in my sentiment for the history and poetry of the Chosen People, almost as much
of a Jew as Heine, and because I was in the same boat
with him, voyaging on the open sea of the modern
spirit.

There is an obvious parallelism between the present
line of Mr. Mencken's effort and the line of Heine, and
it has set me to thinking over some of the reasons why
when the later iconoclast began his critical jehad he
did not bewitch and enchant me as Heine had done.

The first of these reasons Mr. Mencken himself has
just given me by stating that he is a white, blond,
Protestant Nordic and an excessively pure type of the
Anglo-Saxon. I am no sworn lover of the Anglo-
Saxon. Though I have occasionally quoted Mr. Dreiser's theorizings on the intolerable moral idealism of
the "Anglo-Saxons," though, on due and sufficient
provocation, I have twitted various persons for raising
Semitic, Celtic and German banners against the Re-

public, I have always regarded these ethnological speculations as a morass full of will-o'-the wisps which were
not worth chasing. On the one occasion when I did
treat the subject respectfully—in a war tract of 1918
—I dismissed Anglo-Saxonism as a banner of prepos-
terous absurdity, and argued that the only banner
under which the allied nations could possibly unite was
the flag of mankind. The pure Anglo-Saxon, the
white, blond, Protestant Nordic, has never been an
object of my reverence. He never, as such, occupied
ten minutes of my attention till I gave a course of lectures to prove my ancient conviction that in English
literature at least he does not exist. Mr. Mencken, on
the other hand, revels in ethnology, as he proves by his
wild ramblings among the Celts and Saxons in this
volume; and he does assert the existence among us, in
very small numbers, of the pure Anglo-Saxon.

I snatch at this blond Nordicism of his to explain
those characteristics of his work which least captivate
me. The pure, unmodified Anglo-Saxon cannot be
altogether like Heine. As Taine and others describe
the Anglo-Saxon, he is a big white bulk of grobianism
—a hard fighter, a hard eater, a hard drinker, a hard
boaster, reverencing women but keeping them in the
kitchen—a man, in short, with no sentiment or nonsense about him. When I first made acquaintance with
Mr. Mencken's work, his juvenile addiction to Kipling
and the American Navy and his long immersion in
Friedrich Nietzsche had brought all his pure, elemental
Anglo-Saxonism, including his Ur-Germanic grobianism, to the surface. In those days he uttered little soft
stuff about "the civilized minority." His saving rem-
nant was a hunting pack of horny-hearted supermen.
He professed himself a Federalist. He was an atheist

[238]

of the biological type. He celebrated glorious war, like a Prussian professor. He preached the gospel of Herrenmoral. He despitefully assigned women and negroes to the slave class. He emptied dishwater over pretty nearly the whole of American literature, treating with particular ignominy my heroes, the Abolitionists, the Transcendentalists, and the American pioneers of realism. He insulted my grandmother. And I found no compensation for that in his whooping it up for a type of modern German naturalism which had pleased me in my teens but which, when I had found better diet, I had come to loathe.

Mr. Mencken's Fourth Series is still deplorably rich in exulting grobianisms. He rarely faces an adversary, he never argues, he never meets a point, and he never uses one. The only weapons employed by this champion of the civilized minority are bricks and cabbages. But as he hurls these missiles at phantoms and puppets of his own ingenious manufacture, which generally bear no resemblance to the persons whose names he affixes to them, little blood is spilled. Along with these insignificant personal diatribes, he utters much humorous thunder in behalf of universal skepticism and anarchy. In the style with which we have grown quite familiar, he preaches contumacy toward God, the laws, the clergy, the politicians, the courts, the police, the professors, and the farmers; all this as the mark of a civilized minority. He denounces religion, poetry, and romantic love as lies and delusions which can impose on no man of intelligence after the age of thirty. He proclaims the bootlegger the hero of contemporary civilization; and he avows a yearning to see "the whole human race gently stewed," and thereby happy.

Of "cultural progress" in the Mid-West and the

South he is somewhat despondent; but in New York
City he sees cheering indications that multitudes have
quite divested themselves of the fear of hell fire.
"Compared to the revels that go on in New York every
night," he declares, "the carnalities of the West End
of Berlin are trivial and childish, and those of Paris
and the Côte d'Azur take on the harmless aspect of
a Sunday school picnic." New York contains the hope
of a higher culture; it is now an "auction room and a
bawdy house." We have now got all the freedom we
need. There is no longer any earthly reason why
American writers, at last relieved of the moralistic
incubus, shouldn't settle down and produce a great
literature!

Whether Mr. Mencken takes credit for having produced all these improvements—all this ripened spirit of
contumacy and corruption—single-handed, I don't
quite make out. It is clear, however, that he reviews
with satisfaction his performance in a series of leading
rôles; some of which he has quite recently assumed.
He sees himself, of course, as the principal "truth-
seeker" of this generation. He now offers himself as
the defender of the American tradition in letters, the
tradition which includes Poe, Hawthorne, Emerson,
Whitman and Mark Twain—the defender of this tradition as against Mr. Matthews, Mr. Brownell and
others of us who wish "to pass over all these men to
embrace . . . N. P. Willis, J. G. Holland, Charles
Dudley Warner, Mrs. Sigourney and the Sweet Singer
of Michigan." He sees himself as the blond Nordic
assailant of the blond Nordics. He views himself as
the one undaunted voice of the civilized minority. He
is the emancipator of the young from Mr. Comstock.
He is the knight in shining armor going out against

the prohibition demon. He is the man midwife of the naturalistic fiction which makes its bed in the parlor window.

There is not space here to extract the kernel of fact from the bushels of what he calls "pishposh" in which he loves to involve and invalidate all his criticism. I will give but a single illustration. On the soberest page of his book, page 285, he congratulates the young American literatus on the freedom which has been won for him since he, Mr. Mencken, assumed the "martyr's shroud" in 1908; and immediately thereafter he sketches the dreadful condition of American authorship in the period immediately preceding his advent. Before his appearance, he declares, "the American novelists most admired by most publishers, by most readers and by all practising critics were Richard Harding Davis, Robert W. Chambers and James Lane Allen. It is hard indeed, in retrospect, to picture those remote days just as they were. They seem almost fabulous."

Now my animadversions against Mr. Mencken as critic and historian of American letters have been evoked chiefly by the quality which is still regnant in the soberest page of this latest book: I mean his wholly uncritical and grobian callousness about the truth. The "fabulousness" of the decade prior to 1908 Mr. Mencken produces by bringing in H. W. Mabie and ignoring James and Howells, who are, of course, the real way-makers of our realistic fiction; and by bringing in Richard Harding Davis and leaving out Crane's "Red Badge of Courage," 1895; James's "What Maisie Knew," 1897; Frederic's "Damnation of Theron Ware," 1896; Norris's "McTeague," 1899, and "The Pit," 1902; Grant's "Unleavened Bread,"

1900; Mrs. Wharton's "House of Mirth," 1905, and "The Fruit of the Tree," 1907; Sinclair's "Jungle," 1906; O. Henry's "Gentle Grafter," 1908; Herrick's "Together," 1908, not to speak of Mr. Mencken's isolated exception, Mr. Dreiser's "Sister Carrie," 1900. As an historian Mr. Mencken is to be viewed with alarm.

I have sworn to myself not to end this review on the note of detraction, but to bring it back to the note of sincere admiration on which it started. Though Mr. Mencken lacks the patience, the discrimination and the "organ for truth" which the critic of a "civilized minority" ought to possess, he has other great talents. He is, as I have said elsewhere, alive. He has been the occasion of life in others. He has a rare gift at stirring people up and making them strike an attitude, and at least start on the long process of becoming intelligent beings. And he is beginning to quote from good authors. He is beginning to quote shyly from the New Testament in the Latin of the Vulgate. What may that bode? No one who has followed his work as carefully and hopefully as I have these many years can have failed to recognize that his obvious calling is to some form of ministry. From the first, he has exhibited the desk-beating proclivities, the overstrained voice, the tumid phrases and the denunciatory fervor which one associates with the popular orator. Years ago I pointed out the absurdity of his presenting himself as chiefly an æsthetic interpreter when every drop of his blood seethes with moral passion and every beat of his heart summons him to moral propaganda. In his Fourth Series, when Mr. Mencken is not a theologian he is a moralist. His book is properly describable as a moral miscellany.

In the midst of its grobianism there are glimmers of better things. Mr. Mencken, to be sure, still attacks mob psychology with the weapons of the mob. He roars at the populace in the voice of the populace. He still identifies God with the universe, with nature, with the "cosmic process." And his popularity he has won in great part by a demagogic encouragement of the cosmic process, by hurrahing for the liberation in the populace of its natural grobianism. But his radical skepticism has got him half way out of that Serbonian bog. In a brief theological paragraph, entitled "The Goal," he announces that *"the central aim of civilization, it must be plain, is simply to defy and correct the obvious intent of God!"* He is right. *So long as he defines God as he does,* he is right. So long as he identifies God with unimproved Nature, it must be the central aim of civilization "to defy and correct the obvious intent of God." This God is careless, improvident, and lacks a heart.

If he follows that clew, he will inevitably return to the reality of religion, poetry and romantic love and to the sense of their necessity in the culture of a civilized minority. If he follows that clew he may eventually make plain that his faith in science, his allegiance to reason, his passion for music, his devotion to letters and learning and his increasing abomination for mass action and all impositions of brutal force— all the things that he cares most for *are* the religion, *are* the poetry of romantic lovers, created by them and held in existence by their fidelity. If Mr. Mencken does that, he will remind me still more of Heine and will strengthen his claim to the sword of a Liberator.

XIX

Barrett Wendell: Farewell, New England Gentleman

THE most fascinating aspect of American life to-day is the ascent into articulate self-consciousness of that element of our people which Emerson called "the Jacksonian rabble," and the relative decline toward artistic inexpressiveness of that element which Barrett Wendell called the "better sort." I have been reading two recent biographies which, taken together, give one the personal significance and intimate human meaning of this phenomenon. The first records the rise of a Mid-Western waif to success in business, and then his soul-shattering discovery that he is the typical American of our day, and that he is under a kind of divine obligation to become an artist and to reveal his soul in art. I refer to Sherwood Anderson's "A Story Teller's Story," a beautiful book, moving and significant. The second biography records the rise of a well-derived, well-bred Boston boy to be a professor of English at Harvard, and then his gradually strengthening conviction that he is the last of the New England gentlemen—a sobering and saddening thought, mitigated in his case by his belief that a hundred years hence, if all goes well with the Republic, the typical American will be such a man as he has been. I refer to Mr. Howe's life of Barrett Wendell, which is likewise a beautiful book, moving and significant.

I am glad that writing this biography fell to Mr. Howe. He is at the same time the most modest editor and one of the finest masters of the biographic art now practising in America. A New Englander and a Harvard man, full of Latin piety toward the men and *mores* and institutions which for three hundred years have had their center in his corner of Massachusetts, he has sat up there in Boston for decade after decade, like an infatuated and self-effacing recording angel, editing Beacon Biographies, "The Harvard Alumni Bulletin," "The Harvard Graduates' Magazine," "The Atlantic Monthly," the lives and letters of Phillips Brooks and Charles Eliot Norton, the monumental tomes of "The Memoirs of the Harvard Dead in the War Against Germany," "Memories of a Hostess" and the like. In much of this work there has been for Mr. Howe great labor, a beautiful service of commemoration, and a minimum of personal glory. In performing it, however, Mr. Howe has perhaps become the mind of our times most fully and constantly aware of the meaning of Harvard College and New England as elements in the historic, intellectual, literary and social life of the nation. His latest biography proves, moreover, to any discerning eye, proves by all sorts of subtleties in the composition, that he himself has achieved a certain blessed critical detachment from the traditional Boston outlook—or should not one rather say, the traditional Boston inlook—thinking of that rapt and reverent contemplation of the umbilicus which conceivably some colonial Yankee skipper imported from the Orient?

At this point I wish to say a word, by way of side-lighting, about my own feeling for Mr. Howe's subject. I love New England with all my heart, tenderly and sentimentally, and with that protective and jealous passion which resents a slurring word from one who has not so loved her. But since the current mode of contemplating one's grandmother has come in, since several years ago I heard James Harvey Robinson, in the picked diction of Columbia University, characterize all hitherto recorded history as "bunk," I have lain awake night after night foreseeing the devastation which is going to be wrought the moment that it occurs to some young man, bred in Professor Robinson's school, to deal with the "awful majesties" of New England's Great Age as Lytton Strachey and Ford Madox Ford and Max Beerbohm have dealt with the Victorians and Pre-Raphaelites.

If I, or any man who thought of Barrett Wendell merely as a Harvard professor, had attempted to produce his "spitting image," what sort of caricature would our treacherous memories and our still more treacherous "realistic method" have produced? Well, I am afraid we should have seized upon some quite inadequate statement of his idiosyncrasy, trimmed it up in his abundant external eccentricities and thus have made a figure of considerable interest to his former students and perhaps to his colleagues, but of very mild concern to the public at large. To be more specific, it would be easy to make a brilliant caricature of this subject entitled either "A Harvard Professor" or "The Last of the Brahmins"—attenuations of humanity, neither of which could have stirred a deeper emotion in the vast democratic laity than amusement.

Mr. Howe saw both these opportunities. He proved his greatness as a biographer by dismissing them both in favor of a far more difficult task, namely, to show Barrett Wendell attempting to become an honest man, though a professor and a conservative! He has accomplished what he set out to perform. He has consequently produced a far more complex character than most people suspected Barrett Wendell to be—a character far more complex, perhaps, than Barrett Wendell himself thought he was, and certainly far less simple, firm, homogeneous and robust than the impression of himself which in later years he tried to stamp upon his contemporaries.

Mr. Howe's Wendell is no mere glorified schoolmaster but a man rich in humanity, full of temperamental impulses, of humor, of self-questioning, of self-distrust, and, what is most surprising, he abounds in that humility which is one infallible mark of a truly great spirit. I shall perhaps shock some of his friends by this comparison; but I insist upon it as the point of significance in my original juxtaposition of the two names: Barrett Wendell exhibits the same religious humility before his ideal of a good man that Sherwood Anderson exhibits before his ideal of a great artist. The first man's final conclusion is that a respect-worthy human character is the finest work of art. The second man's conclusion is that the finest works of art far transcend in value the most respect-worthy human characters. The conflict between the old times and the new is there. By an adequate and essentially noble presentation of the whole case for the old times, Mr. Howe has made of its representative a figure of almost tragic interest, with an appeal to readers who may never have heard of his classroom, with an appeal to exactly the sense that Sherwood Anderson's narrative so deeply touches—the sense for a high adventure in very difficult circumstances.

In a brief review one cannot even attempt to imitate

the delicate art, intricate, lucid, economical, by which Mr. Howe keeps the soft play of life on his subject from his childhood to his old age in a succession of pictures from all points of view, constantly changing yet cohering in effect like those moving screens which exhibit the unfolding of a plant from seed to flower. The essence of his art is motion and the scrupulous avoidance of a stated thesis and a fixed portrait. I am enamored of the skill with which the thing has been done, but when I try to suggest what has been done I fall at once into violations of the principles which govern the art that I admire. I snatch a single picture from the moving series; to correct its incompleteness I snatch another, and juxtapose the two in a glaring contrast; and truth with her infinite gradations escapes me.

As a small boy Barrett Wendell appears to have been a little prig, encouraged at the age of nine, with the other boys in his private school, to write out for their master "our different opinions about gentlemen, and how to distinguish them from other persons." Mr. Howe quietly connects this childish exercise with the question proposed in the famous "English Composition": "What does a man mean, for example, who asserts that another is or is not a gentleman?" The constant recurrence of that question to Wendell's mind might easily be seized upon by a thesis-writer as his complete and adequate "explanation." It might be said, for example, to explain his "Literary History of America," with its tremendous emphasis upon the pure and blameless Harvard gentlemen who produced "the Renaissance of New England," and its dismissive gesture toward the rest of the country as a territory socially yet unborn and therefore possessing, for literature, no significance, or almost none.

Even within the sacred pale of New England, and among Harvard's own graduates, Wendell draws social distinctions like a lady. He anticipates the absurd snippiness of Mrs. Gerould in finding Thoreau and Alcott underbred and distasteful by reason of a vulgar "self-assertiveness," alarming to people "of sagely conservative habit." He asserts that it requires a hundred years to form a genuine American. He traces his own ancestry to the seventeenth century, revels in his connection with the best families of Massachusetts, delights in adorning the walls of his study with pictures of ten generations of his line, and performs a pious pilgrimage to the grave of his Dutch ancestor. He publishes a tract against the usurpations of the workingman, and hotly resents the iniquity of his standing in a street car while a man with a dinner pail occupies two seats. The death of Queen Victoria occasions in him an "overwhelming sense of personal bereavement"; he regards her life as "surely the most noble in modern times." In the midst of a war "to make the world safe for democracy" he rises in Sanders Theater to deliver as his last message to the Phi Beta Kappa Society his repudiation of the ideal of democracy, his adherence to the ancient, "traditional," aristocratic republicanism. Meeting his colleague, Professor Merriman, he engages in this dialogue:

Barrett Wendell: In all the twenty-five years you have known me, Roger, have you ever heard me utter one liberal sentiment?

Professor Merriman: Not one, sir.

Barrett Wendell: Thank God!

That dialogue suggests pretty well, I imagine, the sort of impression that Barrett Wendell consciously strove to produce: a fastidious, defiantly snobbish and very hard-shelled traditional New England gentleman.

In quite innumerable ways Mr. Howe demonstrates that Wendell was a bigger and better man than that. I don't mean to be paradoxical when I find the most important tokens of Wendell's humanity not in his fortunate and effective and happy external career but in a series of his failures and in the record of impulses which bore little fruit.

The tragedy of his life, and of this he was conscious, was that he became a product of his environment and lacked the initiative, the force, and the courage significantly to alter it. In his early manhood, it is clear that he desired to be a man of his times. At college, perhaps still in a somewhat "cocky" and snobbish fashion, which prevented his attaining the social success achieved there by football captains, he was an iconoclast, an enemy of Philistinism, and, significantly, a founder of "The Harvard Lampoon." Religiously "emancipated," he felt himself as a junior so much out of sympathy with his family that he thought he should "split" if he had to spend his summer vacations with them.

What a young man in that state craves is self-expression and an independent career. His family headed him toward the law, and he humiliatingly failed at the bar examinations. He tried to be a novelist, and he failed. He tried to be a practical dramatist, and he failed. He accepted a Harvard instructorship, and remained in it, because he had been unable to break into the life of his times at any other point, not because he yearned to spend his lifetime teaching boys.

I suppose Harvard is as "free" a university as there is in the country, and only men who have worked there can know how unfree the freest university is, how oppressively it constrains all but the most potent spirits to conform to its type. Barrett Wendell, like William James, was, or became, a potent spirit, and both men were indulged rebels in Cambridge. It is the glory of Harvard that, though she laughs at her rebels and lets them understand that rebellion can never be taken seriously, she does indulge them. Wendell shows little of the self-complacency attributed to the don; he is never proud because he is a professor; he is proud only of being himself, though a professor.

From the outset to the end he was quite out of sympathy with the Germanized scholarship regnant during his time at Cambridge. "God knows," he would say, perhaps with veiled reference to Professor Kittredge, "God knows I am no scholar." At Harvard he always had a feeling that he was "academically out of it"; and till he lectured with plaudits at the Sorbonne perhaps he never had the gratifying sense of being taken quite seriously, by a competent audience, as a man of letters. In 1880 he declared to his friend Stimson:

It is maddening to have to do one's best work in an amateurish way, if not actually on the sly—at the risk of having fingers pointed at you if you are found out.

That was the penalty he paid for trying to be a man of letters in a university. In 1881, struggling over the academically unsanctified business of trying to write a novel, he composes as an epitaph for himself "He lacked the courage to do good or evil." Gradually he resigns himself to doing no evil. In 1893 he regrets his doubtful, reactionary temper: "Such moods as mine are not things that literature demands." A few weeks later he unbosoms himself to Mr. Robert Herrick:

Shut up here in New England, and getting less and less discontented with its daily repetition of things no one outside cares for, I find myself, as I read your letter again, wishing to goodness I had had the luck and the pluck to give and take in a world where something was a-doing.

Returning from lecturing in France, he develops skepticism about his life work, and an acute distaste for teaching: "Harvard stifles me, more than I expected."

It was at about this time, between 1904 and 1906, that I heard him speak on French life, and attended, as a "listener" his course of lectures on the disintegration of the English national temper in the seventeenth century. Mr. Howe describes him well as he appeared in those years:

Well proportioned of figure, of moderate height, shapely of head, tawny bearded, with quick blue eyes, alert and responsive in personal encounter, the man of the world rather than the professor in general appearance.

He entered the lecture room with a cane, in a cutaway coat and spats, with the air of an Anglicized Boston man of letters who had crossed the Charles to speak to the boys about life. As he proceeded to his desk we noticed that his hair was parted down the back of his head to his collar. He plucked his glasses from their hook, somewhere about his waistcoat, and

diddling them on the end of his forefinger, began to
speak in his highly mannered voice, with frequent
breaks into falsetto, something like this:

You can't, you know, always tell the truth. It
isn't polite or expedient. Three-fourths of the time
I don't feel at all like coming over here. And God
knows that three-fourths of the time you would probably rather be anywhere than here. But if we acted
on those feelings you would be called before the dean,
and I should be told that I could devote my energies
to something else.

The formal dress, decorous aspect and little affec-
tations of the man were in delicious contrast with the
opening speech, and, indeed, with the entire point of
view in the course. The man's mind was lucid, honest,
virile, burly and absolutely untrammeled; his speech
likewise. "Literature," he said, "was the meaning of
life"; and he was not afraid to face life's meaning or
to express it in round terms—so long as he dealt with
its meaning in the seventeenth century.

I can suggest the flavor of this series of lectures by a
few extracts from my own memoranda: "In 1642 the
drama was so dead that it stank in the nostrils of
London." "The Puritan thinking himself a sharer in
the will of God believes himself required to force his
will on others." Occasionally there was an excursus:
"Vox populi, vox Dei means that if you can get a
majority of trades unions on your side that's just what
God wants." Speaking of the central figure in his
course, he observed: "It is remarkable that Milton
could approach so close to modern culture and still
believe literally in the Scriptures. How can you take
your Maker and dress him up in pretty verses? I

recall, you know, hearing a discourse on Christ's feeling when he rode into Jerusalem on the ass. I have known a man in the Harvard pulpit who tried to enter into the mind of Christ rather, you know, than into that of the ass . . . Heaven knows we could have spent three years on Milton. . . . Now, Hobbes, whatever else the fellow was, you know, was a big, hot-blooded Elizabethan. When he gets onto God it's rather funny. You can't get the size of God's finger nails; it's no use trying. Abstract right was as purely a thing of the imagination as the finger nails of God. . . . Now, Baxter gives you, like all these Puritans, you know, an account of all his infernal maladies. They fancied, you know, that prayer and fasting could move their bowels. Baxter tried it. In the morning he was saved. There was another case where God interfered. . . . The Puritans were capable of great junks of attention to godly matters; it was as natural to them as eight hours of sleep are to me. . . . God knows what positive truth is. God knows that the effort to make idealism prevail in this world came to grief."

There speaks Barrett Wendell of the later time, being himself in the class-room. That is the Wendell who said: "The dominant figure in any time is sure to be of it." That is the Wendell who recognized Tolstoy as the greatest realist of the age; Wagner as the greatest artist of modern times; Whitman as a man who could "make you feel for a moment how even the ferryboats plying from New York to Brooklyn are fragments of God's eternity"; and "Huckleberry Finn" as "that amazing Odyssey of the Mississippi." That is the Wendell who found our New England literature pallid with our "national inexperience"; who was nauseated by the "fastidious virginity" of A. C. Benson's "Arthur Hamilton"; who found the self-analytic inaction of the nineteenth century "shocking"; who declared that a life of idealistic inaction, though noble, was "tragic"; who yearned for an "active struggle with the life we are born to, a full sense of all its temptations, of all its earthly significance as well as of its spiritual"; and who had to express his longing for adventure and reality by carrying on A. S. Hill's tradition of "clearness, force and elegance" and by play-acting in "Raleigh in Guiana." Do not doubt that he felt the huge irony of his pose as the preserver of the sacred traditions of the historical Puritans, he who expressed his aspiration for an immortal life in a letter to Judge Grant as follows: "If good on earth, I am now persuaded, I may live again as a golden carp in some everflowing fountain of sound French vintage, not too dry."

I never met Barrett Wendell to speak to him till 1918, when I sat next him at a Phi Beta Kappa dinner in Cambridge. He offered me his flask to tincture the ice water which had then come into vogue, and I, in exchange, offered him some compliments on the course to which I had listened in 1904. He flashed on me his quick blue eye and exclaimed, truly enough: "What, you were never any disciple of mine!" Since Mr. Howe's book has revealed to me the man's honest struggle for reality in an environment which almost stifled him, I am ready to revise my relationship to him and to declare myself a disciple of the Wendell who said: "God help me, I don't want to be a humbug!"

[257]

THIRD GALLERY

XX

Mandeville on the Seamy Side of Virtue

THE seamy side of virtue is its origin. Bernard Mandeville, author of "The Fable of the Bees," 1714, was interested in origins. He was a great anatomist of society who transferred to the study of human nature the physician's habit of tracing symptoms to the vital organs. He said: "One of the greatest reasons why so few people understand themselves is that most writers are always teaching men what they should be and hardly ever trouble their heads with telling them what they are." By a merciless probing to the source of social phenomena in the self-preservative and reproductive impulses of natural man, and in the cluster of elementary passions which branch immediately from those two impulses, he attempted to disclose the necessary final basis of morals and politics. In the process he deepened the channels of thought and imparted to his intelligent admirers a relish for coming to grips with reality.

But Mandeville was not merely a social anatomist. He was also a born man of letters with an exuberant personality, which he liked to express. He was no sour misanthrope but, as I take it, a rather hearty, burly fellow who enjoyed the excitement of ideas and the collision of minds. Yet with all his truculent aggressiveness he was a crafty, insidious ironist with a most irritating wit and a capacity for interesting in him a multitude of readers who were sure that they were "on the side of the angels" and that he was not— a multitude of readers who were far from clear what he was about, yet were entirely certain that he was very unconventional, very indecorous, very shocking, and very dangerous. And so Mandeville, who had no Boswell, has come down to us on the tongue of rumor, in an odor of unsanctity, and in a dust of controversy which delays recognition of the originality and penetrating vigor of his mind. The flavor of such a man, however, one gets the better if one comes to him through a little of the dust that he stirred up.

After he had offended the clergy and the masters of schools, as he did grievously—by telling more truth than either class thinks expedient or proper, and in sundry other ways—a number of terrible things were circulated about him. It was said, for example, that he had referred to that mirror of Queen Anne virtue, Joseph Addison, a man who had called his stepson to his deathbed "to see a man die like a Christian"—he had referred to Joseph Addison as "a parson in a tye-wig," which was certainly no proper way to speak of Addison. It was said, and it was openly avowed by Mandeville, that his system of ideas was diametrically opposed to that of the late Lord Shaftesbury; and every one knew that Shaftesbury had devoted his life to proving that man is inclined naturally towards the Good and the Beautiful. It was said that Mandeville was a foreigner, and this was true: by birth and education he was Dutch—out of Rotterdam, the Erasmus school and the University of Leyden.

Mandeville himself had offered to burn his book if anything could be found in it contrary to public morals, and it was said—it was published in the papers

—that a well-dressed gentleman, presumably the author, had been seen carrying "The Fable of the Bees" to the public bonfire. It was said that he had been hired by the distillers to write in behalf of spirituous liquors, and it was given out as his opinion that children of dram-drinking women were never afflicted with rickets. It was said that he lived in obscure lodgings and had little practise as a physician—both serious tokens of moral turpitude in the eyes of the poor in spirit.

Our young countryman, Ben Franklin, on his Wanderjahr in London in 1724, became intimate with a surgeon by the name of Lyons, who took him around to a pale ale house, The Horns, in Cheapside, and introduced him to Dr. Mandeville, who had a club there. Franklin in his autobiography reported that Mandeville was the "soul" of the club and "a most facetious, entertaining companion." But we know that Franklin himself, in those days, was no better than he should have been.

One sees how the legend of the vulgar tavern wit got afoot.

As a matter of fact, at the outset of his literary career, Mandeville himself was at small pains to be taken seriously. His "Fable," as he first launched it on the town in 1705, under the title of "The Grumbling Hive," was not, as it is now, a *magnum opus*, a life-work—comparable with Montaigne's "Essays," Burton's "Anatomy of Melancholy," Hobbes' "Leviathan," Locke on "Human Understanding" or Shaftesbury's "Charactersticks."

He threw out at first but the germ or nucleus about which his meditations were to agglomerate for the next generation. The germ is but a poem of some four hundred doggerel lines, such as splenetic, misanthropic Swift was writing, such as iconoclastic Samuel Butler in "Hudibras" had written to tickle the anti-Puritan fancy of the last age. The pacifists and preachers and little Englanders and the societies for the reformation of morals were actively engaged in their perennial, millennial business, and Mandeville tossed among them a satirical skit, playing inoffensively with the idea that when ambition and enterprise are replaced by frugality, meekness, temperance, and long-suffering, society will cease to "bloom" and expand as it does when its animating ideals are stirring and aggressive.

For nine years Mandeville studied men and meditated on the contrast between what we might call "Christian idealism" and the actual way of the world. He came to the conclusion that all mankind talks about one objective: the kingdom of heaven, and bends the major part of its efforts toward reaching another objective: the power and the glory of this earth. He inquired why people worked at such cross-purposes, and I don't think he quite adequately solved that problem.

But he inquired thoroughly into the reason why the great majority of mankind actually find their pleasure in the pursuit of power and glory. He traced our civilization as it is back to its roots in the savage animal nature—into lust and fear and pride and vanity. His contemporary, Swift, coming on those same roots, became morbid and nasty over them, and was finally driven mad by the discovery. But Mandeville had the phlegm of a physician, and the special sort of robust clean-mindedness of which physicians are capable. He could cut open a patient and grope among his viscera or converse with his excrements, and yet think none

[264]

the worse of him when, a month later, he shook hands with him and passed the time of day.

I conceive that Mandeville thought it would be well for the intelligent adult portion of mankind to acquire a less squeamish habit about facing, recognizing and naming facts of human nature and facts of the social organism. Accordingly he brought out a new edition of his poems in 1714, entitled this time "The Fable of the Bees: Or Private Vices, Publick Benefits," to which he added, ostensibly as a commentary, a substantial body of prose in the form of moral essays. After the lapse of nine years more, he published, in 1723, a second edition, supplemented by defensive dialogues, containing many new speculations, and an extremely provocative "Essay on Charity and Charity Schools," together with a "Search Into the Nature of Society."

If Mandeville desired to bugle forth all the forces of opposition he managed his "publicity" well. Apparently he was attacking everything in sight—especially everything sacred, such as polite society, the army, and charity schools. He displayed a subtitle—Private Vices, Publick Benefits—which attracted and fascinated the mob like the picture of a naked woman—or an advertisement of the Ten Commandments over a moving-picture palace. When the police ran up to see what was going on, he made disparaging remarks about London aldermen and the Lord Mayor —really stinging and insufferable remarks, coming from a foreigner, to the disadvantage of the Lord Mayor as compared with Dutch burgomasters. He explained that his show was not intended for the yokelry but only for the choice few who could think, or at least read and write, that is, what we should call the Intellectuals. *"Apagete vulgus!"* he exclaimed, which was an extremely disrespectful and perhaps almost blasphemous way of saying: "Please rope off the crowd." He might well have added: *"Este procul feminae,"* which, being interpreted, means: "Why don't the ladies go into the drawing-room?" For I suppose no one has ever heard of a woman who was acquainted with Mandeville's book.

Mandeville is for men—he does not flatter. There is, to be sure, something of illicit and "unprofessional" sensationalism in that sub-title; and there is much of sensationalism and economic fallacy in the *mode* of his argument for luxury and extravagance as the pathway to national greatness. But Mandeville's fallacies and his exaggerations have been sufficiently emphasized. Once past his outworks, you find yourself in the hands of a serious and masterly analyst of motive, bent on getting at the savage root of the matter.

Take, for illustration, his treatment of pride. As Christianity speaks of it, pride is to be abased, and as medieval theology regards it, pride is one of the seven deadly sins. Perhaps it is, says Mandeville, in those who are preparing themselves for life in another world, but, as this world goes, pride is one of the indispensable pillars of civilized society. It is, as the ancients regarded it, one of the virtues of the magnanimous man. So far, Mandeville may seem to flatter pride and the pagan at the expense of the Christian virtues, in an effort to bring about, like Nietzsche, a "transvaluation of values." But if you subject yourself to the discipline of Mandeville you will ultimately find yourself left without a rag of pride clinging to you. He cuts beneath all the virtues, Christian and pagan alike, until he has dissected out of civil and polite society that nude, mean, nasty and brutish being in whose passion-

ate selfishness the "cynical" moralists from Hobbes to
Samuel Butler and Mr. Veblen have found the effective
source of polite and civil society.

The fact of the matter is that Mandeville had by
psychological analysis firmly established in his own
mind the conception of man and society as products
of a complex evolution. He hadn't a doubt that man
was an animal of base ancestry and savage relatives.
That this conception has haunted mankind from the
earliest times is often suggested to us by the poets,
who, when they leave off flattering the ladies and depict
human nature as it is, show us lions on the throne,
foxes at court and wolves, bulls, bears, monkeys and
rabbits in the streets. With Mandeville, however, this
conception is not poetically but scientifically and philo-
sophically entertained. He works out his corollaries.
He applies his ideas to the development of languages.
He pries into the physiology of the emotions. He dis-
cards all absolute values, and works out a doctrine
of pure relativity. Before Malthus and Darwin he
meditates on the enormous potential reproductivity of
nature, as exemplified in the shad roe; he concludes
that the shad, if unchecked, would clog up the seven
seas; he perceives that powers which thwart reproduction—pestilence and war—are as necessary to the
"balance of nature" as reproduction: he states clearly
the necessity of the struggle for existence. Without
in the least intending to be a "forward-looking" man
he prepares the way for the philosophical radicals of
the nineteenth and twentieth centuries, whose most important distinction is in the part which they assign
to conscious purpose in altering the terms of the
struggle for existence.

I doubt whether Mandeville suffered much from the

attacks which the ministers made upon him, or even from the heavy guns of Bishop Berkeley and William Law. They started from assumptions about human nature and human origins which he had dismissed as completely as most biologists to-day dismiss the assumptions of Mr. Bryan. He was a very modern type of man: philosophical bishops amused him. But Mr. Kaye, in his admirably learned edition of the "Fable."* has made a large collection of tributes from later writers, which show the wide and deep furrow that Mandeville drew in the thought of two centuries. Most of them are by solid men.

Samuel Johnson said: "I read Mandeville forty, or, I believe, fifty years ago . . . he opened my views into real life very much." Crabb Robinson called the "Fable" "the wickedest, cleverest book in the English language." Lord Macaulay said: "If Shakespeare had written a book on the motives of human actions it is . . . extremely improbable that it would have contained half so much able reasoning on the subject as is to be found in 'The Fable of the Bees.' " William Hazlitt said: "I like Mandeville better [than La Rochefoucauld]. He goes more into his subject." Robert Browning, in "Parleyings" saluted Mandeville as the sage in whom truth triumphs through the harmonious combination of good with evil.

Now, if you look into the ordinary textbook by which English literature is introduced to students in the United States, the probability is that you will not find Bernard Mandeville so much as mentioned, though the author of "Marco Polo's Travels" usually finds a place. In a history of eighteenth century literature,

* *The Fable of the Bees,* New York, 1924, two vols.

[268]

such as that of Edmund Gosse, he is dismissed as a vulgar, if sometimes amusing, fellow, a devil's disciple. Writers like Professor Saintsbury and Dean Inge find him vulgar and foul and unpolished, though Professor Saintsbury, on reconsideration, admits that he is a master of the vernacular. In the great Cambridge History of English Literature he gets a paragraph from Professor Sorley as a reviver of the Hobbesian selfishness theory against the facile optimism of Shaftesbury. The two English writers who have most sought to do him justice are Mr. J. M. Robertson and Mr. Leslie Stephen. The latter, as author of the article in the "Dictionary of National Biography," extensive references in his "English Thought in the Eighteenth Century" and extensive treatment in his essays, is perhaps chiefly responsible for his present English reputation. Leslie Stephen saw clearly that Mandeville was a remarkable man with important intellectual connections, but he was irritated by Mandeville's "detestable grin," and he felt bound to apologize for Mandeville's giving up to the coffee-houses "a penetration meant for loftier purposes."

I have gradually been preparing the way for two announcements. The first is: Mandeville is worth knowing—a man to lay siege to and conquer. The second is: If you wish to know Mandeville you may now, without hesitation, be recommended to disregard everything else, and begin with Mr. Kaye's two magnificent volumes. I speak with emphasis and feeling. In twenty years' observation of the products of higher English study in America I have met with no more exhilarating and satisfying work than this, which originated in the Yale school for eighteenth century letters.

Mr. Kaye gives us an admirable scholarly text of the

[269]

"Fable," preceded by a life of Mandeville, a history of the text, an analysis of Mandeville's thought and studies of his background, and of his influence. The brilliant preliminary discussion is supplemented by extraordinarily rich and illuminating notes and various appendices by the aid of which one sees the naturalistic thought of Europe converging upon Mandeville from the time of the Renaissance, and, from him, coursing on to our own time. The point of view is easily accessible, but the vistas are immense, and Mandeville is steadily at the center of all of them, flooded with light. It is a triumph of technique and of the intelligent, purposeful pursuit of ideas.

XXI

Boswell on His Own Hook

"I wonder how you and I admitted this to the publick eye, for Windham &c. were struck with its indelicacy, and it might hurt the book much. It is, however, mighty good stuff."—Boswell to Malone, 10 Feb., 1791.

WHEN Boswell's mind was not preoccupied and splendidly buzzing with drink, women, friends, celebrities, business, literature and glory, it was occupied with religion. He was no Calvinist, the good Boswell; and he did God the justice to believe him no Calvinist either. From Pope and the tolerant deists of his day he acquired a leaning toward universalism. Of one thing at least he was sure: That the use of religion is to comfort men with whom everything in this world has not gone strictly according to hope and expectation.

How he himself would have governed the universe, with what benignity of temper he would have dealt with sheep and goats alike, one may deliciously infer from his comment on the death of his "poor uncle, Dr. Boswell," who seems to have been, like his poor nephew, what is called nowadays a "yea-sayer to life." Writing to his lifelong confidant, the Rev. William Temple, James Boswell says of his deceased relative, with sympathetic indulgence and a sidelong glance at the complex case he himself was preparing for the last assizes: "He was a very good scholar, knew a great many things, had an elegant taste and was very affectionate. But he had no conduct. His money was all gone; and, do you know, he was not confined to one woman? He had a strange kind of religion. *But, I flatter myself, he will be ere long, if he is not already, in Heaven.*" [My italics.]

Poor Boswell! He hoped all his life for a blessed resurrection, and now he has got one—a resurrection of that quick, curious, eager, affectionate spirit, so scintillant and vivacious, so subject to somber hypochondriac vapors. He has got, also, a resurrection "of the body," according to the aspiration of his creed, with his tied wig, his pointed nose, the fat collops of his double chin, his stomach ruined by alcohol and refusing food, long fevers and shameful diseases clinging to him from nights spent, after intoxication from drinking the health of his intended wife, with girls of doubtful virtue. But all of these ignominies of the unruly flesh, quite unbecoming the friend of Paoli and the disciple of the moral Johnson, as he would be the first to acknowledge, were veiled from a censorious world during his lifetime by "a suit of imperial blue lined with rose-colored silk and ornamented with rich gold-wrought buttons."

Here he is again, the naughty, irrepressible fellow with no conduct, whom the sternest moralist of his day loved like a son; who brought to another stern moralist, Carlyle, more pleasure than any other of the fifteen million souls whose decorum he outraged; and who was declared by Lord Macaulay to be as indubitably the first of biographers as Homer is the first of poets.

Professor Tinker's book,* which every library and every Johnsonian and Boswellian will wish to possess, gives us the most accurate, comprehensive, intimate and scandalous account now available of one of the most captivating figures in the entire range of English literature. There are a hundred hitherto unpublished letters, including a series addressed to the steward of Boswell's estate at Auchinleck. More important than these considerations is the restoration of the original text of the letters to Temple, which are the *pièce de résistance.*

Since 1857, when the series was first published, with the disreputable editing and the grave expurgations characteristic of that decorous Victorian time, apparently no one had studied what Boswell actually wrote till Professor Tinker explored the manuscript treasures in the possession of Mr. J. P. Morgan. After due hesitation, he decided to reproduce with practically immaculate integrity the correspondence in which Boswell shows himself to Temple naked and only intermittently ashamed.

His editorial work may serve as a model to all editors of letters; and all scholars, of course, know that Professor Tinker is much more than a master of editorial technique. In the flourishing Yale school for the study of eighteenth century literature, Professor Tinker has for some years appeared to be, as Boswell said of Malone, "Johnsonianissimus," with his studies of "Johnson and Fanny Burney," "The Salon and English Letters," "Young Boswell" and "Nature's Simple Plan." But his long frequentation of the wits and the blue stockings who bowed to the Great Bear appears at present as but preliminary to the "insidious

* *Letters of James Boswell,* New York, 1924, two vols.

circumvallation" of James Boswell, who now emphatically challenges reconsideration, not as a satellite, but as the fiery center of his own turbulent system.

The impression that Boswell derives all his interest from his relation to Johnson is an error which this edition of his letters will help to explode. This erroneous impression is due, first, to the great biography and then to two famous essays on the biography by Macaulay and by Carlyle. Macaulay, as every one remembers, spitted Boswell on a glittering antithesis: "Many of the greatest men that ever lived have written biography. Boswell was one of the smallest men that ever lived, and he has beaten them all." Macaulay went on to prove that Boswell's achievement was due precisely to the fact that he was an officious, inquisitive, insensible, toad-eating fool, and that he possessed "absolutely none" of "the talents which ordinarily raise men to eminence as writers." Carlyle, himself a biographer of a new style, disrelished Macaulay's recipe for supremacy in the biographical art. He declared this estimate of Boswell egregiously wrong, assured the world that every great work is the fruit of virtues and not of vices, and, in accordance with his own favorite doctrine, he explained Boswell as a man eminently endowed with the supreme virtue of hero-worship. Thus Macaulay and Carlyle both place Boswell in the list of Johnson's dependents.

Carlyle's theory is not, like Macaulay's, positively silly, but it is quite inadequate. It doesn't really touch Boswell's center. Hero-worship certainly was not the mainspring in Boswell. No one can scrutinize intimately his inner workings and fail to recognize that he burns with a flaming desire to be a great man in his own right. He also would rather like, if he could manage it without impediment to larger ambitions, to be a good man in his own right. *Se perfectionner*— to shape and polish his own character: that is an object which already interests him in his teens. With that in mind, he applies for guidance to Hume, to Johnson, to Paoli, to Rousseau, to Voltaire, and he feebly returns from time to time to the consideration of self-perfection amid the growing dissipations of his later years.

But the master passion in Boswell from the outset is for full self-realization and self-expression. He is the supreme biographer because he is a great artist and has a most extraordinary faculty for taking in and giving forth again all the elements in a situation which constitute its life. With much loud ado, Macaulay and Carlyle bring their critical sledge-hammers down on both sides of the nail. Professor Tinker strikes it accurately on the head with this simple declaration in his "Young Boswell": "The distinctive feature in Boswell is the capacity for realizing and using the richness of life to which he was admitted."

Boswell, beyond any man in his time, realized the richness to which he was admitted in Johnson; but in this case he had brisk competition. Fanny Burney, for example, describes an Irish gentleman, a Mr. Musgrave, a member of the Irish Parliament, as glancing up at Johnson's portrait and exclaiming: "What a fine old lion he is! Oh! I love him—I honor him— I reverence him! I would black his shoes for him. I wish I could give him my night's sleep." That is hero-worship, and Fanny, who thinks it is a little foolish, remarks that Musgrave "is a caricature of Mr. Boswell, who is a caricature, I must add, of all other of Dr. Johnson's admirers."

Boswell excelled all the other admirers not because he was a greater hero-worshiper but because he had a far more comprehensive appreciation of the points of interest in the hero. As a biographer Johnson himself was a dry-as-dust professor compared with Boswell. Johnson hadn't, for instance, the dimmest notion why it was worth while to preserve a record of his hoarding of orange peel. Boswell had. From the time he published his "Account of Corsica" to the close of his literary career he was master of a recipe for writing such a book as no one could help reading.

He realized the richness of life that there was in a Corsican patriot before London had heard of him. He realized the richness of life in John Wilkes when England had exiled him. If Johnson had not happened to be the best extant subject for a biographer and the recognized center of literary society, Boswell would not have focused his *magnum opus* upon him, and he would not have wasted his time touring Scotland and the Hebrides with him. He valued his time and he was absolutely sure of the quality of his talent while all the world was laughing at him. In order to prove his possession of a glorious life-enhancing faculty, independent of his subject, it was no more necessary for him to paint Johnson than for Velasquez to paint Philip IV. If Johnson had never lived, Boswell, I think, would still have produced masterpieces.

In the "Letters," the Johnson Biography drops into its place as only a considerable incident in a many-sided, adventurous and ambitious career, full and running over with experience, most of which was zestfully welcomed.

There is the stuff of an excellent novel in Boswell's

relation to Scotland, the Auchinleck estate, and his father, and that "implacable" woman, his father's second wife. As Carlyle recognized well enough, the young James was no insolent toad-eating upstart from nowhere. He has the blood of Bruce in his veins, and social position and culture behind him. His father, an eminent member of the Scottish bar and Lord of Auchinleck, can ride ten miles from his front door on his own land. He wants an heir to his profession and his property and to his position in the country, and he gives his boy an Edinburgh education and tries to make a sound religious Tory and a good Scotsman of him. Sentimentally, the project appeals to James; he always remained sentimentally enthusiastic for his religion, his king, and his family, and he enjoyed drinking port wine and coffee on the 30th of January in honor of the blessed martyr Charles I.

But young James has a pair of the most candid realistic eyes that were ever set in a man's head. At the age of seventeen, precocious, well-read, wide-eyed, he turns his eyes toward London, recognizing that Scotland is going to be more and more irredeemably provincial. With his instinct for the main current, he cannot bear the thought of accepting a Scotch laird's universe, and remaining in the backwater. Edinburgh he knows only too well. He is irked by the study and practise of law as he sees it in the provinces. He loathes the gloom and the dull placidity of country life. His temperamental melancholy craves the stimulation of gay scenes and people. To escape from his manifest destiny and to torment his father, he talks about entering the priesthood and the army. These are but youthful writhings against the study of law. As a disciple of the rational Hume, he has no place in the priesthood. Physically timorous, he has no use for the army, except as the convivialities of the officers' mess entice.

What the young Boswell is really yearning for is the new poetry, the new plays, the new histories, the new skeptical philosophy, hot from the capital; and, as soon as possible, he must be down there in London among the producers of the new age, which his prescient nostrils have scented afar off. His father, almost heartbroken, sees this restlessness, but has outlived his sympathy with it. He talks to James as if he were a silly, stubborn boy—even after James is a man grown and married, he always is made to feel like a "timid boy" in the presence of his father, except when deep drafts of strong beer have stupefied his sensibilities to the paternal snibbing. He reveres his father and would, if given a chance, love him. But his father sheds a black frost on his affection, and seeks to destroy the form which the spirit of his son's young life spontaneously takes. As an incidental consequence, perhaps, of this repressive discipline, when James at the age of twenty-two makes his arrangements to go abroad, ostensibly to study law in Utrecht, he is obliged to set aside £10 of his traveling allowance for the upkeep of the illegitimate child which he leaves behind him.

By heredity and by poetical sentiment and by association with Johnson, Boswell is a Tory, but by a deeper impulse in him he takes to radicalism and revolution like a duck to water. He has in Holland an interesting affair with a young lady of excellent birth, whose skepticism in religious and moral matters shocks him, superficially; but to whom does he run for consultation on the case but to the author of "The Nou-

velle Héloise"! He carries messages from Rousseau
to Paoli, the Corsican patriot. He makes a sensation
at the age of twenty-seven by his "Account of Corsica,"
containing the spirited journal of his association with
Paoli, which first interpreted him to the English world.
He would like to effect a meeting between Rousseau
and Voltaire. Failing at that, he assists at the junc-
tion of Rousseau and Hume; and he pilots Rousseau's
mistress across the Channel. He has an affair with
a lady in Sienna, which pleases him for years. He
courts in Italy the insolent democrat John Wilkes;
and later, as a masterpiece of mediation, he maneuvers
Dr. Johnson himself into a meeting with Wilkes at a
dinner party with the bookseller Dilly. He sides with
the Americans against Dr. Johnson. He pretends to
side with Burke against the French; but Burke's con-
tinually raging against the French bores him to extinction, and he is grateful and happy when the great
man refrains from the subject for an entire evening.

The fact is that Boswell, in the prime of life, hasn't
a political conviction in his body for which he would
shed his blood, nor a moral principle which he isn't
ready to sacrifice at a moment's notice for an enlargement of his experience—unless, indeed, we recognize
as a conviction his impresario's passion for bringing
great artists together; and as a principle, his desire
"to be present always at the focus where the greatest
number of vital forces unite in their purest energy."

Every vital impulse in him is an expansive impulse;
and it is his misfortune, when he is in "good society,"
to live in an "epoch of concentration." His presence
in the sturdy classical circle of Burke, Johnson and
Reynolds is, in a sense, an accident. He paints the
temple of Georgian classicism because it is quite the

finest thing in England. He goes through the political
and religious and social motions of conforming with
the age, and works quite a bit of ardor into his con-
formity. He calls himself a Tory, a Christian and a
gentleman, and he keeps up appearances as well as
he can when he isn't drunk. But his gentility, his
Christianity and his Toryism are garments which he
has got at the tailor's, like his suit of imperial blue
with the rose-colored lining. At heart, one is tempted
to say, the man is a rationalist, a free-thinking deist,
a "child of nature," and far better qualified for discipleship to Rousseau than to Johnson.

If one were bent on proving Boswell a hollow sham
and a contemptible hypocrite one could find abundant
evidence in his outpourings to Temple.

After innumerable previous affairs of the heart
and of the flesh he does marry a cousin and beget three
daughters and two sons, to perpetuate his ancient race.
He thinks an ancient race is a good thing and ought
to be preserved—if it can be done without interfering
with more interesting occupations. But he doesn't
even consider settling down after his marriage to be a
country gentleman. He leaves his "valuable" wife—
his constantly recurring epithet for her—to manage
his estate and the children in the country. He is glad
to pay her an occasional visit, but he is also glad that
she doesn't care to live in town. For his part, he
candidly recognizes that he is "*too many,* as the phrase
is, for one woman, and a certain transient connection
I am persuaded does not interfere with that attachment which a man has for a *wife* and which I have as
much as any man that ever lived, though *some* of my
qualifications are not valued by her, as they have been
by other women—aye, and well educated women, too."

Besides, there is a handsome chambermaid who cheers
him on the way to and from his wife. And on one
of his trips to Auchinleck he has the gout, or some
trouble with his toe; and he easily finds in the post-
chaise an "agreeable young widow" who is happy to
hold his foot in her lap.

These little amours are the byplay of idle moments.
They don't weigh on his mind or fill it. He aspires
for distinction at the English bar. He is trying to
attract the attention of Lord Chatham. He would
like to be English commissioner in Corsica. He is
giving dinner parties and dining out daily with the
most exciting groups of the most stimulating people,
and sitting from 8:30 to 3 in the morning at the Turk's
Head Tavern, gathering material for "the most entertaining book you ever read"—and it is only now
and then in a spare moment that his mind wanders
to his debts and to his "valuable spouse" who, far away
in Auchinleck, is dying of consumption, as he rather
fears from the physician's report of her "severe cough,
sweatings and swelled legs."

Up to the time of his wife's death, Boswell felt,
like another great man, that "he had come to the
ring, and now he must hop." He was hopping in the
London ring when his "valuable wife," who had repeatedly warned him that she was about to do it, died,
uncheered by his presence. He had tarried, with apparent callousness, till it was just too late, and then
had posted to Auchinleck to find her beyond the reach
of his belated consolation. Feebly, at first, he recognized what had happened. Her countenance was so
little disfigured that he almost felt it must all be a
deception. "But alas, to see my excellent wife, and
the mother of my children, and that most sensible lively

woman, lying cold and pale and insensible was very shocking to me." Contrary to the custom of Scottish gentlemen, he resolved to attend the funeral, and got through it very decently. Then he privately read the funeral service over the coffin in the presence of his sons, and was temporarily relieved by that.

But in the next days and weeks gradually there breaks over him such an overwhelming sense of what he has lost that he is "avid of death," and wonders why people are so eager to bring offspring into the world to meet with so much misery and so little real happiness. In his depressed fantastic moods his wife, he now remembers, had been wont to be his comforter and to suggest "rational thoughts" to him. The complex and annoying business of the estate she had in great part taken off his mind. The five sons and daughters—he is terribly attached to them, now that he thinks of them; and he has got to think of them now very hard. Their schooling, for example, must receive attention at once, and what problems for his poor head! The girls are too precocious and too independent to be sent to any ordinary governess; he himself has no "authority" over them and can influence them only by "affection." One of the boys he will send to Eton; the other he takes into his own bachelor apartment in London and provides a private tutor for him; but this arrangement worries him because the poor little fellow has no one to associate with but the old housekeeper and the footman. He rests badly at night, thinking of his sickly mind, his bereavement, the disappointment of his "hopes of success in life," the embarrassment of his affairs, "the disadvantage to my children in having so wretched a father," the uncertainty of being happy after death, the certainty of death.

One can't read the later pages of this correspondence without recognizing that Boswell responds to the elementary moral appeals of life in a way to justify his declaration that, in spite of the romantic aspects of his career, he is "a very sensible, good sort of man." Yet to dull the edge of his misery and his anxiety, he drinks in these last years harder than ever—scarcely gets through a day without sinking into a drunken sleep. In these circumstances, in this half desperate mood between the death of his wife, in 1789, and 1791, in "a dissipated stupor and afraid to think," this Divine Madman, as he called himself, wrote out, polished and published the "Life of Johnson." It was all that held him up. It was enough.

XXII

Laurence Sterne: A Graceless Man of God

ONCE upon a time an old gray wolf had a den in the heart of England, from which he emerged and devastated the countryside, terrorizing travelers, plundering sheepfolds and devouring young children. Parties of men with pitchforks and guns were often organized to hunt the brute down, but year after year, by superior strength and fleetness, he always escaped unscathed, leaving deep scars of these encounters upon his pursuers.

Finally an eccentric country parson whose wits had been turned by drink and disease and by reading curious old books got it fixed in his crack-brained noddle that as there are more ways than one of killing a cat, the same must be true of wolves. He made himself a suit of motley, with cap and bells, and, taking a bladder with rattling beans in one hand and a tear-bottle in the other, went forth to hunt the wolf.

When the fierce creature sprang at him the parson stood fast and rattled the bladder till he saw the whites of the wolf's bloodshot eyes. Then he tossed the contents of the tear-bottle into them. Dismayed by this unaccustomed mode of attack the beast turned tail and fled. The parson pursued, through wood and fen, through hedge and ditch, through bush and briar, still shaking the bladder, till the panic-stricken animal leaped over the cliff at Dover and was drowned.

The poor parson, bedraggled, blood-stained, be-grimed, exhausted but triumphant, returned to the village, carrying the shreds of the bladder and the emptied tear-bottle in his hand. "Why, parson, are you mad?" cried the innkeeper as he passed the tavern door. "Quite!" gasped the parson and staggered in at his garden gate. "Lord-a-mercy," exclaimed the maid who was sweeping off the step, "but you've got yourself filthy, master." "Haven't I!" said the parson, and reeled into the parlor, where his wife sat knitting. "Why, John," screamed his wife, "haven't you torn your breeches?" "Badly!" said the parson, and, stumbling up the stairs, threw himself on his bed. His weak heart having been overstrained by excitement, in a little while he died.

Laurence Sterne was that "poor parson" and the "old gray wolf" whom he hunted with jests and tears was the brutal insensitiveness of the healthy, red-blooded Englishman. It would, of course, be absurd to represent him as conscious of any passion for any sort of reform. If he accomplished any "good" in the world, if he refined the manners of his time, if he introduced into polite society a new form of feeling, it was by indulging and expressing the pleasures in which his own nature found most gratification—like Montaigne, or, for a modern example, like Mr. George Moore.

We mention by way of background that he published several volumes of sermons, goodish in morality, weak in divinity, and embellished with plagiarisms from his illustrious predecessors. The upbearing wings of his reputation are two world-renowned books, "Tristram Shandy" and "A Sentimental Journey," filled with curious learning and sly wit, pervaded by an original humor, concocted of a half maudlin mirth, a half maudlin pathos and acute sensibility to both. He was author also of a journal and of many letters addressed to various ladies not his wife, steeped in the perfume of sentiment and enlivened by delicate intimations that if God should open the gate (and take Mrs. Sterne to himself), he, Parson Yorick, had already in mind the boudoir which he would fit up in his parsonage for her successor.

I don't know just how to go to work to quarrel with people who hold that this sort of thing is infinitely more detestable than the "healthy animality" of Tom Jones. Think it out for yourself, set down your reasons, and balance them.

Judged as a "man of God" or as a "Christian citizen," Laurence Sterne was a ridiculous fellow. It was part of his own absurdity that his great-grandfather had been an Archbishop of York. His father, a poor ensign in the army, was run through in a duel over a goose. His mother—a "fruitful vine" and little else—produced seven children, four of whom died in infancy, and the three others, including Laurence, were, as he remarked of the brood, of delicate frame, "not made to last long." By the kindness of a cousin he was sent to Jesus College, Cambridge, and there he formed a lifelong cronyship with John Hall-Stevenson, apparently originating in their common fondness for idling under a walnut tree, reading Rabelais and swapping bawdy stories. In his senior year he had a hemorrhage of the lungs and got well into debt. And so, by a natural rather than logical process of reasoning, he accepted the advice of his uncle, a canon of York, and entered the Church, which in the mid-eighteenth century, was notoriously a refuge for younger sons, a hospital for lame ducks, a club for bibulous old scholars and antiquarians.

Sterne married early, and, in a country parsonage about eight miles from York, slumped down into the indolent bosom of the Church, precisely as scores of other impecunious, ungodly, place-hunting young men were doing—the feebler ones starving, the stronger reaching out fat, greedy hands crammed full of benefices, to see if they could not, by skilfully crooking a little finger, rake in one more. Sterne vegetated, almost unheard of, in his parish till he was forty-six years old.

What was he doing all that time? Well, he preached twice on Sundays when he had no curate, and when he had a sermon ready, and when he felt like it, though it is related that, crossing the fields one afternoon to deliver his second discourse, he started up a covey of partridges, and, returning to the parsonage for his gun, left his congregation gaping for the sacred word in vain. And then, to eke out his slender clerical living, he dabbled in dairy farming and agriculture, till he found that turnips at £200 the load were too dear. In early years he wrote some political paragraphs for the uncle who had beneficed him, but he thought that dirty work, and he was more congenially occupied with hunting and with fiddling on the bass viol and with painting, mainly copying portraits. Besides, he frequented York society, and was a member of the carousing, free-thinking Demoniacks Club, a society of squires and parsons who drank and jested at Crazy Castle, the tumble-down seat of his crony, John Hall-Stevenson, where there was, furthermore, a library very rich in *Curiosa*, tempting to a parson whom the Lord had not anointed.

We know the reading of this quaint man of God. He had some excellent works of divinity in weekly use—Jeremy Taylor, Joseph Hall, Tillotson, Bishop Berkeley—he *had* to have them in his business. He had also a tooth for all sorts of treatises on military and medical science, and he had manifest interest in the newly developing branch of obstetrics. But, in the long solitudes and silences of that pastoral study the authors most chewed and inwardly digested were meaty, racy fellows—Lucian, Rabelais, Erasmus, Montaigne, Bacon, Cervantes, Robert Burton, Browne, Locke, Beroalde de Verville, Samuel Butler, Swift, Arbuthnot, Tom Brown and Voltaire.

The incongruity of his inner consciousness with his calling grew upon him till, as Gray suggested, he often must have ascended the pulpit, his fingers fairly itching with desire to throw his periwig in the face of his congregation. As an obvious result of his reading and his week-day way of life he was driven to a point of view at which he and his contemporaries, especially those in cassocks, appeared to him unutterably funny in their spiritual decadence, just as the Holy Catholic Church had appeared to Chaucer in the Middle Ages, just as all the churches appeared to Swift in the age of Anne. His humor was born in the stench of a moribund "Christianity."

Finally, in 1759, at the age of forty-six, on the occasion of a clerical wrangling under the shadow of the cathedral, his pent-up amusement burst forth in "A Political Romance," an allegorical skit in the manner of Swift's "Tale of a Tub," exhibiting himself and his clerical friends and enemies contending over an old "watch-coat," which "Trim" wants to take home "in order to have it converted into a warm under-petticoat for his wife and a jerkin for himself." A small edition of this squib was printed at York, 1759, but, on the advice of Sterne's spiritual superiors, burnt— all but a few copies. It did not make for edification, that is, it did not screen, as the work of a good church- man should, the petty greed and folly which mask under the solemn habiliments of the Church.

Seventeen fifty-nine was a momentous year for Lau- rence Sterne. His mother died, but that didn't trouble him. His uncle, the canon, died—but that didn't trouble him—leaving him no legacy, which troubled him so much that he refused to wear the mourning he had prepared in celebration of the event. His wife went mad, but that troubled him little; he humored her in it, for he was engaged in an impassioned flirta- tion—thought to be the cause of his wife's madness— with a professional singer, to whom he was sending wine, honey, sweetmeats and vows of distracted love "to eternity." At the same time he was writing the first instalment of "Tristram Shandy." His hero's name means "the sad crack-brained fellow," and he meant the book to give a true portrait, or rather im- pression, of himself and his peculiar humor.

It does. The characters, the opinions, the novel style—with its discovery of the intimacy-making uses of punctuation and the pause in the sentence—are Shandian, and so are this most outrageous plot and this most absurd of all conceivable artistic "points of view."

Here is an author undertaking to tell what took place below stairs between the time when his mother's pains came upon her and the time of his own birth. With expectation of the poor woman's deliverance to supply "suspense," the discussions of Walter Shandy,

the father, Uncle Toby, Corporal Trim, Doctor Slop
and Susannah run on for three volumes before the
child is born, and he doesn't get into his breeches till
the sixth volume. The "life and opinions" are thus,
as it were, framed in a mystery of obstetrics.

And Sterne seems to say to us that all life is like
that: a child just barely learning to walk and smiling
midway with exultation as he toddles out of the hands
of the midwife and totters into the hands of the
sexton.

If life is like that, Sterne concluded in the teeth
of all the theologians from whom he had plagiarized,
success in life consists not in austere and strenuous
activity and still less in the shows of pomp and cere-
mony, but in expanding to the utmost our consciousness of the smiling interval, in multiplying to the utmost the titillations of moments when birth or death
or the beating of a fair grisette's pulse under our
fingers or a pair of new black silk breeches or a fricas-
seed chicken or burgundy or a jeweled snuffbox or
a pretty act of kindness or a letter from our mistress
has given us a childish joy. If life is like that, says
Sterne, let us follow our happy and our pathetic impulses, "as the fly stings"—on the spur of the moment
—a dreadful notion, of course, unless our first impulses are indeed better than our discreet and cautious
second thoughts.

How is it, madam, in your case, and in yours, sir?

Sterne approved the first spontaneous flow of his
feelings, and so, to supply his own long-felt want,
he invented the word "sentimental" and put it into
circulation. He elaborated, if he did not invent, sentimental relations, and he made an ideal of the life
of "sensibility." In "Tristram Shandy," in "A Senti-

mental Journey," in his letters to his various fair
ones, in the "Journal to Eliza," he devised for it scores
of famous illustrations.

Uncle Toby is sentimental when he carefully puts
a fly that has troubled him out at the window, unwilling to hurt a "hair" of its head, being convinced
there is room enough in the world for both. The Recording Angel who drops a tear on Uncle Toby's oath
in the Book of Life and blots it out is a sentimental
angel. Susannah is sentimental when she bursts into
a flood of tears at Corporal Trim's dropping his hat
to exhibit the transitoriness of life. "God tempers the
wind to the shorn lamb" is a sentimental proverb,
indicating what Sterne himself would have done, had
he been God, and had tempering the wind occasioned
him no great inconvenience. A starling in a cage, a
dead ass by the roadside, may be the occasion of this
new sentimentality. The occasion is nothing; the
quantity and quality of feeling evoked are everything.
Gefühl ist alles. We luxuriate now in emotion for
emotion's sake. We count our tears as they fall, with
a consciousness of our resources in feeling which ren-
ders the pain itself delicious and elevates it to the
level of art.

I think there cannot be a particle of doubt that
Sterne was perfectly honest when he wrote, "Praised
be God for my sensibility." Whether he was equally
honest when he declared that, after all his *badinage*
on the verge of "indelicacy," his heart was as innocent
as when in his boyish days he got astride of a stick and
galloped away—that is a slightly different question.

There is no space here to recall the way Shandian
sentimentalism took fashionable London by storm nor
the opposition to it of a few stalwarts like Dr. John-

son, nor to describe the disgust of a few "immaculate" imaginations like Dr. Goldsmith's and Richardson's, nor the efforts of a few savage critics and shocked clericals to "Nicodemus" Sterne into nothing. The controversy between those who feel intensely and those who hardly feel at all still rages, and is probably destined to rage as long as two sorts of men recur in society.

But to the fashionable mid-eighteenth century in general, sentimentalism came like rain from heaven after a long dry summer. It was such a joy to weep again, and this country parson Sterne had invented a way of weeping copiously over little things; so that, all the time, one could be half smiling through one's tears; and it hardly hurt at all. No wonder he tickled the bluestockings and the great worldly ecclesiastics and the ministers of state; and became the vogue in Paris and the friend of Diderot; and penetrated into Germany and won the plaudits of Goethe and Lessing and later the enthusiastic homage of that kindred spirit, Heinrich Heine.

Sterne was a sensitive, intuitive person. He felt the winds of revolutionary change in European feeling before they had begun to blow. His type of consciousness ran ahead of his age. Sentimentalism seemed merely the fashionable return to superficial emotion. More deeply considered, it indicated "humanitarianism," the discovery of the individual, democracy, the French Revolution, Catholic Emancipation, Prison Reform, the liberation of black slaves and the Reform Bills. More deeply considered, it meant a revolt against the venality, the nepotism, the inefficiency, the selfishness and the obvious rottenness of the ancient régime—in the Church, out of which Sterne emerged;

in the universities; in the entire political and economic system of the State.

One is quite unprepared to understand Sterne in his times unless one sees his crack-brained humor as a product, more or less unconscious—a product, by reaction, of the brutal *insensibility* of generation after generation of upstanding, two-fisted, go-getting Englishmen, whose cities stank with unchanneled slops, whose gin-sodden peasants toiled like cattle, whose children were wasted in mines, whose prisons were crowded with fever-stricken victims driven there by debt and starvation, whose slave ships sailed blithely from Africa to the Indies with hundreds of blacks bound head to foot on the decks and dying in their chains.

It was time for a little "sensibility," high time.

In his "English Humorists," 1851-'53, Thackeray delivered a famous harsh lecture on Sterne as a man who would neglect his dying mother to weep over a dead ass. In 1864 Walter Bagehot, reviewing Percy Fitzgerald's "Life of Sterne," wrote an essay on "Sterne and Thackeray" in which he piquantly argued that "in spite of many superficial differences, there was one fundamental and ineradicable resemblance between the two"—namely, their exacerbated sensibility. Bagehot's essay is, however, in spite of suppressed struggling sympathies, "eminently Victorian," and is now as completely out of date as Thackeray's.

The "Life of Laurence Sterne" is as indisputably Dean Cross's as *the* "Life of Henry Fielding" is his. Since his "Development of the English Novel," 1899, he has been growing steadily more intimate with the subject from year to year through a quarter of a century. In 1904 he edited the Works of Sterne, to-

gether with Fitzgerald's Life, making many revisions
and additions of new material. In 1909, after years
of laborious research, he produced his own "Life and
Times of Laurence Sterne." This work, as he slyly
suggests in the preface to the new edition before us,
seemed to be the special occasion for two new English
biographies within the next two years. By this fresh
and thorough revision Dean Cross reclaims what he
had previously made his own, bringing the book abreast
of the latest discoveries and enriching it with new
materials, especially Sterne's Letter Book, printed from
the manuscript now in the Morgan Library.

Sterne is not an author for all times or for all ages
or for all sorts of people. He is for those who are
ripe and perhaps on the verge of being overripe. He
made, for example, little appeal to me when I was a
young man, though I remember, about 1899, reading
"Tristram Shandy" through one golden afternoon,
lying behind a screen of boughs in a clear space in the
midst of a New England wood, where an eccentric parson had stationed me to wait for partridges, according
to his own mild method of hunting them. I grew tired
of the book long before the parson came to guide me
out of the wood, for I waited till after dark and the
parson never returned at all. He was a Shandian
fellow—irresponsible; perhaps he had left his partridges to write his sermon. But that was no way
to read Sterne, in great gulps. Sterne wrote dainty
little chapters, and for a reason. He wrote them for
tired business men to read between stations in the
subway. Last year I read both "Tristram Shandy"
and "A Sentimental Journey" during leaps of the I.
R. T.; I found them entrancing and wished for more
such alleviants of the rush and jolting of life.

[294]

Sterne is an author for governors who have grown weary in well doing; for secretaries of state who have been baffled at the task of establishing the peace of the world; for judges who have grown skeptical not merely about the possibility but even about the wisdom of enforcing a law; for bishops who find that the Kingdom of God on Earth arrives tardily; and for deans of old New England colleges in hours of relaxation from screwing up the standards. When Dean Cross himself first began to write of Sterne, his sympathy with Sterne's temper and with his form was considerable but not complete. The shadow of Victorianism was still over his author and over him. But Dean Cross, like many other survivors of the august and virtuous Queen, has mellowed with the years, become gently whimsical, mildly epicurean, and now in the perfect sympathy that comes with perfect understanding he takes Sterne kindly by the hand and leads him back to us, and presents him to us as a humorist whom the whirligig of time has made once more singularly in accord with the spirit of a distracted and skeptical age.

XXIII

George Washington as Diarist

IT is generally understood nowadays that George Washington has been poorly transmitted to us— partly his own fault or deficiency, partly the fault of others.

If we assume that he wished to live in the hearts of his countrymen, he had bad luck. He did indeed happen to stand out as the conspicuously fit man for doing two big jobs: commanding the Continental army during the War for Independence and navigating the ship of state on her first two voyages. That may perhaps be reckoned his good fortune. But in consequence of his performance of these two tasks, he was immobilized, marmorealized and demi-godded in his own lifetime.

After the war he never got a chance to unbend, and unbending was not easy to him at the best. Whenever he might otherwise have had an hour off, he was obliged to powder and curl his hair, don his broadcloth and lace, his silk stockings and his silver-buckled shoon, grasp the hilt of his tasseled sword, place one finger upon some epoch-making state paper, compose his features into an expression of august virtue and unutterable majesty and pose for a Roman medallion by Ormsby, a bust by Houdon, a portrait by Stuart, an oration by Patrick Henry, a Latin "Georgii Washingtonii Vita" by Francis Glass, of Ohio, or a biography

[296]

of the perfect statesman by Senator Lodge or President-to-be Wilson.

In olden days people had to have these classicized representations of the Mount Vernon farmer to hang in the legislative halls of the new states, and to erect on public squares, and to exhibit in Europe, and to include in the Statesman's Series. The poor old hero resigned himself in the end to being sublime, just as he had resigned himself to being commander-in-chief and President. He never visibly winced under it. He saw it through, thrusting his prominent chin out further than ever; in which, as Roscoe Thayer suggested, an ill-fitting set of false teeth—wooden—probably assisted. But his eyelids are a little weary.

It is a curious fact that the first great popular biography of Washington, published in the year following his death by the parson of Mount Vernon parish, the celebrated Mason L. Weems, was a protest against transmitting to posterity this classicized warrior and statesman, the official Washington. In the period when Sir Joshua Reynolds was explaining to the Royal Academy that an historical work in the grand style must not be allowed to run into "particularities," but must exhibit the hero only in his heroic aspects and with "as much dignity as the human figure is capable of receiving"—in this grand classicizing period this miserable Parson Weems strongly revolted against demi-godding his neighbor.

Somehow he got it fixed in his poor pious little head that the lovable Washington was the "private citizen," the man whom he had seen year after year planting his turnips and being diligent in business and serving the Lord once or twice a month in Pohick Church, along with Mrs. Washington and Patsy and Jacky

[299]

Custis. And so Parson Weems in the odor of parsonage sanctity excogitated and devised *his* George Washington, a hero whom he and a piety-loving posterity could understand; Washington, the pure-lipped model of all Sabbath school virtues, the boy who could not tell a lie, the friend of the widow and fatherless (didn't he, for example, marry a widow? with $100,000 to be sure), the affectionate son and brother, the devoted farmer, the mirror of industry and frugality. Weems's Washington was an incredible prig to whom school children for a hundred years have been taught to perform lip-service and genuflections.

Since the time, say, of P. L. Ford's "The True George Washington," 1896, there has been accumulating a protest against the heroic demi-god of the classical painters, on the one hand, and the perfect prig of the Weemsian tradition, on the other.

Contemporary biography has learned the A B C's of the art. It is for putting back into the popular conception of the man the "human" traits which the earlier undertakers and sextons of his fame so carefully expunged, including the pockmarks which he got when he accompanied his consumptive brother to the Barbados, where he feasted pretty gaily with the gentlemen of the Beefsteak and Tripe Club and observed that the ladies generally were "very agreeable but by ill custom or . . . affect the Negro style . . ."

Some words are deleted in the diary at that point. Presumably they would have helped the sense and the interest of the passage. But it was a fixed rule with old-school editors to omit everything specially lively. Such a rule obviously bears hard on a diarist like our Father George, who only *verged* on liveliness half a dozen times in a half century.

[300]

Washington, we now learn, had huge hands and enormous feet, and stood six feet and three inches in his No. 13 boots. His big nose got fiery red when the wind blew. His hot temper is now a thing to brag about. He hurled leaden ink wells at dastards, and, in the presence of cowardice in battle, he swore past belief. As for lying, why couldn't he tell a lie? asks one biographer savagely—didn't he have a tongue in his head? Then comes along Mr. Henderson and demonstrates quite neatly, out of the diaries, that George *did* tell a lie—oh, a quite justifiable little white lie, to be sure—in order to be rid of the dust of a troublesome voluntary retinue which persisted in riding before him on his tour through the South. Gradually we recover other little touches of the Virginian gentleman which Weems overlooked; his romantic attachment to an early flame, his dancing all night, his card-playing—losing two to three pounds in an evening, too; his theatergoing, his rapacious appetite for food, his hard riding after foxes, sometimes six or seven hours a day, often ten times in a month, in some years every month.

These are trifling "particularities," but they help destroy the plaster bust.

Now, as I take it, the elaborate publication of Washington's private journals in their entirety is a most significant part of our contemporary effort to recover the whole man.* The importance of this contribution will, I am convinced, grow upon us immensely as the record is "creatively" studied, as its laconic, factual memoranda are gradually pieced together, illuminated from other sources and reasoned upon by biographers and historians who know how to utilize a vast collection

* *The Diaries of George Washington,* Boston, 1925, four vols.

of apparently insignificant detail in the interpretation of a tremendously vital yet bafflingly inexpressive sort of man—an "extravert," I fancy our psychologists would call him, a man with a "reflex mechanism" which expressed itself so adequately in muscular and practical activities that all the forms of emotion and reflection which result in most men from checked impulse are almost non-existent in this record.

But has not the public had access to these diaries hitherto? To certain parts of them, yes—to some of the rare and therefore uncharacteristic purple passages in them. For example, when young Washington, twenty-three years old, returned from his thrillingly venturous mission with his Dutch interpreter and four chiefs of the Six Nations to the French commandant at Fort Le Bœuf, in 1755, Dinwiddie, the Governor of Virginia, gave him just one day's warning to write up his notes of the trip for the inspection of the Legislature, and straightway rushed the narrative through the public printing office, as any newspaper man with the faintest sense of an amazingly live "story" would have done. It has the very whiff and smell of powder and rum and tobacco twist in it, and the intrigue and nervous tension of the frontier at the moment when English, French and Indians were reaching for one another's scalps. Of that hotly printed edition two copies are extant.

There are other fragments, too, that got into print long ago, and contrary to expectation and desire. The notes extending from March to June, 1754, were captured by the French at Fort Necessity, published in Paris, retranslated and published in London, and thence returned to their author. Here again was a great news story of the highest interest to three nations, and the ordinarily dull, incommunicative pen of Washington could not kill it.

The general tranquillity with which the public has regarded Washington's private records seems indicated by the fact that his diaries for the important years 1789 to 1791 waited for publication till Benjamin Lossing brought them out in Richmond in 1861. In 1920 Joseph A. Hoskins published at Summerfield, N. C., "President Washington's Diaries, 1791 to 1799," and much of his material then first came into print.

Within the last two years the diaries have been burrowed into twice by men with imagination. In 1923 Mr. Archibald Henderson made a big and handsome book, "Washington's Southern Tour," all in elucidation of diaries which occupy only fifty pages of our fourth volume in telling the story of the first President's first swing around the circle. As indication of the relative novelty of the material, Mr. Henderson notes that "neither Woodrow Wilson nor Henry Cabot Lodge," two of the chief biographers, "even so much as makes mention of the Southern Tour"—which one hopes is an extraordinary instance of historial indolence. In 1925 P. S. Haworth made a fresh attack upon the august sphinx in a book called "George Washington: Country Gentleman," which was based on the Mount Vernon farm journals.

Obviously within the last five years the suspicion has got abroad that those forty or fifty old diaries in the Library of Congress and elsewhere are worth a thorough working over. And yet Editor Fitzpatrick informs us that till the Mount Vernon Ladies' Association of the Union put its fair shoulder to the task *"hardly one-sixth of the available record"* had been published. These four fine volumes, therefore, very greatly augment the dimensions of Washington as a diarist. They will greatly augment our consciousness of the real nature of his personality and his career if we have the wit and the imagination and the industry to use them—and only so.

Let us be plain about this. There is a little batch of diaries, perhaps half a dozen, which are of vivid interest throughout—to anybody. But for hundreds of pages an unprepared and incurious reader will regard Washington as the "dumbest" diarist who ever employed the line-a-day method. There is nothing which Greville would have called a "character" in all the four volumes, and upon all the famous men that he met in half a century he utters only with the utmost rarity a two-line judgment. In general, neither births nor deaths nor weddings nor funerals nor good fortune nor calamity nor pestilence nor hurricane betrays him into the recording of the faintest emotion of elation or sorrow or hope or regret. He almost never attempts a picture or reports a conversation. Of himself as a dramatic object of consciousness he seems to have been aware on only two or three occasions in the course of his life. There is virtually no indication that he ever felt the slightest curiosity regarding the "subjective" condition of any other being. He seems to have been absolutely uninitiated into the pleasure of associating ideas. And these characteristics make great tracts of the record—months and years of it—as dry as chopped straw, as dry as Aristotle or Euclid, as dry as the fossil teeth of a dinosaur.

Nevertheless the only way to give this man a chance to reconstitute for us his character and career is to take a clear week and plow straight through the diaries systematically from end to end, going just as slowly and working the imagination just as hard through the long desert places as in the occasional astonishing oases.

We start from an oasis. The first diary begins early Friday morning, March 11, 1748, when in his sixteenth year George Washington set out with his neighbor, young George Fairfax, on a jolly surveying and turkey-shooting expedition in the wild lands of Lord Fairfax beyond the Blue Ridge. At sixteen George had high spirits and a sense of humor, such as he seldom betrayed during the next fifty years. He relishes the joke on himself when, in a backwoods lodging, he strips "orderly" for bed, to find himself lying on a little matted straw under one threadbare blanket "with double its weight of vermin such as lice, fleas, etc." He gets up, dresses and lies, "as my companions," outdoors by a fire. Next day: "We cleaned ourselves (to get rid of the game we had catch'd the night before)." The next week, meeting thirty-odd Indians with a scalp, the boys give them some liquor: "it elevating their spirits put them in the humor of dancing." Then follows the first and last description of a dance in all George's four volumes.

If I were bent on making merely a readable article about the diaries, my cue would be to dwell at length on this first batch of them, written when the young fellow admitted finding a charm in the whistling of bullets. Then I should pass swiftly to the diary kept during Washington's attendance at the Continental Congress in 1775, and I should pause there and say that the diarist disappointed me bitterly in that emergency. Specimen entries during the month of May are here presented:

12. Dined and supped at the City Tavern.
13. Dined at the City Tavern with the Congress. Spent the evening at my lodgings.
14. Dined at Mr. Wellings and spent the evening at my lodgings.
15. Dined at Burnes and spent the evening at my lodgings.

Something happened; for Washington was made commander-in-chief; but the incident gets no more space or comment in this singular journal than planting turnips back of the garden. During a considerable period of the war he was too busy to write at all.

On entering Philadelphia for the Constitutional Convention in 1787 he was for a few moments impressed with his reception by his old officers and by his own conduct and appearance. But his memoranda of the sessions are perfectly barren. We learn the names of a great number of Philadelphia ladies and gentlemen with whom he "drank tea"—at one place he "drank tea in great splendour"; we learn that he sat to Mr. Peale for his portrait, attended charity concerts, visited Morris at his country place, went trout fishing and rode away from his fishing companion to visit the site of one of his old cantonments.

What did he feel on August 19, 1787, standing on the old camp ground from which he had marched to his winter quarters in Valley Forge? I do not know. All that he says is: "traversed my old incampment, and *contemplated on* the dangers which threatened the American Army at that place." All that he says of the faintest color, when the great business of the four months' convention is over, is that the members adjourned to the City Tavern, dined in good humor and he, after he had finished up some odd jobs with the secretary of the convention, "retired to meditate on the momentous work which had been executed." Those eleven words indicate about the extent to which the soul of the man will expand and flow—on paper.

The diaries of the first years of the Presidency seem, relatively speaking, of an absorbing interest to one who is trying to press nearer to the man. Of course, there was a big budget of national business without guiding precedents: diplomatic missions to be established, Moroccan affairs, Indian affairs, national militia, finance, ratification of state constitutions, Quaker slavery agitation, Spain and France threatening the flanks of the new nation, problems of uniting the seaboard and the Western frontier by land and water and by the ties of commerce. But, after all, this was nothing but national housekeeping, of which Washington had mastered the principles at Mount Vernon, in the Virginia House of Burgesses, and in the army. He conducts business now with Cabinet officers instead of overseers; but he goes at it in precisely the same thorough, methodical, orderly, realistic fashion. An able, unagitated executive.

What strikes the student of the diaries is that the Presidential office made Washington conscious of himself and of Mrs. Washington as parts of a dramatic exhibition, which they were "putting on" for the edification of their countrymen. The Father of His Country obviously gave anxious thought to all the details of the visible spectacle when he made his appearance to deliver his first message before the two houses of Congress; and the diarist records the picture—his equipage and his costume, his entrance and his exit—

with evident feeling that the little show, now set up
to rival the performances at Versailles and the Court of
St. James, came off fairly well.

One feels this new self-consciousness of his with almost pathetic poignancy in his notes on the success of
his Tuesday levees and of Mrs. Washington's Friday
teas. He is particularly sensitive about the "Fridays." One day: "The visitors to Mrs. Washington
were respectable, both of gentlemen and ladies"; another day, "not numerous, but respectable"; another,
"rainy and bad; no one but the Vice-President." On
the 29th of December, 1789: "Being very snowing,
not a single person appeared at the Levee"; but on
the following New Year's Day, thank goodness, "all
the respectable citizens" turned out, and the Federal
Union once more seemed secure.

When one considers what George Washington had
been through without turning a hair—such things as
having two horses shot under him and his clothes rid-
dled with bullets in a single battle, and when one considers the events in which he participated without leaving a word of them in his daily record, one is almost
justified in guessing that the very deeps of his nature
must have been troubled on those Fridays when he
set down for everlasting remembrance the reason why
the attendance at Mrs. Washington's tea was light.

The two of them liked it superficially when there
was a big gathering of "respectable" persons, but inwardly I think they both hated the officializing of
their social intercourse, and were unspeakably happy,
when the second heavy term was over, to be back again
in the easy casual coming to and fro of their Virginia kinsmen and neighbors.

I have been dwelling on what, as it seems to *us*,

must have been the high spots in Washington's life. How did they seem to him? Well, there is no emphasis or proportioning in the diaries to suggest that Washington himself regarded his soldiership and statesmanship as *living* and the rest of life as débris and dross. On the contrary, the Revolution and the two Presidential terms dwindle and sink in this long record—sink into troublesome but by no means overwhelming incidents in the half century. So far as the record goes, the planting of a consignment of Chinese flower seeds in his garden made a vastly greater impression upon him than meeting Benjamin Franklin in Philadelphia; and I am certain that he took more pleasure in making inventories of his stock, servants and tools in preparation for the spring planting than he did in making inventories of his regiments in preparation for the spring fighting. It is only when his public life is set in his private that one can see it as he saw it.

All that one knows about Washington gets a new value when one comes at it faithfully in its place amid the long routine of his country life. The first obvious reward of reading straight through the diaries is that one receives an almost oppressive sense of *lapsing time*, filled with the ordinary "inanities" of existence— so important an element in "artistic illusion." One gets the sense of streaming time not merely or mainly in the crowded years of war and statecraft but most richly and sumptuously in the long, quiet, orderly flow of the years on the Mount Vernon estate in the '60s and the early '70s, when one follows the crops and the weather, the first haul of shad in the river, the breeding stock and the litters of puppies, the blossoms in orchard and garden, the harvesting of hay and wheat, of apples and of ice, and the fleeing of hunted foxes, or of ducks in the swampland, day by day, month by month, season by season, year by year—up at sunrise, breakfast with guests who have spent the night, then off on horseback to visit "my mill," "my ferry," "my fishlanding," "my swamp," "my sick people," or to see what Cupid and Sambo, "my Negroes," two or three hundreds of them, are doing on "my" remoter plantations.

"A better farmer ne'er brushed dew from lawn," as Byron remarked of George III. Our "Farmer George," as you see, had a lively sense of property. He liked branding his stock "G. W." It expanded his sense of being. And he enjoyed all the details of good husbandry. Twice he made actual experiment with tallow and spermaceti candles and recorded in fractions his demonstration that tallow is cheaper. And so on.

The last diary ends on December 13, 1799—a snowy day with the mercury falling from 30 to 28 and a northeast wind blowing. On that day the Father of his Country developed an acute sore throat from the previous day's exposure, having come in from the farms with his neck wet and snow hanging in his hair. On the next day he died very quietly under the bleedings and blisters and wheat-bran cataplasms of the attending physicians. He expressed a desire not to be put in the vault till he had been three days dead. Beyond that he betrayed no anxiety about the hereafter.

XXIV

Brigham Young: A Fundamentalist Who Got What He Wanted

MY devotion to American biography has been rewarded and exhilarated by Mr. M. R. Werner's
"Brigham Young."

In the production of a classical work, we are told,
everything depends on the choice of a subject. This
is Mr. Werner's subject: An impecunious Vermont
boy with only a few weeks of schooling rises to be
prophet, priest and king, head of a church, general
of an army, governor of a territory, possessor of an
estate worth $2,000,000, husband of twenty-seven
wives and father of fifty-six children. I should like
to say that this subject is of "epic sweep"; but since
critics have got the habit of describing every mid-
western novel which shows a section of cornland under
cultivation as of "epic sweep," the phrase has become
a little colorless. What one has in mind about Mr.
Werner's subject is, that it begins in Vermont, ascends
to heaven, descends to western New York, and travers-
ing the great West to the Rocky Mountains presents
such events as the councils of God, the revelation of
laws to man, the founding of cities, the martyrdom of
saints, the building of temples, the waging of wars,
the massacre of infidels and the establishment of
civilization in the wilderness.

To whom hitherto have most "Gentiles" been in-

[311]

debted for their conception of Mormon leaders and Mormon civilization? To Congressmen viewing with subconscious envy the efficiency of the theocratic "machine" in Utah and the Oriental prerogatives of the Mormon "boss." To lone, lorn hysterical women, without even a thirtieth share in a husband, seeking to free the Mormon wives from "bondage." To clergymen diverting their minds from domestic troubles by proposing a foreign war—like the Rev. De Witt Talmage, who, as Mr. Werner reminds us, paused in interpreting the Gospel of Christ one Sunday morning in 1877 to suggest to the national government that the time was ripe, now that Brigham Young had died, to send Phil Sheridan to Utah and to confiscate as much of the rich Mormon lands as would pay for their subjugation. To comic journalists like Artemus Ward and Mark Twain, who in quest of copy and a national guffaw, interviewed the Governor of Utah, and led off with such questions as this: " 'You air a married man, Mister Yung, I bleeve?' sez I."

We are officially under obligation to think of a man with a non-monogamous mind as a monster. But deep in the sinful heart of man lurks a kind of atavistic sympathy and curiosity regarding the private life of Brigham Young: he had a human experience so rich and so varied. He had the wisdom possible only to one who has the comparative point of view. While this subject is before us it should be said that Mr. Werner goes into it as carefully as one can desire in three really instructive chapters on "Puritan Polygamy," "Brigham Young and His Wives" and "Polygamy and the Law."

In the palmy days of plurality Heber Kimball, eminent saint, declared in the pulpit: "For a man of God to be confined to one woman is small business." Kimball was a sincere man; he married forty-five wives. Brigham Young and his associates believed that a man "cannot be saved without a woman at his side." Young avowed that he was a "great lover of good women." He liked them plain and honest, clean and chaste, with their hair parted in the middle and combed smoothly back from the forehead. He said, I think honestly, that there were "few men who care about the private society of women as little as I do.

Everything that he did bears that out: his marrying three or four on the same day, his assembling them in large numbers so that the intimacy of his family life was less like a *solitude à deux* than a church social. With much justice he contended, in that great vacant territory, that the purpose of matrimony was to replenish the earth with saints. Mr. Werner notes that in 1851 Brigham Young became a father in January, February, March and April, and in 1852 in March, April and May. He seems to have been a "natural born" father. There is something heroic in the way he faced the consequences of his beliefs. There was little romantic sentiment about him. To women who whined for love he said in effect: "What difference does it make?" If they had a child, they ought to be content, and to exclaim with joy: "Hallelujah! I am a mother—I have borne an image of God."

Brigham Young's uxoriousness can be overemphasized, his philoprogenitiveness, not. But let us pass to other matters by way of a quotation from Young's "Journal of Discourses," giving the public reflections of the Governor on Gentile curiosity relating to his domestic arrangements. I make this extended quotation to emphasize my own chief discovery about Brig-

1847, not by praying for rain but by introducing the first extensive irrigation system in the United States. It is impossible, if I may judge by my own experience, to visit Salt Lake City without a thrill of pride in the Mormons.

Professor Young's book is charming. It glows with affection and pride in the state, based upon intimate extensive acquaintance with it. It is free from offensive chauvinism: one-fourth of it is devoted to the history of the Great Basin before the Mormons entered it. It begins with an account of Rocky Mountain sunshine, flowers and topography and proceeds in successive chapters to a generous appraisal of the native Indians, the Cliff-dwellers, the Spanish adventurers, the fur-traders, the scientific explorers, who made the old trails and endowed the territory with ancient and romantic human associations. Then, as an integral part of the general westward migration, comes the tale of the Mormon colonization, made rich and vivid by many choice excerpts from the letters and journals of the pioneers, illustrating their trials and adversities, their courage, industry and enterprise. In all this Brigham Young figures largely.

Two silences are impressive: there is no mention of Joseph Smith or of polygamy. For all account of Mormon religion, Professor Young says: "The leaders of this religious people were men whose ancestors had lived in the pioneer districts of New England, and were Puritans and Methodists in belief." Incidents like the Mountain Meadows massacre are passed over quickly as among the things mainly attributable to the Indians, "which we wish had never happened." The object of Mormon missions is described as "the conversion of the Indians to Christianity." Professor

Young leaves the impression that political, religious, ethical ideals in the state to-day are democratic and idealistic and essentially indistinguishable from those of any other enlightened American commonwealth. He concludes his narrative with a picture of "Utah To-day" as a highly civilized state, with a notably low percentage of crime, insanity, pauperism, and illiteracy, but with high school attendance, flourishing agriculture, manufactures and mines and lively interest in the arts and sciences.

Professor Young has liberally whitewashed the founding of Utah. But I doubt whether he has whitewashed it a whit more than the average non-Mormon historian whitewashes the foundation of Massachusetts when he prepares a book for the use of Boston schools.

Mr. Werner's book ends with the death of Brigham Young in 1877, but as he has envisaged his biographical problem, the scope of his work and its larger purpose are not very different from Professor Young's. That is to say he too is interested in the founding of Utah, and he sees the divisions of his hero's life as steps in that long epical process. Before he is done with it he makes a nationally important and most impressive figure of Brigham Young. If he came to scoff he remained to quote respectfully Seward's remark that "America had never produced a greater statesman."

Unlike the Mormon historian, however, Mr. Werner does not suppress Joseph Smith. He appears to believe that Smith was a drunkard, a profligate, and, what was worse in the circumstances, a very poor business man, even when God had carefully revealed the plans for Smith's financial campaigns and had dictated in extraordinary detail the organization of his

[317]

stock company. Smith's religious leadership, he holds, originated with deliberate humbug and childish flummery; but he suspects that after long imposing on others Smith finally imposed on himself. But Mr. Werner does, I think, make an honest and fruitful effort to understand and explain the man as a "product" of his times and of the rather weedy Puritan culture of the New England village.

The prophet-martyr was born, without any celestial notification or portent, in Sharon, Vt., in 1805, to an old and poverty stricken but fertile American family—there were eventually nine children—with epileptic tendencies on both sides, and various relatives subject to religious visions. Both his parents were visited, as all Puritans from the time of Wycliffe to the present day have been, by dreams assuring them that none of the existing churches was truly representative of Jesus Christ and the ancient Apostles.

The old people didn't know what to do about it. Old people in Vermont never know what to do about anything. For example, old people in Vermont have abundant streams of pure water flowing from the mountains past their back doors—have had for three hundred years. But old Vermont villagers still pump their water from driven wells, a teaspoonful at a time. That is the way the Vermont mind works on its native heath. It is only when the Vermonter is transplanted to southern latitudes that he is transformed into a Yankee Mahomet. Utah is in the latitude of Virginia and Spain. There is hope for young Vermonters if they migrate early.

Joseph Smith, like his parents, had visions; unlike them, he had ingenuity and considerable "creative imagination." In one of these visions he was visited by two mysterious presences. One of them proved to be God, for "pointing"—probably in the rustic village manner, by way of introduction—to the other stranger, he said: "This is my beloved son, hear him." At this interview God bore it in upon Joseph's mind that He had no true church in the world, and confided various other matters which were not then, as Mr. Werner puts it, "released for publication."

Joseph, for a time, went on with the ungodly life of a Vermont villager. But he meditated on these things. He also, it is reported, studied the memoirs of the itinerant clerical scalawag, Stephen Burroughs, and the autobigraphy of Captain Kidd. Kidd seems to have set his mind running on buried treasure, and Burroughs on the undeveloped resources of heaven, open to exploitation by an enterprising Yankee. When his family moved to western New York, then the asylum of footloose religions, he went out on a treasure hunting expedition. On Cumnorah Hill, near Palmyra, in 1830 he dug up the famous gold plates, subsequently returned to heaven, on which the book of Mormon was written. Together with them he found the "celestial spectacles," called Urim and Thummim, with the aid of which he was able to translate the "Reformed Egyptian" of the original "caractors" into somewhat broken Elizabethan English. God directed him to get the book printed and to offer it for sale at $1.75, but later advised that the price be lowered to $1.25.

Non-Mormon analyists of this book and of Joseph Smith's other translations from the "Reformed Egyptian" writings of Abraham, etc., regard them on the whole as very puerile flummery, full of ignorance, superstition and absurd anachronisms. I think they are. They were written before the Mormons had done any-

[319]

thing notable. The true sacred books of the Mormons are their own chronicles. They have histories comparable with Genesis, Exodus, Leviticus. They lived in "bondage," they suffered ferocious persecution, they wandered in the wilderness, they entered "the land of Canaan," they built a tabernacle to their God, and the story of these deeds is a moving, heroic and often majestic portion of our national narrative, which deserves all the reverence due to any great chapter in the tear-stricken, blood-stained annals of mankind.

It is to be remembered, however, that Joseph Smith's "revelations" were not a substitute for the Bible in Mormon culture, but a supplement to it. They had a special work to perform in their time. *They worked!* They achieved their purpose. In the minds of Joseph Smith's followers, they established as flaming truths two grand propositions which were of utmost value in converting a democratic mob into a marching militant nation: that God still lived and spoke to men; and that Joseph Smith was his prophet and must be obeyed to the letter.

Mr. Werner, after expressing his skepticism of prophets, appropriately quotes Carlyle's heated assurance that no hollow quack ever founded a religion. Joseph Smith was a quack, but not hollow. He gripped with both hands two mighty principles of order: the principle of absolute authority and the principle of absolute obedience; and he held them fast, through all his vagaries, till he was assassinated in the jail at Carthage, Illinois, in 1844. His apostles recognized that Joseph had got hold of something invaluable, and they upheld him through thick and thin. On the rock of his principles, Joseph Smith built his church, organized his militia, governed his curiously chartered

city of Nauvoo. If it was destined, as it now seems
to have been, that several thousands of superstitious,
credulous, hungry, pioneering "democrats" should be
drawn out from the unruly American rabble of 1840,
disciplined, drilled, welded into a firm homogeneous
religious society and planted in the wilderness as the
seed of a new state, then Joseph Smith was a truly
"inspired" man.

He was killed at just the right time, retrospectively
speaking. His work was done. His principle of
authority and his principle of obedience were firmly
implanted among his followers and his martyrdom
sanctified his work. He turned over to his successor
a political-religious machine which was in admirable
running order and surpassed Tammany Hall by the
inclusion of polygamy. Polygamy, though not openly
promulgated in Nauvoo, was extensively practised,
and so far as spiritual affairs were concerned, Brigham
Young had little to do but to "carry on" and work
out details. Mr. Werner draws a sharp line between
the character of Joseph and that of his successor, and
nearly all his admiration goes to Brigham Young.
Being a very skeptical, very modern biographer, Mr.
Werner, I think, rather undervalues "fire from
heaven"; and consequently rather underestimates the
"genius" of Joseph Smith and tends to overlook the
strict adequacy of his response to his opportunity.

I share, however, Mr. Werner's admiration for
Brigham Young and think him in most respects immensely Joseph Smith's superior. He was not spiritually as impressionable as Joseph, but he had a vast
deal more of common sense. He was born a governor
of men and women and he was always working at his
job. It was said of him that he slept with one eye

open and one foot out of bed. He encouraged his
people to come to him with their pettiest troubles and
he *required* them to consult on every undertaking of
importance. He had at their disposal a sagacity which
frequently dictated counsel of which Benjamin Franklin might have been proud. A woman rushed to him
in tears to complain that her husband had told her
to go to hell. Brigham Young looked at her solemnly
and said, "Well, don't go; don't go." As advice it
is perfect.

The outstanding virtue in Brigham Young by which
he insensibly modified the entire character of Mor-
monism and modernized it was this: He knew how to
do everything himself and he thought and preached
that it was disgraceful and unmanly to ask God's
assistance until one's own resources were entirely exhausted. He didn't like whining. "If you have any
crying to do, wife, you can do that along with the
children, for I have none of that kind of business to
do." Discoursing on prayer he said: "While we have
a rich soil in this valley and seed to put in the ground
we need not ask God to feed us, nor follow us around
with a loaf of bread begging of us to eat it. He
will not do it, neither would I were I the Lord." He
had received the prophetic mantle from Joseph Smith
and might at any time have asked, as Joseph had done
constantly, for divine revelations about the organization of his masterly exodus from Illinois and about a
thousand details concerning the foundation of his city.
Except on very rare occasions, and then mainly for the
look of the thing, Brigham Young dispensed with
special revelations. They really were not necessary,
and so he could dispense, too, with flummery. He had
a bland forehead and serene and humane eyes, but his

head was as hard as a keg of nails and his mouth closed like a bear trap. He, too, had his vision. He gripped with both hands two vital principles, the preservation of life and the perpetuation of the species. "I am very kind," he said, "but know how to rule." Unquestionably he did.

XXV

Interpreting Jesus

JESUS was born in the artisan class and rose to be an original teacher among a people who made a rigorous religious ritual out of the way their ancestors had washed the dishes, and that sort of thing. His imagination was molded by the history and traditions of his own people, but the fresh life in him revolted from the suffocatingly traditional forms in which academic minds attempted to fix the spiritual activities of the time. Though at maturity he did not hold with the ascetic sects, in early middle life he was much influenced by the preaching of John, an ascetic in the style of the elder prophets. John was attempting to produce a penitential movement in expectation of a savior of the people, whose coming was a matter of ancient prediction.

Jesus became convinced that he himself was the foretold savior. He fostered that belief in his followers. Of the bystanders, some said that he was "a good man" and others said that he was "misleading the people." Indisputably, they were both right. Jesus was a good man. Jesus did mislead the people in ten thousand tragic ways.

It seems clear, however, that he himself contemplated no such exodus from the power of the Roman law as the multitude hoped for, but rather an escape into an inner world of "spiritual freedom." He desired less a refuge from Roman taxes than from the dead hand which the Jewish rabbis laid upon his spirit. It is obvious that his conception of new birth and new life in a loving creative activity was understood by few, if any, of the men and women who trooped after him, craving mental and physical healing, bread and fish, and power and place in the physical kingdom over which they persisted in believing he was to reign.

He was unable to explain his idea to the satisfaction of his own family. Even his most intimate friends misunderstood him absurdly, quarreled over left and right hand places in the throne room, and on one occasion went so far as to suggest that they should call down fire from heaven on a house which had refused them hospitality. As for the leading representatives of the established order among his countrymen, they regarded him as a dangerous radical, an habitual Sabbath-breaker, a blasphemer and a fomenter of sedition against the state—not to mention the fact that in his hotter moods he had designated them personally as liars and vipers.

From the Jewish point of view there was abundant evidence to support all these charges. Furthermore, the cures and resurrections attributed to Jesus seem not to have impressed the hierarchy as they impressed the common people. They regarded them as orthodox physicians regarded the miracles of M. Coué. That the Roman Pilate was not offended by his breaking the Jewish Sabbath or by his identifying himself with the Jewish God or by his assumption of the Jewish kingship, temporal or spiritual, was irrelevant to the Jewish case against him.

Jesus, as we must suppose, did his best to explain and justify himself to his own generation. On the

whole, he failed tragically. He spoke puzzlingly, para-
doxically and poetically, and failed to find any common ground with most of his hearers. He died leaving
no written testament.

In the course of time four of his followers wrote
short biographies of him, comprising recollections or
hearsay as to what he had done and said, amid which
they mingled the guesses of "average" men—tax col-
lectors, physicians and the like—as to who he was and
what he really meant. Three of these biographers
got their leading idea largely from traditional sources;
and accordingly they made much of the supernatural
birth, miracles and fulfillments of prophecy. The
fourth, who seems to have written much later, was a
mystic with access to experience and forms of thought
which appear to have been quite alien to the harlots
and publicans and the Scribes and the Pharisees to
whom Jesus had tried to convey his message.

Yet whether or not they fully comprehended his
mission, from the earliest time to the present day,
people in increasing numbers have believed, or suspected, that there was focused in this obscure Naza-
rene an extraordinary power, perhaps a unique power,
to relieve hearts of their burdens and to replace the
burdens with a sense of abundant life and happiness.
The four little biographies, for example, make mention of a number of persons, both men and women,
who seem to have troubled themselves little about the
fulfillment of prophecy or difficult questions regarding
the Logos or the Godhead; but they went straight,
by a kind of bee instinct, to the source of the Master's
fascination for them.

They did not attempt to fathom or explain him.
They loved him and they loved one another, as he

had loved them; and thus instinctively they fulfilled what the adorable mystic who wrote the fourth Gospel called his "new commandment." In this love, clearly a new sort of love to most of them—especially to women like Mary of Magdala and the Samaritan water drawer —in this love, characterized by a peculiar sense of "light" and "life," they found themselves at the center of a strange power which enabled them to operate all the necessary laws of conduct from within, and to bear all the pain and sorrow of life—and death itself— smiling.

The quality and intensity of their devotion, at once childlike and passionate, is suggested to us by recollection of the woman who sat on the floor kissing the feet of Jesus all through the dinner while the host performed the usual courtesies. She had become quite literally childlike, and was therefore qualified for this extraordinary new "kingdom," and was a fit companion for the beloved disciple, for the ecstatic St. Francis, for Thomas à Kempis, for Saint Theresa, for Saint Joan, for Vaughan, for Blake singing his songs of innocence, and declaring to the organized church:

> The vision of Christ that thou dost see
> Is my vision's greatest enemy.

It is possible, of course, that if Jesus had reappeared many centuries later, he might have concluded that a man's ability to do good work in the world is dependent on his wealth and his membership in various powerful organizations. He might have taken to bishops and deans who mixed in politics and wrote filthy satires and edited old plays and fought for the perpetuation of ancient creeds and doctrines devised by the savage bulls and frantic eunuchs of the church during the duskier ages of the world.

But if he looked to-day for the ardor of his first friends and for the childlike spirit which he declared was prerequisite for admission to his fellowship, one is rather at a loss to know where he would find it, unless, perchance, in the radiant face of some Salvation Army lass in the street, with the "bread of God" on her lips; or in the chant of some Negro woman, toiling all day over the tubs and singing with serene pathos:

> Jesus knows all about our sorrows,
> He will tell us when the work is done.

In the lack of a lucid and completely intelligible explanation of his ability to make his lovers radiantly happy, the humbler laity and the learned theologians connected his power for centuries with interruptions of the order of nature and with certain business transactions in heaven. A few theologians still survive who attempt to account for magic by logic. And some simple folk still believe that the power of Jesus to confer a sense of abundant life and happiness is somehow dependent upon and knit up with his power to make wine out of well water.

But the plain people of my own acquaintance regard most of the Oriental interruptions of nature as puerile when compared with the wonders that any Occidental farmer can work when he gets into harmony with nature by the aid of half a dozen modern inventions. And so the once fiery miracle question is rather fading away. The theological questions, too.

And yet religion, as Mr. Irwin Edman shows in a remarkable article on "Religion for the Faithless," * an article beautifully glowing with the mystical ardor of the intellect—religion is something that we don't get away from; it is a necessary and inevitable form and mode of our innermost living.

Only the intelligent layman, when, like the curious Greeks, he "would see Jesus," when he wishes to draw near to a master of religious living, turns more and more away from the theologians to the accredited interpreters of magic—turns to men who use their imaginations when they attempt to explain that colossal imagination which imagined Christendom and dreamed of a kingdom of heaven within the realm of Herod Antipas and in the city of Mayor Hylan.

But these literary men, object historical students and serious pious people, we don't want them and their unlicensed imaginations filling the space between us and Jesus. We wish the truth and nothing but the truth. "Renan, indeed," says William G. Hutchinson, prefacing "The Life of Jesus," "is a good instance of the egoistic historian, the narrator who is rather lyrical than dramatic; the Jesus with whom he presents us is a Renanized Jesus—a Jesus who is gentle, ironical, at times almost gay—a Jesus, in short, who in many features resembles M. Ernest Renan. But what would we have?"

What, indeed? So it has been from the beginning. The Jesus of Matthew was a Matthewized Jesus, of John a Johnized Jesus, of Paul a Paulized Jesus. Every man finds his own Jesus as he finds his own God; and in neither does he discover aught that was not previously patent or latent in himself. This is

* *Bookman,* April, 1925.

as true of generations as of individuals; and this explains why Jesus enjoys a resurrection at every Easter when the lilies come up, and at the beginning of every generation, when young people appear with new culture and new hearts.

I can remember the appearance, a generation ago, of the æstheticized Christ, who was developed out of Renan's Jesus and out of Pre-Raphaelite art by young men without Renan's immense Semitic scholarship, but with more than his allowance of sentiment and sensuousness and sensibility to Syrian wild flowers. I can recall the exotic passions of the Salome, the Herodias and the John Baptist of Oscar Wilde and Sudermann; and Rostand's Jesus, "æsthetically" comparing the lines of the Samaritan woman's figure with the jug which she rests on the well-curb; and Oscar Wilde in "De Profundis," hymning Jesus as the exquisite esthete, the romantic artist, and setting the tragic story of the passion to the flute and oboe music of that period of life when he snatched at vice as an enlargement of experience, a lifting of the horizon—and then at repentance, as another enlargement of experience, a fresh lifting of the horizon.

You may argue all day and perhaps prove by sunset that the Jesus of Wilde and of Rostand was utterly inconsistent with the Jesus of Matthew, Mark, Luke, and John; but it would be rather vain to attempt proving that the esthetic sensibility of these poets and their period was utterly inconsistent with the Son of God. Instinctively as I resent the intrusion of *fin-de-siècle* estheticism between me and the conception of the Holy Land and its characters, which I inherited from Puritan interpreters, I am constrained to admit that my

[330]

doctrinal treatise on the "Book of Jonah" by the Arch-bishop of Canterbury cannot compare with the sensuous studies of these esthetes for bringing alive in my imagination the heat and fragrance of the Palestinian spring.

Gabriel Miro's "Figures of the Passion of Our Lord," though not published in Spain till 1917, and only now translated into English, belongs in spirit to the period of fervently esthetic interpretation, and is more impressive as a work of creative imagination than as a work of piety. Its author is of Jesuit upbringing, enamored of landscape and mountain scenery, and temperamentally enriched with the esthetic melancholy of the later romanticists. His imagination is passionate, colorful, sensuous, with a touch of Latin *morbidezza*.

In painting the scenes and telling the stories of the Passion, he seizes, like Flaubert, in his Carthaginian picture, upon all its exotic possibilities, its luxury, its cruelty—like the merciless painters of the early Renaissance, he counts the blood drops under the lash. He revels in the Herodian pomp and the sumptuous softness of the Roman procurator's palace and in the subtle degeneration of his mind. Not in isolation and in little companies does he see the protagonist moving toward his doom, but with his pitiful broken humanity poignant against the riotous springtime, drenched in odors of tropical fruits, winding toward Calvary against the buzz and brilliance of Oriental bazaars, and all the scent and hum and murmur of the Roman East.

As a specimen of his quality, consider this passage in which Claudia, the wife of Pilate, her hips partially thrust forward from the bedstead of marble and lemon-wood, tells of her warning dream:

[331]

Upon me his eyes did shed a feeling of sorrow, but a sorrow that was like the soft comforting of a precious ointment. . . . And had it been said unto me: "Give that Jew the kiss of love," and I had given it him, I still should not have been kissing that in him which so beguiled me, as though I had been kissing thee, O Pontius, who art in very truth my love and my beloved. Rather would it have been as though, to kiss music, I had kissed my lute in music's stead. For music is in my flesh already, and standeth apart from it and from the lute alike. . . . O Pontius, conspire not against this man!

Pontius wrapped about him the softness of his fleecy white bathrobe, and smiled.

And the slave-woman drew back the curtains from before a window of Syrian glass, and the Roman passed to his bath, with the sheen of the blue sky striking reflections from the *amphimallum's* glistening folds.

And presently Pontius's feet were heard cleaving the bath water.

Giovanni Papini, in his voluble, not to say garrulous, and, as I find it, almost unreadable "Life of Christ," turned away from all that ornate estheticizing, with execrations on the "decadents," because he had become a good Catholic and wished to become a best seller.

Mary Austin turns away from all that because it really does not interest her. In "A Small Town Man," published originally in 1915, and now republished with revisions and a more explicit statement of her conclusions, Mary Austin comes to the interpretation of Jesus, as every sincere interpreter must, with just what she has of her own that can give her an original and personal view. She has, she assures us, studied her Biblical literature, topography, ethnography, etc., patiently, carefully, like other scholars. She gives God thanks and makes no parade of that; she even, with a slight ostentation of superiority to scholarship, calls attention to her deliberate omission of footnotes.

She comes to her task, as I take it, with these special preparations of her insight: birth and upbringing in a small Illinois town at just about that stage of religious petrifaction, of stiff-necked killing literalism, which Jesus encountered in Capernaum. To this she adds years in the rainless places of California and the Southwest, studying Indian folklore, poetry and religion—in short, the elements of barbaric culture, such as Hebrew tradition carefully preserved from the ancient times when Jehovah first entered upon bloody competition with the gods of the heathen, whose fat of rams and oxen smoked over against his. She brings an intimate, almost a first-hand, acquaintance with the universality and the deep natural significance of spring festivals and of the atoning sacrifice among primitive peoples, without which no modern commentator can speak with authority of the Doctrine of Atonement. Furthermore, Mrs. Austin has been for years a student of the psychology of "genius," a phenomenon which she keeps under constant observation. Finally, as she reminds us, she has the intuitions of a woman, and she is proud of it.

Mrs. Austin comes to Jesus as an equal and treats him as such. I mean precisely that. She comes to him as a small-town mystic and she treats him as a small-town mystic. Her writing here is clear and free from the pseudo-scientific jargon into which she sometimes lapses. Her insight appears to me remarkable, and her treatment of the problem far more illuminating, consistent and persuasive than that of Signor

Papini. Her book deserves wide reading. I suspect
there are many people whom it, together with a
thoughtful reading of the Gospel of John, would persuade that they are not altogether "faithless." Certainly her "psychological" approach brings us infinitely nearer to the magic of Jesus—to the source
which inspired St. Francis, Thomas à Kempis, and the
haunting negro "spirituals" than either the "esthetic"
approach of the "decadents" or the cold ethical approach of rationalizing churches. She has as good a
right to her Jesus as St. Augustine had to his, or as the
Rev. Dr. Haldeman has to his.

What Mrs. Austin possesses above any recent commentator that I have seen is a sense for the "mystical
moments" in the experience of Jesus, without which he
is inexplicable—moments when he followed "the inward
voice, followed it instinctively with the freedom of a
river in its natural channel, with no fretting of the
flesh. But where the voice left him uninformed he
was simply a man from Nazareth: his social outlook
was the outlook of a villager." Only a person who has
known some of these moments when the mind with
light on its wings goes straight to the mark "like a
homing pigeon through the pathless"—only a person,
I think, with such experience can make Jesus come
alive for us in his most exalted moods, as thus:

At this latitude the sky retains its blueness on
until midnight, the stars are not pricked in on one
plane, but draw the eye to the barred door of space.
A man praying here all night on one of these open
hill-fronts might think he heard them swinging to their
stations, might hear without any fancying, the heavy
surge of the Mediterranean roll up along the western
buttress of the Bridge. At dawn the fishing fleet would

break out of the lake towns like doves out of a dove-cote, and caravans, starting early to avoid the heat of the day, begin to crawl along the Wâdi el Haman. Hours such as this God flowed into him, filled and over-filled him.

The peril of the mystic is fire without an altar, which is a more splendid peril, though none the less a peril, than an altar without a fire. Mrs. Austin's study of the mystical Jesus needs to be supplemented and completed; and an excellent supplement is at hand in Dr. James Moffatt's "Everyman's Life of Jesus." Dr. Moffatt is a distinguished Biblical scholar who has made a modern translation of the Old and the New Testaments. In this book he makes one continuous narrative of the life of Jesus in the words of the four Gospels, arranging the incidents, however, freely in accordance with his own sense. I have long been pro-foundly averse to revised versions and rearrangements, being firmly convinced that I did not wish my reli-gious poetry "improved" by a modern hand. Dr. Moffatt has temporarily converted me, which means that his Jesus comes alive for me, as for him.

The worth and persuasiveness of this little book reside largely in the introductions which precede each chapter and interpret the material of the Gospel nar-rative from a point of view which, Dr. Moffatt be-lieves, should make his Jesus accessible and appealing to every man. Jesus himself always implied, he de-clares, "that true religion is more endangered by 'reli-gious' people than even by the irreligious, and his moral indignation burned against religious leaders who were responsible for the sin of misrepresenting God."

Dr. Moffatt, though both religious and scholarly,

[335]

shuns the dead phrases of the scholar and the pietist, and when he has occasion to cite another authority he rarely brings in an orthodox believer. He turns by preference to those men of imagination, spiritually quick, who from time to time have had glimpses of Jesus as fresh and strange as the vision seen early in the morning by those women, who, through their tears, mistook him for the gardener. Dr. Moffatt appeals to Emerson, to Jefferies, to Renan, Pascal, St. Francis, Blake, Mill, Shorthouse, De Quincey. He rescues Jesus from our own Scribes and Pharisees, and assorts him with men who use words sensitively.

His Jesus differs in important respects from the mystical villager of Mary Austin. Dr. Moffatt has studied the cause through its historical effects, and he does not pretend to divest himself of the impressions derived, for example, from having in his ears the Latin hymns of the Middle Ages. Every man's Jesus to-day is, as a spiritual force, what the "Christian ages" have made him, and his effect upon Renan is as truly an aspect of his personality as his effect upon Matthew. Dr. Moffatt's Jesus is less instinctive than Mary Austin's, more intellectual, more consciously the iconoclast and the moral revolutionary. He aims at a radical and democratic regeneration. He definitely makes light of dietary regulations, Sabbatarianism and all caste feeling. He sweepingly substitutes the spirit and custom of forgiveness and pardon for the custom of judgment and the ancient law of retaliation. He aspires toward a society in which racial prejudice and nationalistic ambition shall disappear in a brotherly comradeship embracing all men who are active for good in the world.

Great experiences like to be met half way. If we

desire the "realizing sense" of this personality, of which the faithful used to speak in former times, we shall have to use, I fancy, the "means of grace" available to our times. Even if you reckon yourself among Mr. Irwin's "faithless," you are fairly certain to find, if you let Dr. Moffatt throw his light on the ethical substance of Jesus, and if you let Mary Austin kindle that substance with a core of mystical fire, and Gabriel Miro paint the scenes and portray the visible drama of the Passion—you are fairly certain to find Jesus walking in your imagination through the Easter lilies— toward you, full of grace and truth.

XXVI

The Known Soldier

IN "Memoirs of the Harvard Dead in the War Against Germany," Mr. M. A. De Wolfe Howe has built quite the best war memorial that I have ever seen —better than cannon and monuments in parks, better than crossed swords and flags in museums and armories, better than the yards of inscribed brass plates which are crowding the epitaphs of deans and bishops from the walls of English cathedrals, better than groves and chimes of bells, better than flowers and the flickering flame which quicken emotion by the grave of the Unknown Soldier lying under the shadow of the Arc de Triomphe in Paris, emblazoned with the victories of Napoleon and the names of his famous marshals.

I call this the best form of war memorial because it is intimately personal and holds us in lively remembrance of the young lives that are gone. It does not allow the mind to relax and rove among vague grandiose conceptions of military glory and embattled nations and warring machines and angels and horsemen of the Apocalypse, but keeps it closely fixed upon the spirited, lovable, gentlemanly boys from Groton and St. Paul's and the Roxbury Latin School, with a Harvard finishing, who, so far as Harvard is concerned, seemed necessary for conducting the most dangerous parts of the dirty and bloody business of bringing peace on earth and good will to men by the sword.

[338]

I am well aware that an increasing number of people nowadays resent all reference to dead soldiers which gives any satisfaction to the survivors. They will not admit that there are *any* good war memorials, except such narratives as those of Latzko, Duhamel, and Barbusse, such dramas as "What Price Glory?", such poems as Sandburg's "Unknown Soldier," such novels as the "Three Soldiers" of John Dos Passos and Thomas Boyd's "Through the Wheat," which expose the futility, horror, and degradation of war and bitterly and scornfully asperse every one responsible for sending men into battle. There are even extremists who hold that dead soldiers should be asked to make one more sacrifice for the living and consent to oblivion. I do not hold with them. But their presence and the diffusion among us of mordant skepticism regarding "military glory" render it difficult to write or even to feel quite simply and happily any longer about those who gave "the last full measure of devotion."

Mr. Howe himself has recognized this difficulty. His thin volume of verse, almost privately distributed, "The Known Soldier," from which I have borrowed my title, shows him to have been through the war decade a supporter of the war President, a militant pacifist, who swallowed in good faith the slogan "the war to end war." When in 1918 he undertook these truly monumental memoirs, it was not generally considered an index of subnormal intelligence to believe that benign consequences would flow from the World War. In the preface to his first volume, which appeared in 1920 and dealt with the thirty men who eagerly ran to meet their death before the United States consented to enter the struggle, it was still possible for Mr. Howe

Critical Wood Cuts

to write with fervent simplicity of the vanguard, ever to be remembered with gratitude—"the men who sealed with their blood the pledge of that overwhelming sentiment in favor of the Allies which was to make our country an active participant in the fight."

But in the preface of his fifth and final volume, which appeared in 1924, Mr. Howe's ardor for fighting along the path to peace has been sicklied o'er with the pale cast of current thought. "In the ten years since the World War began," he observes, "and especially since it ended, the very theme of war has taken on a new aspect, both for those who read and for those who write about it." He suspects, has had occasion to suspect, that the fruits of victory have been devoured by "the damned politicians"—Mr. Howe *quotes* the phrase.

As a biographer and as a citizen he begins to surmise that he will have to take his satisfaction less in what these young heroes actually achieved than in the fine gallantry and unselfishness which they exhibited. He indulges in little glorification of the abstract fighting spirit. He can't make himself happy any longer by murmuring "It is the cause, my soul." More and more he finds the cause which moves his heart in the individual. He bends over the known soldier, studies him as a son, as a school boy, in college among his clubs and "activities," as a sportsman, as a young man in business, in law, medicine, dentistry, as a comrade and friend in desperate enterprises and in the agony of death. The individual stands the test. He rejoices to think that the three hundred and seventy-three men whose memoirs he and his associates have written are but specimen Americans—are, indeed, but

[340]

a thirtieth part of the Harvard men who were in the war.

My predominant desire is to emphasize the fact that the best way to regard these memoirs is not as *obituaries*, but as *lives* of the American educated class, edited by a capital biographer, the first three volumes wholly written by him—lives of all sorts of American college men drawn into one tragic story by their relation to one college and to the war, but even more profoundly unified and linked with all of us by their relation to one country, its culture, and its ideals. Every American university has materials for a record similar to this. This record happens to be—no, such things, alas! don't happen—this record is extraordinarily rich, and it has been handsomely made. I should like to persuade skeptics that they had better not pass it by as designed for a special audience or for respectful repose amid the dust of university archives. I wish to assure readers who feel no special interest in Harvard men as such, and who wish to forget the dead and to "study war no more," that here is an astonishing collection of materials for study of the great human qualities available for American life and the tasks of peace.

If, however, you are not in the skeptical class, which requires conciliation, you may be assured that Mr. Howe and his associates have brought out in these memoirs everything that can be said in honor of heroic virtues and fighting men and to the glory of Harvard and America militant. If your belief in the World War is unabated, if you instinctively honor young men who die at the behest of their country, if a relative of yours is commemorated here, if you feel an unmodified traditonal satisfaction in the military exploits of the sons of Harvard, you will read these volumes from first to last with intense interest and proud emotion, and you will be astonished that such a magnificent library of adventure has received so little attention from the press.

Here you will learn of one dead hero that he came of a long line of Harvard scholars; of another that he was sprung from excellent fighting stock; of another that his grandfather fought in the Civil War; of still another that his ancestors distinguished themselves in the Revolution and in the French and Indian wars. This young officer's father was a Mayor; that one's a President of the United States; the sire of this one was a famous New York clergyman; the grandfather of this one was Lincoln's Secretary of War; this boy was of the tenth generation from Elder Brewster; this "ace of aces" was descended from the colonel who crawled into the den after the wolf. They bred true, these fine old stocks. There are memoirs here which read like Pindaric odes, pouring a splendor of death and glory upon ten generations.

Here you will find, on the part of soldiers and their fathers and mothers, expressions of faith, of dedication, and of solemn sacrifice—sometimes even of joyous sacrifice. So great a hope, so clear a sense of duty, animated most of these volunteers that they felt bitterness only when the influenza or the pneumonia, more deadly than the bullet, made their free-will offering unavailing. "For many of them," says Mr. Howe, "Howard Rogers Clapp spoke when he wrote:

'It is much more than *patria* that we are fighting for now; it is the ending of such horrible pain and sorrow for all the generations that are to come after

us. It is a religious war, greater far than any of
the old Crusades in its principles—principles that are
greater and larger than Christianity itself.'

This is not a speech from the sidelines but from
the firing line, and it may be set against that of the
realistic politician who insists that "we merely went
in to *strafe* the Hun."

Some of these men went into battle in mortal fear.
Of one it is said: "He had a horror of war and was
always very nervous when he went to the front, and
yet he always volunteered for any dangerous mission."
Others developed the *sang-froid* of Mercutio, fighting
and taking their own death with a jest on their lips.
Happiest of the dead, probably, were the first thirty—
sportsmen, many of them, football and polo players
and big game hunters, eager for the thick of the
scrimmage.

For Victor Chapman, entrance into American aviation, declares his father, was "like being made a knight.
It transformed—one might almost say transfigured—
him. That the universe should have supplied this spirit
with the consummation which it had sought from infancy and should have given in a few weeks complete
happiness and complete fulfillment—the crown of life
to which one can imagine no other perfect ending—
is one of the mysteries of this divine age."

Of the same Hotspur breed were Hamilton Coolidge,
Quentin Roosevelt, Norman Prince and young David
Endicott Putnam, a boy of twenty, who had had some
difficulty entering aviation on account of his youth,
yet brought down five German planes in a day and
gayly wrote to his mother on the evening of June 30,
1918:

"Dearest Mother: I wrote to you this morning and said that I would try to 'get' another boche in the evening. I did!"

Others there were, but, so far as these records show, few, like Alan Seeger, of brooding poetic temperament, with a fiery thirst for experience, snatching at death as if it were the last untasted cup of intoxication, and luxuriating in danger for the fuller, intenser sense of life that it gave in the allotted interval. After a year and a half of war, knowing well whereof he spoke, Seeger wrote that he saw all life revolving about the twin poles of Love and Strife, in the macrocosm, and in the microcosm of his own emotions. Love was good, he held,

as far as it goes, but it goes only half way, and my aspiration was to go all the gamut, to "drink life to the lees." My interest in life was passion, my object to experience it in all rare and refined, in all intense and violent forms. The war having broken out, then, it was natural that I should have staked my life on learning what it alone could teach me. How could I have let millions of other men know an emotion that I remained ignorant of?

Doubtless there were a few men in this company with blood so hot or heart so fully satiated with ordinary experience that death in battle was, indeed, to them, as Mr. John Jay Chapman puts it, "the crown of life to which one can imagine no other perfect ending"; but the total impression that one gathers from a war memorial in which three hundred and seventy-three intelligent men are allowed to speak is very different from that.

The crown of Life? They imagined many other crowns!

Says André Cheronnet-Champollion, enlisted as a private in the French Army, and the third Harvard man to die in the war:

I often feel like a fool instead of like an honest man trying to do his duty. . . . I often wonder if I will ever come back to see René grow up, to be his first guide in the park and to watch his progress through St. Paul School and Harvard. When I compare my attractive New Hampshire home to the terrible gloom of the barracks and cantonments and I see the park in all its splendor and loveliness, even New York, which I used to curse at a good deal, now seems like a paradise that is out of reach. Never has America seemed so beautiful.

Writes Francis Reed Austin a couple of months before he got death and his Distinguished Service Cross for "extraordinary heroism in action near Haumont, France, November 11, 1918," at the age of twenty-one:

By candlelight in an old French fort. Oh, it is lovely here in a little living room for the officers, made just as homelike as any place I have ever been in. . . . You forget everything except home as you listen to the piano with the two big candles on each side of it, and then dark all around. The wonderful old tunes resound up into the towers and down the dark corridors. They are playing "Memories." It is wonderful, and I think of my childhood, and my family gave me the very happiest. Wouldn't it be great if I could give them just as happy an old age. Believe me, this war makes you really appreciate everybody

and everything. . . . Thank God, they know naught
of war down here. . . . I don't know why I have written all this stuff, but the music has just guided my
pencil, and after battered towns, dead bodies, suffering
families and devastated fields all you most think of is
love and beauty.

Says Captain Roger Fulton Goss, who died of influenza at Camp Greene, in North Carolina:

You feel that you are getting a good deal out of
yourself—your physical organism and your mental
and moral capacities—but you are sacrificing, nevertheless, the imaginative possibilities of unregimented
"individual life," where a man is the focus of many
demands and is the agent of many enterprises—and
can play "the great lover."

In the last memoir to which I shall call attention,
a rather ordinary or "average" boy is commemorated
—so I infer from an introductory paragraph in which,
with inveterate Harvard condescension, the author
reminds us that a certain number of undergraduates
come from the "central states," with nothing but "the
local high school" behind them, and yet have a "wholesome" influence in Cambridge.

Osric Mills Watkins, an Indiana boy in the American aviation section, aged twenty-one, who died of
pneumonia at Bar-le-Duc in 1918, wrote three letters
from France which constitute the body of his six-page
life in the "Memoirs." In the first, in which he announces to his parents his decison to enter the air
service, he says: "I promise you that I will do well
in this; that I will face all things unafraid, both physical and abstract, as I have always tried to do in the

[346]

past." The other two letters were prepared to be sent
in case of his death. To his mother he begins: "This
isn't to be mailed until I've gone where all the good
aviators go, honey. You are so wise and brave and
cheerful that I know you can be as proud as you are
sad at my death." But I can quote no more of this.
It will be found in the fifth volume. The letter for
his father I will quote in full, with no other comment
than this: It has suggested to me more poignantly
than any other page in these five volumes, packed with
poignant suggestions, the incalculable costs of war:

Dearest Dad: When you get this I shall have gotten
into a spin too close to the ground or something else
equally foolish. I can faintly conceive of your grief,
as I, too, have dreamed of sons that might one day
have been mine. But if a man has lived well he dies
well, as I believe; then know that I shall have held my
head high before the Judgment Seat. I have committed my sins, but I am deeply ashamed of them,
and I know that God will forgive them. I regret that
I might not have lived to lighten your old age, father
dear, and that I might not have given you a grand-
son; but it was not to be.
We have not written each other much, dad, but it
has been somewhat unnecessary. We understand each
other sufficiently well that we may leave things unsaid.
You have been a good father to me, dad. You'll
never know how much I have loved and respected you.
Even as I write I think of a hundred little ways in
which you guided my faltering steps and molded my
character. "I before E, except after C." I doubt
whether I could ever have become as good a man as
you. Evil desires followed me much. That was one
reason I wanted to live.
They are just passing the window with the dead

[347]

body of a boy who fell while I was writing the first
page of this. The poor boy never got his chance at
the Huns. I hope I do. Whether I do or not, I shall
be proud to have died for America.

I'll be with you in spirit, father, in the days to
come. I hope it will be in my power to make you
happy.

Your devoted son,   OSRIC.

It was very obliging for these boys to die for us.
But after a careful study of these three hundred and
seventy-three personal records, I must say that it
strikes me as rather a florid figure of speech on our
part to declare that death was "the crown of life"—
for them.